Economic Forecasting for Management

ECONOMIC FORECASTING FOR MANAGEMENT

POSSIBILITIES AND LIMITATIONS

Hans Georg Graf

QUORUM BOOKS
Westport, Connecticut • London

Library of Congress Cataloguing-in-Publication Data

Graf, Hans Georg.
    Economic forecasting for management : possibilities and limitations / Hans Georg Graf.
        p.   cm.
    Includes bibliographical references and index.
    ISBN 1–56720–601–8 (alk. paper)
    1. Managerial economics.   2. Economic forecasting.   I. Title.
 HD30.22.G696   2002
    330′.024′658—dc21   2002017765

British Library Cataloguing in Publication Data is available.

Library of Congress Catalog Card Number: 2002017765
ISBN: 1–56720–601–8

First published in 2002

Quorum Books, 88 Post Road West, Westport, CT 06881
An imprint of Greenwood Publishing Group, Inc.
www.quorumbooks.com

Printed in the United States of America

The paper used in this book complies with the
Permanent Paper Standard issued by the National
Information Standards Organization (Z39.48–1984).

10 9 8 7 6 5 4 3 2 1

Copyright Acknowledgment

Originally published as *Prognosen und Szenarien in der Wirtschaftspraxis*, © 1999 Buchverlag NZZ,
Zurich.

Contents

Part III: Scenarios for Strategy Development

Part IV: Short-Term Economic and Market Forecasting

Illustrations

FIGURES

TABLES

PREFACE

For more than 30 years the St. Gallen Center for Futures Research (SGZZ) has been conducting studies analyzing and forecasting the macroeconomic, sector-specific, and regional developments of Switzerland. Such studies of a small, open economy cannot deal solely with that country. Rather, they must also have a European and ultimately a global perspective because the development of these general conditions is of considerable importance to our country. However, if a holistic image is to be developed, no matter how important or even crucial, long-term forecasting for developing macroeconomic or corporate strategies cannot occur without taking into account short-term trends or investigating individual sector-specific and market-related trends, respectively. For this reason many aspects of forecasting have always been worked on at the SGZZ, in terms both of methodology and subject matter, so that—with a view to economic issues—an almost complete pool of expertise is available. This formed the basis for a publication by Kneschaurek and Graf in 1984.[1] Additional experience gained since, along with expanded and newly developed methods, have also been included in the present publication.

While SGZZ's work is based on economic fundamentals, many studies are positioned at the boundary between economics and business administration. This means that they focus on the general conditions in which corporate activities occur and are therefore, in their long-term orientation, directly related to normative and strategic management. However, with respect to short-term economic forecasting, they shed light on the macroeconomic and market-related areas of operative management. For these reasons this book deliberately seeks a connection with the St. Gallen management concept. Therefore, it describes how finding information via forecasting can be incorporated into the concepts of integrated management. The conceptual framework of this book is based on the holistic systemic approach, as pursued by Ulrich and his students. Therefore, the studies conducted to date at the

St. Gallen Center for Futures Research, along with the previously mentioned book by Kneschaurek and Graf, form the basis for this book. Because of its connection to the 'integrated management approach,' this basis is augmented by the tradition of research and reasoning continued by Knut Bleicher at the University of St. Gallen.

Due to the increasing complexity in companies large and small, and particularly with the accelerated change of these environments, the limitations of traditional forecasting efforts are being reached and exceeded noticeably faster. Therefore, the usefulness of this instrument for obtaining information appears at first glance to be decreasing for all levels of management.

However, this observation does not mean that this traditional instrument can simply be 'thrown overboard' and replaced by new approaches. Rather, it is important to combine such instruments in a useful manner by taking advantage of their respective strengths, so that the possibilities and limitations of future-oriented information can be expanded. Such information will continue to be absolutely essential for structuring planning tasks.

This book has three objectives. First, it is a textbook to give students in economics and business administration degree programs an introduction in dealing with questions about the future and the conversion of future-oriented information into a basis for decisionmaking relevant for companies. Second, it gives users of future-oriented information hints not only about the possibilities and limitations of such information but also about the variety, even diversity of statements made by forecasts. This book seeks to help them handle forecasts more expediently. In operative management a thorough forecast with only a long-term perspective leads to planning deficiencies, while in strategic management the time horizon of short-term forecasts leads to excessive planning effort and misunderstandings. Third, the book gives the general public an overview as to the different ways and possibilities of dealing with the future from an economic perspective. For this purpose, its content ranges from product forecasts to working with global models and also from time-series extrapolations to futures seminars.

In addition, recommendations are given on methods. However, this book does not go into detail about mathematical/statistical tools and the various methods and possibilities of empirical economic research. Rather, an attempt is made to kindle an understanding of the various methods. An effective forecast for a company—as well as a national economy and government or administration—must ultimately always be 'custom-made' because both a company's business idea and a country's identity have to be regarded as unique. In addition, the book develops an understanding of the fact that, especially with forecasts, an isolated view of a subject under investigation usually leads to incorrect results, particularly when dealing with longer-term trends. The time, subject, and space dimensions of forecasts, which differ depending on the problem, require as a rule a far broader approach than simply that of economic 'tunnel vision.' In so doing it has to be kept in mind that people always are, and must be, at the center of economic activity, so very quickly rendering mechanistic ideas about the future that assume a purely rational view of humankind superficial.

As already mentioned, this book reflects the author's experiences over the course of more than 30 years working at the St. Gallen Center for Futures Research. While working on my dissertation I took the first steps into the area of market forecasting. In this connection I would like to thank my academic teacher, colleague, and friend Francesco Kneschaurek, who provided assistance during my first steps into this area of research. With him I have been able to carry out a great number of highly interesting, although in part politically explosive, research projects that were nonetheless in most cases exciting. This work ultimately led to futures research in Switzerland—at a very early stage by international comparison—receiving a lot of attention on the political level. Nonetheless, the fact that neither we nor anybody else possesses prophetic talents—which we have emphasized repeatedly—has not by any means been universally accepted. Mechanistically rational models with unilaterally economic orientations have therefore again been happily revived. Not least, this book emphasizes how little information such approaches can provide.

I would also like to express my thanks to my personal assistant, Dr. Roland Sütterlin, who lent his expertise and great commitment to the development of this book, suggested corrections and additions, and provided valuable support while I was working on the manuscript. During many conversations, my at times overly academic and in part abbreviated line of reasoning was expanded. In addition, he suggested various lateral connections to legal and management questions and finally was in charge of editing references and footnotes. I would also like to thank Stephan Kummer, Dipl.-Wirtsch.Ing., who, during the course of his dissertation supervised by me, prepared an overview on working with global models. His article was included in this book in an edited form. My wife and my assistant, Michael Artho, have prepared the manuscript and the figures for the English edition of this book with great care. Especially I would like to thank my wife for her patience with her husband, who was frequently lost in thought, and for her careful work and repeated checking of the manuscript for possible errors. Despite all this assistance, any remaining discrepancies are, of course, my responsibility.

Special gratitude is extended to several persons, firms, and institutions for their generosity in making it possible through their financial contributions to have this book translated into English. These contributors are: The Duke of Liechtenstein, Avina Foundation, Credit Suisse, Model Holding, Philips (Schweiz) AG, Swiss Re, Helvetia Patria Insurance, SAir Group, Banca della Svizzera Italiana, HUWA Finanz AG, Nord-Ostschweizerische Kraftwerke, Confiserie Sprüngli AG, Ernst Basler & Partner, Sarna Verwaltungs AG, Winterthur Versicherungs Gesellschaft. The German original was translated into English by IBC German Translations, Dublin, Ireland. The final preparation of the print-ready version was effected by Deborah Whitford. I am grateful for her diligent work.

BOOK STRUCTURE

The development of companies, sectors, and entire economies is determined significantly by their demographic, social, political, economic, technological, and ecological environments. However, the relevant questions in dealing with future oriented information are not addressed in a comprehensive manner in economic or business administration degree programs. What is missing in particular is an overview of the necessary instruments for developing a future-oriented basis for decisionmaking in practical, everyday management situations. Such a basis for decisionmaking *cannot* start primarily from *theories* operating with abstract models and the various, in part opposing versions of such theories. Nor can the various mathematical/statistical approaches be a central focus. Rather, the specific relevant *possibilities and limitations of forecasting*, from the point of view of a company or government, have to be the focus of attention.

These considerations determined the structure of this book, which is divided into four parts. Part I sheds light on the *various dimensions* associated with the examination of the future that lead ultimately to great diversity in the contents, assessment, and interpretation of future-oriented information.

It becomes apparent that an informative forecast can, in the end, be meaningful only when developed via dialogue and a combination of the diverse knowledge and experiences of forecast developers and users. Only when the two sides understand each other can forecasts be used in a targeted manner.

Part II addresses initially the question as to whether, in the long term, forecasting is possible at all and then sheds light on the various methodological approaches of traditional, long-term, *macroeconomic and global economic* forecasting. The approaches for long-term issues, that is, the Delphi and cross-impact techniques, are—as a transition to thinking in terms of scenarios—introduced briefly in separate chapters.

Part III describes the *scenario technique* as a central instrument for long-term economic forecasting, in the course of which particular attention is given to the question of using and implementing scenarios in companies. The previously familiar planning process based on 'knowing about the future' is replaced by 'thinking in terms of alternatives,' as required by the scenario technique. Through the opening of perspectives, this approach allows the discovery of interesting future directions, which would not otherwise be recognized at all or in time.

Part IV is devoted to *short-term economic and market forecasting*. The focus here is on describing and evaluating the various approaches of economic forecasting as well as the requirements for meaningful market forecasts and their application at the corporate level. Also important in this part are the possibilities and limitations of such forecasting efforts and adequately interpreting and using their results, instead of simply providing recipes or instructions. This part concludes with a short overview of the aspects relevant to handling future issues.

NOTE

1. Kneschaurek, F. and Graf, H.G. (*Wirtschafts- und Marktprognosen*), 1984.

PART I

FORECASTING AND FUTURES RESEARCH—AN UNEQUAL PAIR

1

Fundamentals of Human Behavior

THE NECESSITY FOR A HOLISTIC APPROACH

It has recently become more and more widely recognized that many aspects of problem solving can no longer be tackled in a targeted fashion using conventional procedures and methods of thinking.[1] The perceived condition of a world that is changing at an ever faster rate as well as the depth and severity of the problems to be overcome have led to a search for fundamentally new approaches and a new way of thinking. What is needed is a new holistic and integrated way of thinking based on a wide horizon that investigates relations and associations, taking into account a great number of influential factors. Increasingly, this means turning away from a mainly analytical and therefore isolating (reductionist) approach.

This new approach proves sensible and useful not only for major problems. Many solutions to small-scale problems developed in a perfectly logical manner according to conventional thinking cannot, in the end, be implemented, or they trigger side effects with consequences at least as unwanted as the original problem. Especially because of these circumstances, it has often been possible to 'attach blame' to 'forecasters' for undesired results either because they did not achieve the paradigm shift or because the respective user of the forecast did not take note of their overall view.

It has been postulated, therefore, that, particularly for longer-term and complex issues, we should depart from the idea of forecasting and start from the more comprehensive approach of futures research (Graf, 1988, p. 34). This is because the future problems that are becoming apparent have really reached a new, more comprehensive dimension, meaning that their characteristics are completely different from those in the past. In particular, it can be observed that the dynamics and degree of change have increased significantly such that the problem situation itself has to be reassessed. Otherwise, failures are basically preprogrammed when solving difficult problems. It can happen that a problem-solving method that in the past definitely led to success no longer meets the requirements for solving the problem situations of today and particularly those in the future. 'The idea of forecasting proves too narrow in any case for long-term investigations that deal adequately with problems. It has to be replaced by the more comprehensive idea of futures research' (p. 36).

In a general sense this can be regarded as a radical change in scientific perspective. According to Fritjof Capra[2] this change has the following three characteristics: a reversal of the relationship between the part and the whole; a shift in focus from searching for structures, to considering processes; and abandonment of the idea that knowledge consists of building blocks on a solid foundation like a building that can be locked, in favor of the idea of a network of knowledge. This view leads to a way of thinking that contrasts significantly with the conventional idea of scientific working and thinking. It requires a real paradigm shift in the perception of problems. Analytical thinking that focuses on details and the search for the smallest units that shape each image is replaced by integrated thinking that focuses on the whole. At first glance such system-oriented thinking loses in sharpness and clarity during analysis; however, it has been shown that a considerably greater degree of explanation can be attained with such an approach than with even the most detailed single analysis. Following this logic, thought no longer consists of small, linear causal chains with a definable beginning and end, but rather of circular connections. What cannot be measured, quantified, or formulated in mathematical terms is no longer banned from science as in the past but is instead consciously included in the investigation process. This procedure turns our focus to the dynamics of events, while at the same time we are looking for patterns of order in such processes.

Consequently, the conviction loses its validity that the human 'mind' can grasp reality completely and objectively by means of rational thinking. Many questions of crucial importance cannot be solved by traditional approaches. Conventional analytical and isolating thinking is the product of several centuries of scientific, technical, and economic development and therefore seems to be the only natural, logical way of thought (Capra, 1988). However, the new way of holistic thinking[3] contradicts thought patterns that have been imprinted in people's minds, so making it rather difficult to use this new way of thinking. Especially more highly educated people have to overcome particular difficulties on their way to holistic thinking.

It is by no means a coincidence that with systems theory a new thought pattern has evolved that takes into account increasing complexity and dynamics. Systems theory raises the question as to what dynamic, complex, comprehensive systems actually have in common and how such systems behave and are able to exist at all. Involved here is an interdisciplinary level on which conceptual instruments for characterizing such phenomena and a 'systemic way of thinking' are being developed that have by now led to a learnable 'systems method.'[4]

Holistic thinking and systems theory are very closely connected. The concepts, knowledge, and methods of systems theory form indispensable instruments for rational and learnable holistic thinking. In this way a postulated, comprehensive view of problems becomes a rational, logically comprehensible method for solving problems. It should be noted that the term 'systemic,' not 'systematic,' is being used consciously because the latter term is used in the classic way of thinking for logical, linear-analytical procedures.

However, not every method for solving problems using the term 'system' has departed from the conventional paradigm. It should also be mentioned that by no means can, or must, the systemic way of thinking be applied to all problems. Systems theory approaches are used mostly in complex situations where, in addition to a complicated investigation subject, there is a significant dynamic element or when the degree and speed of change of the investigated subject are of major importance (Chapter 2). When preparing forecasts, they can range—depending on the issues addressed—from simple to highly complex problems. Accordingly, different methods have to be employed.

Following, therefore, are, on one hand, classic instruments of analysis and forecasting for cases that definitely have to be regarded as complicated and where, however, it can be assumed that the structures are relatively constant, that is, that the degree of change in the fundamental composition of the whole system investigated is small. On the other hand, it is obvious that with complex problems, such as the long-term change of the world economy, the degree and speed at which the structures in this system are subject to change have to be examined; in addition, the level of a specialized field (e.g., economics) has to be surpassed and additional levels (society, politics, technology, ecology, etc.) included in the thought process.[5]

Holistic thinking is, however, only one—although a necessary—initial step toward holistic behavior. The danger continues to be that, while insights are gained into the big picture, and conventional behavior is criticized due to the holistic perspective, only measures following conventional ideas of 'feasibility' are often derived. These are exactly the ones that will not achieve their goal because they are unconnected to the system.

This means that, in addition to a holistic view, a holistic method for solving problems will have to be found allowing implementation of the insights gained. It follows from this that what is important is by no means only the description of a method for solving problems but that normative and strategic future issues can really be addressed only via a comprehensively focused dialogue. This dialogue must have a sufficiently flexible structure such that it corresponds to the great variety of possible futures and can show adequate solutions for each of these problems. This definitely refutes the idea that a forecaster can announce the 'truth,' that is, that therefore some people have prophetic talents.[6] However, to date many of those who use forecasts have not (yet) been able to give up this idea in their thought processes.

PEOPLE AND THEIR ACTIVITIES AT THE CENTER

In essence, economics and therefore also economic forecasting, as part of social science, always deal with people. As a result we can assume a dual situation of people and their activity in an economy. On one hand, we have to keep in mind that economic activities should serve people, that economic activity is for their benefit, and that economic activity is not an end in itself.[7] Economic activity is at the service of people to procure life's essentials and to satisfy their wishes. As a result, economic activity evolved from the fact that many of people's wishes run into a shortage of availability of the goods and services that they desire such that complete satisfaction of their insatiable wishes is ultimately not possible (cf. Binswanger, 1994).

On the other side of this dual study of people from the point of view of economics is the fact that economic activity always has to take into consideration human behavior. Herein lie the fascination and at the same time the difficulty of social science, for human behavior is not firmly predetermined but varies greatly with social development and the associated interactions. So, what matters from the point of view of a company is understanding as precisely as possible consumer demand and how it changes, in order to work out an activity margin through its function as a go-between providing goods and services to the ultimate consumer, which in turn allows the company to meet consumer needs. Therefore, the essential point in this study is the question as to which social, cultural, and political environments shape the individuals in question, that is the central characteristics of the system surrounding a company that have to be taken into consideration within the scope of economic activity.

Thus, people play a central part in the economic process, be it as potential buyers or suppliers of goods and services. When groups of individuals interact as consumers or suppliers of goods and services, a market is created, which through a balance between preferences and prices allows both satisfaction of needs and compensation for work during production. Especially due to the effects of globalization on management activities, investments, competition, and new locations, it is often overlooked that people, who behave neither rationally nor mechanically, are at the center of events, so mechanistic approaches and mentalities—particularly in the longer term—are doomed to failure.

While structures and patterns of behavior may be quite stable in the short term, we cannot definitely exclude unexpected changes in direction over the longer term. These could occur very abruptly and at short notice, so rendering things familiar to us completely useless. This can be illustrated by numerous examples, ranging from the replacement of long-playing records by compact discs, to the removal of the Iron Curtain. In every case all rules were turned on their heads at one blow.

However, there are often indications beforehand for such changes in direction—although often only by comparison with basic theoretical ideas or by means of looming social or political conflicts.[8] In addition, various conceivable types of change have often to be expected, so a general view of the situation is obtainable only through a comprehensive approach and by working with various futures (scenarios), which in turn can be regarded as the basis for necessary decisions.

HUMAN BEHAVIOR IS FUTURE-ORIENTED

People constantly find themselves in the situation of having to decide how to behave or what to do. There are several alternatives available for virtually every problem, so a decision has to be made each time as to which alternative to chose, in the course of which the decision not to do anything also qualifies as a decision. At the same time, making decisions in a problem situation is always oriented toward the future.[9]

People judge a situation based on their values, whereby the very short term, practically immediate future is of concern (i.e., a situation is not satisfactory and should be changed).[10] It can, however, also be about evaluating a future condition that we hope for or fear and that we would like to occur or prevent, respectively. In order to reach a decision, it is not reality that is being changed; rather, possible alternative behaviors are being simulated by imagining the respective situations. By means of a simulation, the effects of various alternatives are rehearsed, and only then is a decision made. These are routines that happen daily and of which we are often totally unaware.

Simulation of alternative behaviors in our minds by means of mental models of reality therefore tests in advance the effects of our future behavior. In this respect, each decision practically presupposes a forecast, with which the anticipated future effect of our behavior is evaluated. When making a decision, the point is therefore always to either achieve something that still lies in the future or to adjust to expected future events. Consequently, forecasting enhances the information available when trying to make a decision.

At first glance numerous decisions are made daily that are apparently not based on forecasts. However, this is only true insofar as no formal, formulated, and/or empirically testable forecasts are used for such decisions. A forecast is made in the back of our minds, so to speak, during the course of mentally simulating possible alternative behaviors. Also, these decisions do not require real instructions in the sense of showing the best way; rather, the point is overcoming our indecision when selecting an alternative as opposed to not doing anything. Of course, such a decision can also be arrived at by tossing a coin, for example, which is by no means new. 'The ancient Greeks and Romans were not more naive than we are, they were wiser by paying a little money to a soothsayer so that he would flip the coin for them or do some equivalent hocus pocus. We are so cheap that we pocket the nickel after it has shown head or tail!' (Iklé, 1965). According to this, decisions having the sole purpose of helping us overcome our indecision usually do not require forecasting information.

POLICY SHAPES THE FUTURE

Respect for time is called for when we examine future issues: history, the present, and the future are a continuum. The present, which becomes part of the past the moment that we experience it, is the transitory element; the future is uncertain;

history burdens us and has to be overcome. From this perspective, we as individuals, our national economy, even the entire world and its people are constantly challenged by minor and major future issues that put us under an obligation internally and externally. They do not do us the favor of following theoretical classifications or economic disciplines. Problems are by nature always interdisciplinary. As defined by the responsibility that we all carry for the future, these have to be solved as they arise. This is called for particularly in the interest of increasing not only our chances of being able to act freely but also those of future generations (cf. Lendi, 1995, p. 8).

In the end, the future is always a question. We cannot regard it passively, no more than we can escape it. A fatalistic understanding of the future would basically release us from any actions and decisions and, at the same time, lead to totalitarian subjugation. A fatalistic belief in a predetermined future would also release us from the ongoing necessity for forecasts because decisions would then essentially be unnecessary. Future development can, however, be shaped, at least in part, on an individual as well as a collective level. However, feasibility is, to some extent, very limited; the belief that a perfect future can be reached will always turn out to be a false expectation. Nevertheless, a 'better' future is possible. But one of our's primary abilities is to actively shape our own future and that of our descendants. This was the only way possible for hunters and gatherers to develop into an industrial and learned society. Of course, nobody knows what is correct. There are always many possible solutions.

Therefore, restraint is particularly called for in policy making. Solutions can and should not be forced; rather, the general conditions have to be set such that a better future becomes possible. In this context Lendi[11] uses the term 'national planning.' However, his understanding of planning has nothing to do with the planned economic understanding in the Marxist sense but rather means dealing creatively with the future. He defines planning as 'a systematic outline of a rational order on the basis of available, pertinent knowledge; its implementation is developed through targeted, generally agreed action and carried out in an ongoing process of evaluating objectives and measures' (Lendi, 1995, p. 9). The basis for such planned activity is carefully considered images of possible futures, which have to be created by means of the previously mentioned process. A selection ultimately has to be made on a macroeconomic level in a democratic process.

Therefore, policy in particular is, to a large extent, oriented toward the future. On the basis of this understanding government policy becomes one of fulfilling public tasks, which, due to its bearing, is inevitably oriented toward the future. Fulfilling public tasks requires a longer-term vision of the future, whereby the extent to which various possible actions contribute to the optimal fulfillment of these tasks has to be evaluated. Inevitably, the planning environment (i.e., the context in which such planning is to be carried out) has to be made clear during such evaluation of possible actions. In addition, statements are necessary as to where realization and implementation should occur and the effects that the planned measures may have on the various areas possibly effected. In this context the apprehension of politicians about the future has to be considered. The reason for this lies in the fact that government measures are nearly always related to the present; that is, policies have to be justified in the present. A politician is judged much more by his or her current actions than by any results expected in the future. The discrepancy between connection with the present and obligation for an orientation toward the future—a decision made has to be legitimated in the present, although it will not show any effect until later—burdens a politician's perspective, which is tied to the desire for reelection.[12]

CORPORATE POLICY ALSO SHAPES THE FUTURE

Within the scope of normative and strategic management, the main focus is on ensuring a company's ability to survive and develop (Bleicher, 1996, p. 53). The capability for development also includes a qualified change in the direction of a positive, useful transformation. It is therefore—almost tautologically—a future-oriented process that is carried on in anticipation of changes in the company's environment or in order to attain new, successful positions in the future. Consequently, corporate policy actions and behavior start from a company vision of the future; this vision forms the beginning of all managerial deliberations (Bleicher, 1994, p. 101). Bleicher refers to this vision as a guiding star, that is followed during the formation and development of companies in a social environment. It focuses on a realistic view of the future that fundamentally has scenario character. However, it deviates from classic scenario development insofar as with this vision a clear selection of the various scenario images has already been made, and a comprehensive, forward-looking idea of the purposes and ways of reaching them has been derived (Bleicher, 1994, p. 102). Consequently, visions are much more binding for individual companies than scenarios, the latter representing an environment for deriving company-specific visions. What matters, therefore, is to creatively convert information about the future and possible alternative futures described by scenarios into a vision that is specific and binding for the company in question. This vision would also ultimately incorporate the social role (i.e., the 'corporate identity' of the company) and define the environment for normative/strategic and operative management.

In order for a company to ensure its capability for development, it is forced to show corporate policy behavior, which 'always has to have a dual orientation in the tension field between, on one hand the past, present and future, and on the other the environment and the internal world' (Bleicher, 1994, p. 119). Therefore, if promising management is to be achieved, fundamental corporate policy decisions have to take into account the essential (future) problems of the environment and their interdependence, as well as possible inconsistencies with internal objectives and measures. Often of importance is a management team that summarizes its own view of the objectives, actual situation, and general conditions for implementing the objectives in the form of a systemic image. Management, together with the employees, represents the most important resource for coping with changes to be expected in corporate environments and individual national economies and even the global economy as a whole. Especially during a time of profound change, management has to carry out a clear and comprehensive evaluation of alternative actions and their effects, on both a government and corporate policy level. This is the only way that it can face its tasks in a future-oriented way and also meet them in future.

TRADITION OF FUTURES RESEARCH

Depending on the definition used for forecasting, either a long or, by contrast, a very short history can be assigned. Basically, in Western cultures there is very great continuity in the various forms of dealing with the future (cf. Hatem, 1993b, p. 27). It is definitely alleged in part that essentially nothing has changed in dealing with the future since the endeavors of the Phytia of Delphi or Cicero's 'de divinationem.' This means that in dealing with the future in this way, we are, of course, using the term 'forecasting' in a very wide sense (Cazes, 1993, p. 29). In contrast, the development of futures research in the contemporary sense can be understood as a very young phenomenon, in the sense of an institutionalized activity drawing on scientifically inspired methods. Dealing with the future in this manner can be found in the literature of the late 19th century and later in the work of H.G. Wells.[13] However, real institutionalization of futures research did not start until after the end of the World War II, initially in the United States, followed by major international organizations and, eventually, also in other industrialized countries.

Here the United States played a really pioneering role, in the course of which, initially following the World War II, defense strategy studies were at the forefront, leading to the creation of the famous Rand Corporation. Starting around 1960, university and independent research groups followed in the footsteps of these efforts (e.g., the Hudson Institute under the leadership of the former Rand employee Herman Kahn). In 1970 the American president and Congress, respectively, started a specific initiative and formed a comprehensive research group by creating the 'Commission for the Year 2000.'

These initiatives were later taken up by large international organizations. For example, at the Organization for Economic Cooperation and Development (OECD) the 'Interfutures' project was started under the direction of J. Lesourne; these models were advanced by W. Leontief within the scope of the United Nations Organization (UNO). The World Bank also participated in these research efforts. Finally, these efforts took hold in individual countries to varying degrees. In the Netherlands, research work that is still in progress today was advanced within the scope of the Centraal Plan Bureau, not least on the initiative of J. Tinbergen (Zalm, 1992). In France the Commissariat du Plan was created. Also in many other European countries—usually at the university level—similar initiatives were started or research institutes created, for example, the SGZZ in Switzerland[14] that examine to this day the long-term issues related to global economic and national development.

Also, during recent years several ways of dealing with the future have been clearly distinguishable that determine the most recent developmental history of forecasting. While the initial focus has been primarily on extending the past into the future (extrapolation), exceptionally strongly disaggregated 'bottom-up' approaches were employed in a second phase that almost aimed at prescribing progress.[15] In some cases utopian ideas were developed leading immediately to antiutopian ideas.[16] Eventually, approaches based on an increasingly holistic, systemic point of view moved to the forefront and today determine the environment for longer-term forecasting.[17] Ultimately, eclectically designed expert systems assume that for each question to be examined, the respective methodological approaches have to be combined, and therefore there cannot be any standard recipes. In any event, a wide spectrum of methods has to be applied and adjusted to each issue.

Significant Publications

In disseminating future-oriented ways of thinking in the 1970s and 1980s the following publications have made a significant contribution:

Kusnets, S.: *Concepts and Assumptions in Long Term Projections of Income and Wealth.* Princeton, NJ, 1954.
Ruggles, R.: *Long Range Economic Projections.* Princeton NJ, 1954.
Fourastié, J.: *La grande métamorphose du XXe siècle.* Paris, 1961.
Commission on the Year 2000: *Working Papers.* Boston, 1965.
Jantsch, E.: *Technological Forecasting in Perspective.* Paris, 1967.
Kahn, H. and Wiener, A.J.: *The Year 2000, A Framework for Speculation on the Next Thirty-Three Years.* New York, 1967.
Bell, D.: *Towards the Year 2000: Work in Progress.* Cambridge, 1968.
Flechtheim, O.K.: *Futurologie, Der Kampf um die Zukunft* [The Fight for the Future]. Cologne, 1970.
Toffler, A.: *Future Shock.* New York, 1970.
Forrester, J.W.: *World Dynamics.* Cambridge, 1971.
Meadows, D. et al.: *Limits to Growth—A Report to the Club of Rome.* New York, 1972.
Bell, D.: *The Coming of the Postindustrial Society.* New York, 1973.
Jungk, R.: *Der Jahrtausendmensch* [Man and Millennium]. Munich, 1973.
Mesarovic, M. and Pestel, E.: *Menschheit am Wendepunkt* [Turning Point for Mankind]. Stuttgart, 1974.
Herrera A., Skolnik H. et al.: *Grenzen des Elends* [Limits to Misery]. Frankfurt, 1976.
Kahn H. et al.: *The Next 200 Years.* New York, 1976.
Galbraith, J.K.: *The Age of Uncertainty.* London, 1977.
Laszlo, E.: *The Goals for Mankind.* New York, 1977.
Leontief, W. et al.: *The Future of the World Economy.* New York, 1977.
Tinbergen, J.: *Reshaping the international order.* London, 1977.
OECD (Lesourne, J.): *Interfutures, Facing the Future, Mastering the Probable and Managing the Unpredictable.* Paris, 1979.
Vester, F.: *Neuland des Denkens* [New Ways of Thinking]. Stuttgart, 1980.
World Commission on Environment and Development: *Our Common Future.* Oxford, 1987.

Pestel, E.: *Jenseits der Grenzen des Wachstums* [Beyond the Limits to Growth], 2nd ed. Stuttgart, 1988.
Schwartz, P.: *The Art of the Long View.* New York, 1991.
International Commission on Peace and Food: *Uncommon Opportunities.* London, 1994.
Bell, W.: *Foundations of Futures Studies*, 2. Vols. New Brunswick, 1996.

It should be noted that with most of these studies, an interdisciplinary approach was chosen, which has led to a substantial deepening of the information base for future-oriented decisions. At the same time the range of information has been significantly expanded by a variety of issues. It has remained unresolved, however, whether, following the decisions taken so far—particularly on a macroeconomic and global level—frequently raised problems have actually been tackled, whether the problems made evident through projections have in the end really been understood correctly, or whether the developments forecast have indeed displayed the alleged negative effects.

INFORMATION AS THE BASIS FOR DECISIONS

As explained earlier, forecasts are indispensable to decision making. Accordingly, the purpose of forecasting is to contribute significantly to increasing the information base for decision making. Therefore, knowledge of the general future macroeconomic conditions can be designated as one of the most important pieces of executive information for both managers and politicians. However, as soon as we speak of forecasting, we are confronted with deeply engrained skepticism, because the only thing that can be forecast with certainty is that the forecast is wrong (cf. in Chapter 3); one only has to have the right 'nose' or the right 'knack,' which is what really makes a good entrepreneur or politician.

This so far commonly held idea has probably had its day due to the effects of the increasing complexity of the general macroeconomic conditions. We can probably also assume that, in the past, managers who were better informed made better decisions. Only those having the correct and relevant information about the environment can take the correct decisions and actions. The quality of decisions taken today depends largely on the correct assessment of the future, because the effects of decisions become evident only in the future. Corporate management requires in any event—as do governments—future-oriented information. At the same time the idea prevailed for a long time that it was important to understand future developments in as precise detail as possible in order that the right decisions be taken on the basis of such 'knowledge' of the future. The realization that *the* future cannot exist has become generally accepted with the increasing complexity of the general conditions and the use of holistic ways of thinking. It is therefore clear that we have to think in terms of various 'futures.' Normative and strategic management, which is confronted with a number of future developments, therefore has to develop instruments suitable for adjusting to these circumstances.

Therefore, only when we know the possibilities for the future (i.e., what could happen) can corporate management, politicians, and people in general make a choice between various alternatives. On the other hand, those without any idea of the future can therefore not choose what they would like to see happening, not to mention develop policies and take measures in order to make such a future come about.[18] Accordingly, the first step for creating a better future is to identify developments and trends that could happen in the future. Once these possibilities are known, we can go about bringing desired developments closer to reality and curbing or avoiding the realization of undesired processes.

Farsighted people are therefore agreed that forecasting is unavoidable in order to be able to prepare for alternative future developmental trends and events. This can be illustrated by a great number of examples of brilliant successes. Based on careful analysis of what could happen, and particularly of what could develop in the future, carefully considered strategies were developed in order to cope with situations and problems that became evident.[19] However, it should also be pointed out in this context that the actual course of events could not be forecast precisely in any of the cases (i.e., complete knowledge of the actual course of events was therefore really never available). With a carefully considered, flexible strategy, the respective margins for action could, however, be clarified and used in the end. Such successes can be clearly proven both on a political and military level and also in economic and technological environments.

Nevertheless, a forecast can by no means guarantee success. The intricacy and complexity of social processes, as well as the fact that people often do not behave rationally, can have the effect that actual development takes a different course from the projected alternatives. In the same way, the influence of other decision makers regarding the realization of their future goals can be greater than one's own, so that the future takes a different course than individually desired. Also, the lack of forward-looking thoughts does not necessarily lead to failure. Sometimes misfortune can turn careful planning on its head. Fortunate coincidences can equally well turn fools into geniuses. In most cases, however, victory belongs to those who think ahead, not to those who fail to do so.

NEED FOR A WIDE RANGE OF INFORMATION

In accordance with the breadth of the issue 'future,' decisions can be distinguished according to their importance and meaning, a differentiation that finds its expression in economics in the terms 'business cycle' and 'growth' and in business administration in the terms 'operative' and 'strategic (normative) management.' At the same time this differentiation means that for each of the processes addressed, we have to consider differences in their distances into the future, reflected in variations in the required information. With a view to a forecast, the number of assumptions that must be made also increases, and the demand for a systemic perspective becomes all the more important.

Figure 1.1
Schematic Depiction of Information from a Time Perspective

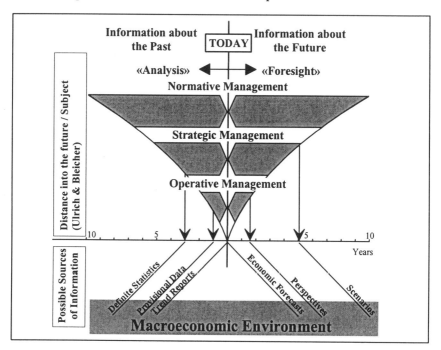

Depending on the level in the decision-making hierarchy, there are different requirements for an information system (both at the level of companies and at the
level of national economies). This means that there have to be different kinds of
forecasts of varying information depths in order to be able to provide information
adequate for decision making. For long-term basic decisions on a corporate policy
or strategic level, information about the environment is required that has a
long-term structure and focus in order to reduce the uncertainty of decisions and
to better estimate their long-term effects on the ability of companies to survive and
develop.

Figures 1.1 and 1.2 compare such an information-based concept with the 'integrated management concept' of Bleicher (Bleicher, 1996, p. 76) and show clearly
the parallelism of the two approaches. It has to be taken into account that naturally
what matters is not only forward-looking information but that the system in question also has to be positioned in its previous environment. For such a purpose, its
reactions in the past to changes in the previous environment can be investigated in
order to be able to obtain information as to the effectiveness of measures and possible effects of alternative actions. At the same time this comparison indicates that
the amount of information also has to increase with a growing time horizon (i.e.,
increasing complexity of the environment with increasing distance into the future
and subject complexity).

Figure 1.2
Interrelationships between Normative, Strategic, and Operative Management

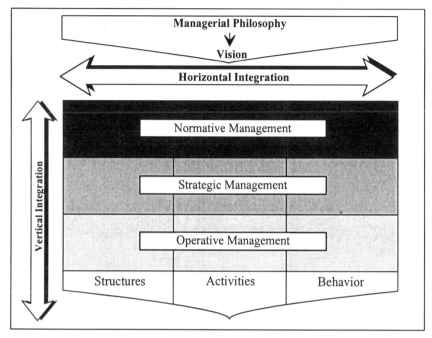

Source: Bleicher, *Konzept,* 1996, p. 76.

Finally, Figure 1.1 indicates the information that has to be drawn upon in order to answer the respective issues investigated. We can also relate the three major issues in economics to these three levels of management. While the level of normative management focuses mainly on issues of growth and evolution, strategic management pays particular attention to structural changes in the economy (Bleicher, 1996, p. 76). Finally at the operative level, the state of the economy and short-term changes in an economy's utilization of capacity (business cycle) are at the forefront. This is where the respective views of business administration and economics meet in such studies. The view of economic forecasting also has to be in keeping with that of business administration and economics.

LEVELS OF DECISION MAKING

A decision's distance into the future, as previous mentioned, is closely connected with the importance of the subject matter for an economy's or company's ability to develop. It can be assumed that the depth of required information increases with increasing distance into the future because, in the long term, the number of (structural) changes increases rapidly. So—as will be shown later—there is a rapid increase in the degree of complexity of the subject investigated and therefore

Figure 1.3
Levels of Economic Activity

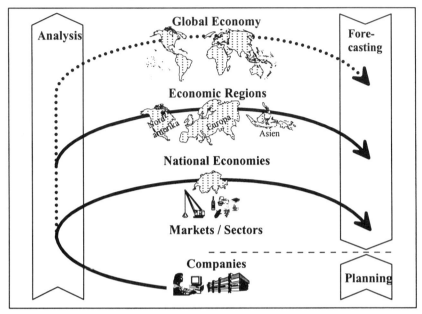

also of the decision itself. Figure 1.3 shows the various levels of economic activity, which, starting from a company, cover an ever-widening range, even extending as far as the global economy. At the operative level identification of short-term developmental trends in markets, sectors, and national economies is usually sufficient, while at the strategic level additional information at the level of global economic regions is indispensable. At the normative level, general global economic conditions have also to be taken into account so that, due to the effects of growing internationalization, sufficient information is made available for decisions having long-term effects.

In each case it has to be kept in mind that, from an economic point of view, phenomena are being investigated that definitely differ. In the normative area, the focus is mainly on issues related to growth potentials of national economies, world regions, even the global economy as a whole. The issue of a sustainable evolution of the global economic system is also considered particularly important. In contrast, the operative level deals mostly with issues of short- and medium-term fluctuations in the utilization of production capacity (of growth potential). Finally, with strategic management it is also important to take sufficiently into account changes in composition (mix of goods, range of sectors, regional breakdown, etc.).

Figure 1.3 also shows that an analysis related to the positioning of a company (national economy) within its general conditions progresses from the bottom to the top, from the specific to the general, and consequently it is also being determined during analysis what information is *relevant* for each issue. Therefore, operative issues will have a significantly 'smaller scope' than issues of normative management. In contrast, forecasting does the opposite (i.e., goes from the more general to the more specific and progresses from top to bottom in Figure 1.3).

Finally, Figure 1.3 indicates that in such a study, forecasting applies exclusively to the issue of the relevant images of development of a company's environment (i.e., strives to clarify those general conditions crucial for a company's development). Consequently, an environmental forecast forms the indispensable basis for managerial decisions. However, it is in our opinion not very useful to speak of 'corporate forecasts,' even though there have been, on various occasions, approaches referred to as 'economic forecasting' in the literature under the title 'corporate forecasting' (and also 'business forecasting') that, in the end, turned out to be budget calculations. Such attempts start from the wrong assumptions about the nature and possibilities of economic forecasting. At the corporate level it is inevitable that the planning or budgeting ideas of management regarding the future development of business are included. In such cases we consider it wrong therefore to use the term 'forecasting.' Forecasting—in our understanding—always refers to future development of a company environment: as indicated in Figure 1.3, forecasting at any rate ends at the markets/sectors level. This is where corporate planning begins.

NOTES

1. See among others, Capra, F. (*The Turning Point*), 1988, and Forrester, J.W. (*World Dynamics*), 1971.

2. Capra, *The Turning Point*.

3. Ecologists claim to have invented this way of thinking. We can go as far as saying that the failure so far to take the effects of human activities on the rest of nature into account can be regarded as an important trigger for the development of a holistic method of viewing the world. 'On the other hand, it would be wrong for ecologists to believe that they have the exclusive rights to using holistic thinking in their field of knowledge.' Ulrich, H. and Probst, G. (*Anleitung*), 1988, p. 19.

4. Ulrich and Probst, (*Anleitung*) as well as Willke, H., (*Systemtheorie*), 1991–1996.

5. Such an approach, where a company with its primary economic problems is imbedded in other environmental spheres, is part of the St. Gallen Management Model; Ulrich, H. and Krieg, W. (*Managementmodell*), 1974. Cf. also Graf, H.G., (Instrument), 1988, p. 31.

6. It has been attempted many times before (unsuccessfully) to point out this fact; cf. Kneschaurek, F. and Graf, H.G., (*Entwicklungsperspektiven*).

7. Peter Ulrich also demands an economy that is useful to life and that has to orient itself toward the needs of people; Ulrich, P. (*Wirtschaftsethik*).

8. Early warning systems within companies aim at registering such weak signals and making them available to management; cf. Krystek, U. and Müller-Stewens, G. (*Frühaufklärung*), 1993.

9. At the latest, since people started settling, virtually all human behavior has been directed toward future expectations. This is evident in all forms of investment, which are made particularly because higher earnings are expected in the future.

10. According to von Hayek, it was particularly a sense of wonder, in addition to unsatisfied wishes, that drove people to scientific research. Questions arise when a person comes

across something that is familiar. This can be a certain regularity (pattern or order) or a 'similar characteristic in otherwise different circumstances'; Hayek von, F.A. (*Muster*), 1996, p. 282. With Popper, on the other hand, all knowledge starts with a specific problem: 'Knowledge does not start with perceptions or observations rather, it starts with problems. This means that it starts with the discrepancy between knowledge and the lack of it'; Popper, K.R. (*Logik*), 1969, p. 104. Consequently, according to Popper, it is not the observation of a new pattern or the deviation from something familiar that is the cause for knowledge, but a specific problem.

11. Lendi, M. (*Nationalplanung*), 1995.

12. Regarding 'Public Choice' and the associated 'political business cycle,' cf. Gwartney, J.D. and Stroup, R.C. (*Public Choice*), 1997, p. 753.

13. Wells, H.G. (*Anticipations*) 1990 and also (*Découverte*), 1902.

14. Created in 1968 with its work for the 'Perspektivstab' of the Swiss Federal Administration; see Kneschaurek, F. and Graf, H.G. (*Entwicklungsperspektiven*)

15. Cf. the Link Model, Bodkin, R.G. et al. (*History*) 1991.

16. Cf. the approaches by Henderson.

17. Cf. Chapter 11.

18. Cf. Alice in Wonderland's statement cited by Bleicher: (*Konzept*) 'If you don't know where to go, any way will lead you there.'

19. The advantages of farsighted planning were illustrated by the example of the Kuwaiti crisis and the Desert Storm campaign; on a corporate level, cf. the Shell example; Wack, P. (Uncharted Waters), 1985, p. 73.

2

DIMENSIONS OF FORECASTING

OVERVIEW

The considerations about the corporate level discussed in the previous chapter also have their equivalents at the macroeconomic level. Here again the distance into the future of forecasts is a crucial criterion for determining the information obtained and also for the choice of approach and forecasting method. These distinctions are derivable in part from the developmental history of scientific economic forecasting. However, they are, for the most part, related to the various objectives. Short-term economic forecasting—with a forecast horizon of one to one and a half years—is faced with a relatively narrowly defined target system, which has been described by the term 'magic triangle' (full employment, price stability, foreign trade balance/exchange-rate stability).

In contrast, the target system for longer-term macroeconomic development is considerably more comprehensive and complex. It is not only economic terms that are summarized under the topmost objective of 'increase in welfare' but also, increasingly and with growing importance, other factors (e.g., preservation of resources and reduction in environmental pollution). The reason for widespread criticism of the concept of quantitative growth was (and still is today) its simplistic view. In addition, it is separated more and more from the nation-state setting by the effect of economies' growing together into a 'global economy.' From this comprehensive point of view the term 'magic hexagon' can be used, which in addition to economic policy objectives, includes 'accumulation of wealth,' 'sustainability,' and 'fair distribution' (cf. Figure 2.1). Global developmental problems and the vicious cycle of poverty and destruction of the environment therefore expand substantially the target functions of long-term forecasts compared to those of economic forecasting in terms of both time and content. An intermediate position

Figure 2.1
Objectives in Economic Policy

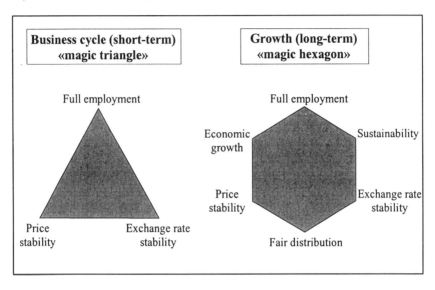

Source: Following Basseler, U., Heinrich, J., and Koch, W. (*Volkswirtschaft*), 1999, p. 34.

with respect to target functions is assumed, in a sense, by structural shifts in the developmental processes of individual economies, specific instabilities in individual economic areas, or saturation phenomena in individual markets—including their consequences for structural composition (Graf, 1988, p. 34).

THE TIME DIMENSION

Problem Situations

People are forced as mentioned previously, to make decisions in problem situations on virtually a continuous basis. Moreover, an increase in a decision's distance into the future often coincides with an increase in subject complexity, such that the degree of difficulty of a decision frequently correlates with its effect over time. Problems are easier or more difficult to access depending on the intensity of their elements and their interrelationship. In this sense Ulrich and Probst distinguish between simple, complicated, complex, and extremely complex systems and situations (Ulrich and Probst, 1988, p. 108).

Many everyday problem situations are so simple that we are practically not aware of having made a decision; if it is a simple problem, we can solve it routinely. As a rule, such a procedure leads to the expected result if we are dealing with a situation that is based on a stable structure or for which the rules of change remain constant. The knowledge necessary for making a successful decision does, however, always relate to future circumstances.

But when the information necessary for a rational decision is not easily obtained, then we face a difficult problem. This can be attributed to the fact that either the situation consists of a great number of elements that have to be taken into account or the interrelationship between the individual elements is unknown, so making it difficult to predict the effects of our behavior. Also, various possible behaviors are conceivable, so making it difficult to select the best alternative. Nonetheless, in reality there often exists a rather stable order of relationships between effects that change little, so that even in such complicated situations the actual difficulty consists of acquiring the necessary knowledge. It is therefore an information-related problem that is fundamentally solvable but requires a lot of time and effort.

However, there are certainly often situations where it remains impossible—despite all efforts—to acquire all the information required for an important decision; these are referred to as complex situations. The specific attributes of complex problems are structures with a high degree of cross-linking and processes that are highly dynamic (i.e., they change both rapidly and in varying ways, as well as at irregular intervals). In such a case it is never possible to provide complete information.

These considerations, which are borrowed from systems theory, are very suitable for application to the question at issue. As the different situations and levels of decision making outlined earlier are characterized by varying degrees of complexity, they can, therefore, from a systems theory point of view, be solved only by applying different approaches. 'Complexity depends on the composition-type of a system. This complexity is, on one hand, determined by the number and diversity of the elements and relationships that it contains. On the other, its typical dynamics (i.e., change over time) are determined by the various possible behaviors of its elements and the variability of the courses of action between the elements' (Schlange, 1995, p. 8). The combination of these characteristics and their possible expressions leads to the classification diagram in Figure 2.2.

According to our considerations on complexity, simple and complicated situations are trivial systems, while complex situations are nontrivial systems. Although this sounds like hairsplitting, it is of crucial importance for answering the question as to how to proceed when solving problems. If a situation is simple or just has a complicated structure, then we are well advised to analyze it very carefully, to carefully record the relationships of effect between all elements, and to quantify the individual factors as precisely as possible. Because the system behaves according to fixed rules, we can come up with sufficiently reliable forecasts with respect to the expected changes in the situation.

However, things are completely different when we are dealing with a complex situation (i.e., a nontrivial system). Due to the great variability over time, we will never succeed in grasping the situation exactly and forecasting precisely future circumstances at a particular time. Nonetheless, we have to make a decision if we do not want to become paralyzed. Therefore, when dealing with such situations, the general question arises as to how we should handle complexity mentally and in reality. (Ulrich and Probst, 1988, p. 109)

In following this classification, we can basically assume that, although national-level decisions with a short-term reach are as a rule complicated, they have,

Figure 2.2
Complexity of Systems

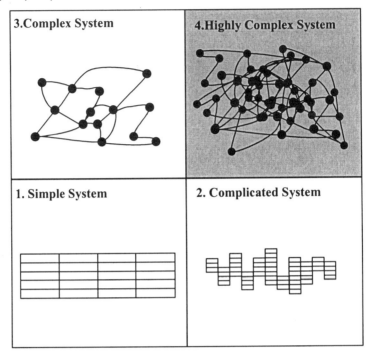

Source: Following Ulrich, H. and Probst, G. (*Anleitung*), 1988, p. 61.

however, virtually stable structures. This means that the dynamics of the system are rather limited, making it possible to develop a sufficient information base for decision making with traditional, quantifying approaches. By contrast, longer-term decisions with greater subject complexity are characterized by increasing importance of the dynamic component. Here we are ultimately dealing with highly complex issues, for which traditional instruments of knowledge are no longer sufficient, and entirely different approaches have to be followed. Kusnets[1] deduced the strict requirement in assessing forecasting approaches that fundamental relationships have to be stable in terms of time in order to be able to draw a satisfactory connection between the future and the past. Consequently, this requirement can be, at most, fulfilled partially with long-term approaches—if at all.

Previously, such highly complex situations were approached by means of simplification strategies (complexity reduction), followed by attempts to solve them with traditional quantitative methods. However, this rarely proved successful because reality could not be influenced this way, not to mention behave in such a way. Mostly only one problem was solved precisely via thought processes in each case, which had never presented itself in this form originally. Also misleading is the idea that we could first develop a simple model and solve the problem with it theoretically in order to then—through additional introduction of variables or mechanisms of effect—reach an approximation to reality. Traditional complexity reduction has to be replaced by an expanded point of view. Within the meaning of the comprehensive way of solving problems, it is essential to create internally a variety of problem-solving approaches matching the diversity found in the environment.[2] This is the only way of meeting the qualitatively entirely different characteristics of nontrivial systems.

Forecasting and Complexity

For decision-oriented information retrieval, such problem assessment proves almost vital. We can refer to a problem as trivial if we assume the following: (1) short-term economic and market forecasts have 'only' a high degree of complexity because they involve only slight changes in structure (i.e., the idea of structural constancy), (2) it is possible to obtain a sufficiently well founded basis of information for the decisions at hand, and (3) the effects of planned measures can be deduced rather precisely. This can be largely tackled with the traditional approaches of market analysis and forecasting or with economic forecasting as such. By contrast, long-term forecasting has to be included in the category of highly complex issues because of the increasing importance of process dynamics, increasingly faster and more significant structural changes, and uncertainty as to the effects of planned decisions and the behavior of the actors in the system involved. Here the traditional, quantifying approaches must fail, especially because the notion that complete information can be provided has to be excluded.

For company management this means that it has to 'master' the various requirements of trivial and nontrivial issues, respectively, through 'the interplay between complexity-decreasing stabilization and complexity-increasing change.'[3] Accordingly, other methods also have to be found for nontrivial questions, which aim mainly at achieving a comparable level of information for assessing alternative behaviors. In so doing, it will be possible to describe alternatives with considerably less clarity from the traditional point of view.

Figure 2.3 shows that the degree of predictability decreases with increasing distance into the future (Heyden, 1996, p. 93), because, on one hand, the system's stability decreases; that is, the system's dynamics, speed, and extent of change of structural components (predetermineds) become more important. On the other hand, uncertainty also increases from the outset according to the type and extent of decisions made in the future as well as their effects. Therefore, in the short term the degree of predictability is high, and so forecasting is the usual planning mode. By contrast, in the very long term the uncertainties are so great, and the stability of structural components is so small that only the 'hope principle' can be applied. In the medium term, uncertainty and the assessability of change of the structural components are such that information can be gained by working with various images of the future, that is, the creation of conceivable futures (scenarios). Referring to business cycle or market forecasts as a trivial problem may be surprising, be-

Figure 2.3
The Balance of Predictability and Uncertainty in the Business Environment

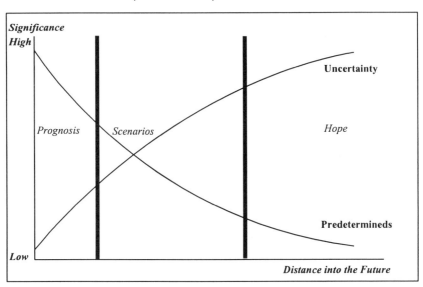

Source: Heyden (*Scenarios*), 1996, p. 92.

cause we are often dealing in such cases with larger social systems involving a multitude of people. By the same token, in the private area a decision is not made, and actions are not taken for an individual in an isolated fashion but always in connection with the decisions and actions of other people. Therefore, the term 'complexity' can certainly be used.

However: these situations are simpler because they have already been largely prestructured via decisions (legal provisions, regulations, and existing infrastructures, etc.) that are practically unchangeable during the time period of the forecast. So, ultimately we are dealing with a complicated problem that requires extensive knowledge and skill. However, these are not highly complex situations because they can be fully controlled by thought, because structural change is limited, and because successful action can most likely be taken.

In contrast, with a view to longer-term problem situations showing great dynamics or instability in their structural components, it seems imperative to depart from the term 'forecast.' This is because no longer can *just* one likely development be expected; rather due to various alternative behaviors also in the structural components, various futures are possible.

Therefore, with such longer-term, nontrivial considerations dealing with far-reaching subjects, the focus can by no means be on forecasting future events. Rather what matters is shedding light on general future conditions that are important to the problem under investigation. An image of the future, within the scope of such an approach, has to be adequate for the problem insofar as it makes evident the shunting positions for the various required resource allocations, so making possible deviation of the developmental paths. At the center of such an approach is specifically showing junctions and the prerequisites for moving safely along one or another path of development.

In accordance with the St. Gallen tradition, management should be understood as a contribution to coping with the complexity of social systems. Management wants to direct and shape the 'corporate' social system in institutional, functional, and personal terms in order to ensure its ability to develop and survive and at the same time to balance external and internal interests (Ulrich and Krieg, 1974). This is obviously a complex task, particularly because the human capacity to recognize and process structurally complicated systems is limited, especially those systems that are confronted with dynamic changes at the same time. People habitually respond to highly complex problem situations by reducing complexity (i.e., through simplification and abstraction). Such a process generally cannot be adequate for meeting objectives, considering today's general conditions for companies and human activity. In this regard management requires a switch between the reduction and increase in complexity that is adequate to each situation. While a reduction in complexity can be achieved through a managerial decision based on knowledge, an increase in complexity is a process in itself. This process must be concerned with analyzing the outside world and shaping the internal world of a company, in the course of which management itself and ultimately the entire company have to be regarded as a 'learning organization.' In so doing, with dynamics becoming an increasingly important factor in determining complexity, the interest of management has to shift from coping with structural, to process-related complexity (cf. Bleicher, 1994, p. 34ff.).

The ability to work with such approaches, to generally understand complex situations, and to behave successfully is—as experience has shown—rather limited. Here we are dealing with interference in dynamic networks. In such cases, the immediate effect aimed for, on the basis of measures taken according to the usual linear point of view, is often achieved. However, frequently, additional unexpected and undesired side effects arise that call for further interference. The reason for this circumstance is that we usually think along short, linear chains of effect, not circular networks. In this way, from the start, an image is taken of a situation as a basis for making a forecast that does not correspond to reality. This means that with an unsuitable model, even when the greatest effort is taken to provide an exact logical analysis, success is not possible. Of course, identification of this problem situation also means that for such circumstances there is no exact method for decision making in the sense of a complete program. Rather, the focus should be on a series of procedural rules that can increase the probability of finding a good solution, even though this cannot be guaranteed. Also important is not blindly following rules, as ultimately only a pattern can be shown because the specific expression of such a problem situation is always unique. Instead, the pattern developed should be constantly interpreted and filled out in our minds.[4]

Imperative of Integrating Short- and Long-Term Forecasting

As shown previously, it is important to distinguish between short- and long-term forecasting from the point of view not only of time but also of subject and space and the information required at the various levels of management. Consequently, our objectives cannot be met solely, for example, via an examination of the economic cycle phenomenon that is detached from the longer-term general conditions and developmental trends (i.e., from the level and development of capacity utilization of an economy). In the long term, short-term economic activities should also not have a damaging effect. This applies both to the microeconomic level of companies and to the economy as a whole. Thus, to coordinate individual decisions, numerous feedforward and feedback processes have to take place between the various levels of management. It is obvious also at a macroeconomic level that the cyclical vulnerability of an economy cannot be independent of the pace of growth of this country. Business cycle and growth surely are different phenomena of economic activity that have to be treated differently—especially because they have different target functions (see Figure 2.1)—however, they necessitate and influence each other.

Excursion: 'Output Gap' as an Integrated Growth Concept

A good example is the 'output gap' concept (Dornbusch and Fischer, 1990). In this concept each country's position in the business cycle is assessed on the basis of a comparison between actual economic output and the so-called potential output (cf. Figure 18.2). This should be understood as the resulting production level if all input factors were utilized to their optimum, that is, capital (machinery), labor, knowledge, and natural resources. Optimum utilization should not mean complete disappearance of unemployment, as this would have a negative effect on structural change. Also associated with this concept is a long-term path of growth along which longer-term, sustainable economic development of an economy would progress.

In such a model of thought, cyclical fluctuations lead, on one hand, to underutilization of productive capacities, that is, a gap between the actual and possible (dependent on capacity) total volumes of output, a so-called output gap. On the other hand, it may also happen that overall economic activities overshoot the path of growth in the short term, leading to the associated inflationary stimuli. To date, any positive growth rate in gross domestic product (GDP) has been interpreted as a sign of economic growth in studies of economic activity. In contrast, with the new concept, a GDP growth rate lagging behind the long-term path of growth means missed growth opportunities. Even positive growth rates in GDP can be accompanied by further widening of the gap between effective and potential economic growth. The assessment of inflationary risks is also different in this concept: only when an economy is in danger of facing capacity constraints due to excessive demand is the seed sown for rising prices.

Admittedly, it is not easy to define exactly the long-term growth potential of an economy. Usually—also at the OECD and International Monetary Fund (IMF)—the calculation of growth potential is based on a Cobb-Douglas production function with labor and capital as the production factors (Giorno, 1995). However, this approach has been shown to be implausible when compared to the actual development over the last few years. A course of economic activity where underutilization persists for five or more years could be explained only on the assumption that monetary policy has a persistently restrictive effect or that countercyclical stimuli emanate continuously from financial policy. Usually, however, such behavior cannot be observed. It is therefore questionable as to whether a development calculated in this fashion can still be regarded as a downturn in economic activity. Rather, it can be assumed that continued stagnation is mostly an expression of a structural problem. Important criteria for this are the many inflexibilities on the supply side that have markedly limited growth in capacity. On the basis of other methods of calculation, the Kiel Institute of World Economics has come to the realization that underutilization of productive capacities barely exists anymore in most industrialized countries. This means that the slowdown in output increase in industrialized countries at the beginning of the 1990s has to be interpreted as GDP moving toward alignment with its potential path. These calculations prove that the development in industrialized countries has to be interpreted as a structural and not a cyclical problem.

Nonetheless, this concept proves increasingly relevant to economic policy despite the difficulties associated with precise quantification of the long-term path of growth of an economy. This is because no country can afford any longer being too liberal with its growth opportunities with impunity at a time when competition between nations for capital investments within their territory becomes increasingly fierce. It is particularly such considerations that lead discussions in our country about deregulation and liberalization (i.e., revitalization of our national economy, mostly with a view toward sustainability in the long term). Points of discussion include site attractiveness, competitiveness of regions and entire economies, the increasing importance of a qualified workforce, and the availability of other production factors and their cost (e.g., capital). This discussion, which determines economic policy responsibilities, will ultimately have to be looked at against the background of the question of the interplay between economic activity and growth of an economy.

THE SUBJECT DIMENSION

Types of Forecasting

The differentiation between short-term forecasts, on one hand, and long-term predictions, on the other, discussed in the previous chapter, covers in addition differences from the subject point of view (i.e., the scope and depth of information). However, it is fundamentally important to also consider other types of forecasting used for various purposes. These not only have divergent objectives but are also based on various methodological approaches that ultimately also include significantly different information. However, the clearly important differentiation of forecasting according to explorative and normative approaches (from a methodological point of view) also includes definitely subject-related aspects. This also applies to differentiation according to duration, even though it seems to relate only to time.

The *explorative approach* differs from the normative approach mostly because of its 'direction of view.' With the explorative approach the view is directed from the past into the future. In contrast, the normative approach looks in the opposite direction: the view is directed from the future back into the past. Figure 2.4 illustrates these concepts graphically.

Accordingly, explorative approaches follow the traditional route of 'prognosis being simply good analysis' (Bassie, 1958); that is, the development of the variable investigated in a future time period is derived on the basis of trends and associations so far observed. In so doing, both time-series and also causal-analytical methods can be employed. With the latter, assumptions as to important variations in the exogenous variable(s) are absolutely conceivable (see Part IV for questions related to methodology).

On the basis of more or less thorough analysis of the relationships and factors determining past development, such an approach therefore investigates mostly the issue of the future trend that can be expected on the basis of *assumptions* about the development of these determinants. Such an explorative-investigative approach has given this procedure its name.

Figure 2.4
Forecasting Approaches

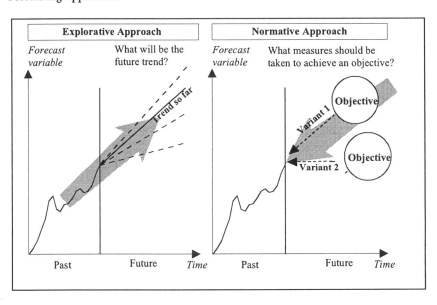

By contrast, *normative forecasting* is characterized by a view directed from the future to today's conditions and—starting from the objective of predicting one or several future conditions of the subject investigated—examines the question as to what measures have to be taken or what events have to happen in order to connect these two points in time.

Consequently, while with the explorative method the focus of interest is the issue of the final condition and path there based on certain assumptions, with the normative approach the focus is the measures that have to be taken to reach a desirable (conceivable) final condition. The normative approach is obviously very similar to the planning process. Planning can be regarded as part of the process of forecasting when the measures that have to be taken to reach specific objectives point out, at the same time, future conditions of the object of planning (Graf, 1988, pp. 35ff.). But the direction of view again differs between planning and forecasting: 'While with planning, reference to the future would have inevitably to be from the organization outwards, in future studies the orientation would be from the environment to the organization' (Shani, 1974) (also see Figures 2.7 and 2.8). Normative forecasting proceeds from an idea (norm) about the future state of development, target, or desirable vision without primarily shedding light on the path that leads, or could lead, to such an objective. Only when looking 'back' is the issue of how such a vision can be implemented in the foreground (Bleicher, 1994, pp. 503ff.).

Subject of Forecasting

Another differentiation, based on a forecast's subject matter, arises from a contents point of view. In economic forecasting it seems practical to distinguish between macroeconomic forecasting, on one hand, and market (product) forecasting, on the other (see Table 2.1). Following Figure 1.3, macroeconomic forecasting also includes the areas of information on global economics, economic regions, and individual or several national economies. Within individual economies various sectors or markets are frequently of specific (economic or trade association policy) interest, so that for such areas forecasts are often also developed based on developmental trends in superordinate areas.[5] Forecasts for such sectors of an economy can—as they often address a specific market directly—already be grouped with market forecasting. However, in most cases markets are additionally defined by product specifics or regional specialties, so that it makes sense to include these forecasts for sectors and markets at the macroeconomic level.

Real market (product) forecasts relate to company-specific issues and investigate an individual product or range of products satisfying specific needs with respect to their past and future positions in a (possibly regionally demarcated) market. Such forecasts ultimately also include considerations about competition in the respective markets (i.e., one's own market position is compared with that of relevant competitors within the scope of the actual economic context). Such information usually follows corporate planning processes directly; however, it is still

Table 2.1
Subject Areas of Economic Forecasts

Macroeconomic Forecasts	Market and Product Forecasts

• Global economy/economic regions
• National economies
  —Business cycle (labor market, prices, foreign trade)
  —Structure (adjustment processes)
  —Growth/evolution (sustainability, demographics, potentials, demand)
• Markets/Sectors
  —Food chain
  —Construction industry
  —Transportation and energy
  —Education and health
  —Distribution
	• Analysis of causal chains and mechanisms of effect
	• Forecasting on the basis of the development of general macroeconomic conditions
	• For (examples):
	  —Consumer nondurables
	  —Consumer durables
	  —Capital goods
	  —Intermediate goods
	  —Output chains
	  —Financial services
	  —Personal services

considered part of forecasting rather than actual budgeting because integration of the respective market in the general conditions has to be seen as a central element of such investigations. With this comment we would again like to draw attention to the fact that forecasts relate exclusively to the issue of the future image of the corporate (economic policy) *environment.* That is, they relate to the issue of developing those general conditions that are of crucial importance to the development of a company (economy or economic region). At any rate, actual corporate budget calculations should not be covered by the term 'forecast.' We believe that operative budgets, which to a large extent include decisions of corporate management, are not part of the forecast category because they are greatly influenced by individual actions and decisions. Therefore, particularly the issue of an individual company's future market position cannot be the subject of a forecast in the true sense of the word. Forecasts—as we understand them—always relate to the future development of a corporate (economies) environment (cf. Figure 1.3).

INTEGRATION OF VARYING POINTS OF VIEW

This categorization leads to various types of forecasting that differ significantly in terms of the information that they provide. A central issue when working with forecasts is to find out in each case the type of forecast to use and the intended forecasting information. This is because the information from different forecasts has to be used at varying levels of the decision-making hierarchy. As described later, the three differentiation criteria previously developed can be combined into a cube consisting of eight individual parts.

Let us first look only on the macroeconomic level at the classification into short-/long-term and explorative/normative approaches. Figure 2.5 shows the information provided by these four forecast subcategories. The explorative short-term forecast is a traditional economic forecast with which we attempt to predict the degree of utilization of the production factors of an economy during the following one to two years. The information provided here is: 'This is how it *will* be, if . . . !' In this case the assumptions that have to be made ('if') relate to a relatively narrow segment of macroeconomic and economic policy factors because it is assumed that the structural components are largely constant.

Basic normative attitudes can often also not be overlooked with economic forecasting. In this case the rationale behind expressing a desire (particularly by 'opinion leaders') and with it the attempt to influence economic development are based on the fact that economic activity is often guided by expectations and that the 'sociopsychological core process' (Jöhr, 1972) is largely responsible for economic fluctuations.[6] The statement of such a 'forecast' is: 'As it should be, if . . . ,' with the if relating to the expected effect of specific (political) measures taken.

At the long-term level the explorative procedure deals with various images of the future that describe conceivable possible futures with the statement: 'This is how it could be, *if . . .* !' We have particularly emphasized 'if' in this statement, as with such an approach the spectrum of assumptions has to be more extensive. Also required, in addition to the economic perspective, are demographic, social, technical, ecological, and political assumptions and at the same time, analyses.

Figure 2.5
Information Provided by Different Forecast Types

Time \ Subject	NORMATIVE	EXPLORATIVE
LONG-TERM (more than 5 years)	As it has to be!	As it could be, if ...!
SHORT-TERM (up to 1 1/2 years)	As it should be, if ...!	As it will be, (if ...)!

Ultimately, a distinctly interdisciplinary approach has to be used as the basis. In so doing, the central focus is on designing a system of assumptions that forms a consistent framework within itself and allows for the development of informative scenarios. At the same time, the fact that the composition of the system examined (its structure) is shifting requires that allowance is made for the dynamics of change. At any rate, it is particularly significant that no probability of occurrence can be allocated to the alternatives developed via this way of thinking from an objective point of view.

Finally, with longer-term normative approaches, the statement is: 'This is how it has to be!' According to this, such images of the future describe a desirable future situation (of the world, an economy, a market, a region) from a subjective point of view. Usually dispensed with here is a description of the necessary prerequisites or the path leading to such a situation. Self-contained evolutionary theories (such as that of Marx) describe a final condition of society and the economy that can be regarded as ideal from the subjective point of view of the author. There is also no shortage of such examples in the literature (Morus' *Utopia*, Plato's *Politeia*). However, such 'utopias' are also conceivable for individual economies, sectors or regions, whereby in this context the term utopia is by no means meant disparagingly but rather ultimately describes a positive vision.[7]

If we supplement these two differentiating features with the third category (i.e., the differentiation into macroeconomic and market/product forecasts), then basically a similar statement results at the market/product forecasting level as was identified earlier for the macroeconomic level. Here, macroeconomic forecasts serve—at least in part—as input variables for deriving the information necessary at the company level. Accordingly, the database provided at the macroeconomic level is used in part for processing the information base for market and product forecasts or serves as a basis for corporate policy considerations and deriving the corresponding objectives. Apart from macroeconomic information there is also other, more detailed or product-specific, relevant information that is usually no longer provided via official statistics or includes only very specific segments at the macroeconomic level. Figure 2.6 illustrates these interrelationships in three dimensions. A cube was chosen to point out, on one hand, that macroeconomic forecasts are an indispensable prerequisite for deriving information about the markets and products relevant to a company. On the other hand, macroeconomic trends arise due to individual economic results.

The purpose of the classification proposed here is to categorize existing or wanted information and to make it available in a targeted way. As set out in Chapter 1, information about the future is one of the most important pieces of executive information as long as it is used appropriately. In that regard it is imperative that adequate information be made available for each problem. Thus, for example, the use of detailed economic forecasting models for long-term issues leads to excessive planning effort and exaggerates the reliability of the forecast provided. In the same way, working with scenarios in short-term situations leads to insufficient operative planning because structural restrictions are not considered adequately.

Figure 2.6
Types of Forecasting

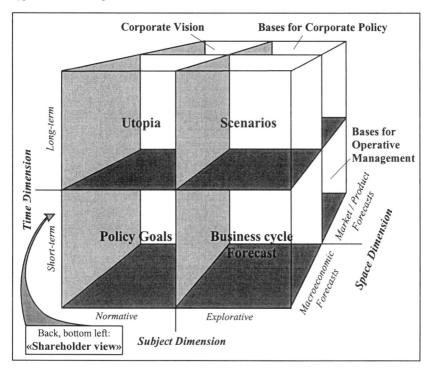

THE SPACE DIMENSION

Corporate and National Economic Perspective

Forecasts essentially always relate to the viewer's environment (i.e., a company, individual, or national economy). However, we would like to use the term 'planning' for the implementation of decisions made on the basis of such environmental forecasts. During planning, knowledge of future general conditions is converted into targeted activity and brought to completion. Here the term 'environment' should not be interpreted in the more widely used ecological sense. When looking at a company's environment from the usual business point of view the relationship between the company and its environment is described such that the company is located at the center of the relational system (Figure 2.7). There are close relationships of information exchange between a company and sales markets that make use of the company's range of services, along with less detailed relationships with business segments showing potential for the company that have not yet been opened up. Equally, on the supply side, information is required on input markets (e.g., the cost and availability of production factors) so that here also what matters are not just business segments already established. This system is sur-

Figure 2.7
Environmental Information from a Company's Point of View

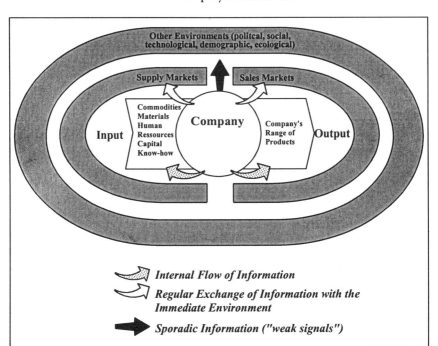

rounded by further environments that contribute, however, only quite sporadic and mostly weak information to the corporate decision-making process.

However, such a diagram gives a limited view of the actual situation. In the real world even the largest individual company represents only a small particle in a vast, multidimensional cosmos, whose development it cannot change of its own accord. From a national economic point of view, a company's environment consists of a great number of interconnected systems that influence companies via reciprocal relationships and substantially influence business development. Figure 2.8 illustrates these relationships schematically in greatly simplified form. First of all, every company is imbedded in its sector. Sectors are subsystems and constitute a national economy in their entirety. This economy is, in turn, part of the global economy. The latter included 190 sovereign states, about 6 billion inhabitants and a potential output in 2000 of approximately U.S. $ 40,000 billion. These magnitudes are summarized in Figure 2.9, which at the same time roughly shows the structure of the global economy and draws attention to the vast differences in distribution of global economic output and income in the year 1995.

The global economic system is very closely connected to other systems whose networks of relationships are equally dense, such as shown already for the economic environment. This system also refers to the ecological system, which in-

Figure 2.8
A Company in Its Environment

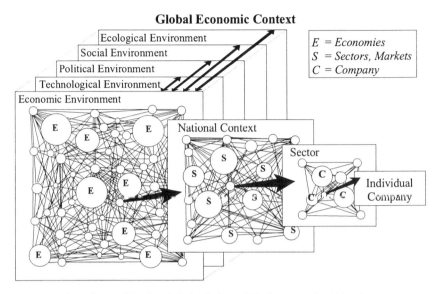

Source: Kneschaurek, F. and Graf, H.G. (*Wirtschafts- und Marktprognosen*), 1986, p. 3.

cludes the entire household of nature and so therefore the supply system of the global economy with all kinds of resources (air, water, soil, raw materials, etc.). Furthermore, it refers to the political system, showing the political structures of individual countries, the structures of trading blocs and farther-reaching integrated structures such as the European Union (EU), and their (political) relationships with one another. It also refers to the social system, which captures the positions of people as individuals and social beings in individual countries along with all their social values, norms, priorities, attitudes, and ways of behavior. Finally, it refers to the technological system, showing the scope of activities of science and technology in relation to humans living together in all its aspects and relationships. (cf. Graf, *Global Scenarios*, 2002).

From this perspective the systems view of the various levels of economic activity, shown in Figure 1.3 in its economic expressions, has to be interpreted much more widely. This is especially so because the relationships and links are as varied and tangled in the third dimension, shown in Figure 2.8, as at the economic level. It can be derived from these considerations that for an individual company and essentially also for practically all economies of the world, the focus can only be on finding one's way and maintaining one's ground in such an environment. This means adjusting optimally to the constantly and rapidly changing economic, social, ecological, political, and technological environmental conditions.

Accordingly, it is of primary importance for each corporate or economic policy decision that the environmental conditions, particularly the correct evaluation of

Figure 2.9
Global Population and GDP in 1995

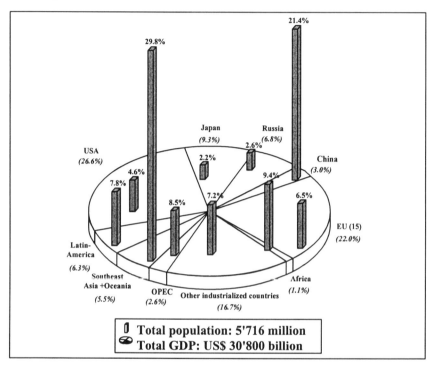

Source: UNO (*World Survey*), 1998; OECD (*Economic Outlook*), 1997, calculations by SGZZ.

future developments, be assessed correctly. In this respect deriving policy objectives at the corporate and national levels is one of the most important tasks of corporate management and governments, respectively. These objectives can be derived on the basis of information on future developmental trends in the relevant environments and the general developmental courses outlined by such information. Corporate management and governments can try to implement these objectives using the instruments available to them.

Dwindling Importance of the Nation State

We pointed out earlier that policy is aimed at shaping the future (of a company, national economy, etc.). On one hand, this concept refutes the historical determinism supported by Marx, among others, according to which every national economy reaches ultimately a predetermined final condition (i.e., ends in the condition of a communist economy). On the other, it justifies the existence of government administrations and politicians and also corporate chief executives. With the significant change in global economic structures and the accelerated speed of change at almost all levels of human activity, the demands on the imaginative powers of politicians increase, while new limitations emerge with respect to the degree to which, for example, economic policy can be shaped. The demand for more markets, which is presently also frequently uttered by politicians, is astonishing insofar as politicians limit their own room for maneuvering this way in that it is markets, no longer politics, that should drive matters.

As an example of the importance of the space dimension when looking into the future, we would like to refer to increasing internationalization. The fact that the nation-state is losing importance as a player in the economic environment can be labeled as an important result of the globalization of economic activity; that is, alliances and company networks contribute to building bridges between nations in a way that governments cannot. Most alliances have led to an increase in competition and contributed to a greater degree of consumer satisfaction. The increasingly reliable and stable network of global company networks ultimately leads to a pronounced cohesion of the global economy that is almost independent of the stability of the governments of the countries involved.[8] Nonetheless, stability is of crucial importance for maintaining the competitiveness of individual economies.

It is obvious, however, that government activities (i.e., policy) can now occur only with the market and not against the market. This is why national governments share powers with other governments, companies, international institutions, and nongovernmental organizations (NGOs). Former core functions of national governmental sovereignty at the political, social, and security policy levels are creating a new 'transgovernmental order' (Slaughter, 1997, p. 183) that can be regarded as the possible answer to the urgent international challenges of the 21st century. (Graf, 2002, pp. 69ff.) Basically, more market does not mean doing away with rules but rather removing the crusts of excessive intervention from liberal market economic principles that often rendered ineffective or limited market mechanisms.[9]

The frequently prevailing view today that the global market represses political activity or even replaces it is, however, essentially monocausal and economic in nature and reduces the multidimensionality of globalization to only one (i.e., the economic) dimension. Because of this linear way of thinking, all other dimensions—ecological, cultural, political, social, and international trends—disappear behind the dominating global economic system. This is by no means an attempt to deny or diminish the central importance of economic globalization at the corporate or macroeconomic levels. However, what tends to be overlooked is that with such an attitude, the central task of policy (i.e., to lay out the general legal, social, and economic conditions in which economic activity becomes possible and legitimate in society) disappears from view or is suppressed completely. According to this, governments would have to manage companies under an (economic) optimum criterion (Beck, 1997, p. 196).

This has led to calls for 'new rules for a new game' (Neue Zürcher Zeitung). According to these, the change to a global society would be linked inevitably to the creation of global law (i.e., international law for business as well as social, environmental, and security policy, respectively). In particular, the international competition for efficiency would have to be curbed via a global social constitution. However, these advocates of 'government' and 'control' beyond national borders have to be confronted with the fact that companies, in their own interests, certainly establish and control certain rules, without this having to be ordered by some jurisdiction or international entity.

Nevertheless, with globalization, companies have more room to maneuver, while at the same time they are subject to fewer rules. In order to make sure that this ethical vacuum does not have any negative effects, companies have to be encouraged to treat all concerned and their environment with awareness (Sorrosal and Sütterlin, 1998, p. 32).

Of the conditions named by Kant for 'perpetual peace,' the principle of cosmopolitan law, of hospitality, is surely central in this context: recognizing others as individuals and not preventing contact with foreigners as well as not misusing the right to visit. This means that a company can continue following the profit principle in order to ensure its viability in the long run. However, these abilities have to be subject to the restriction of ethically justifiable trade and so go further than just considering interested 'shareholders.'

It can be assumed that globalization (i.e., intensification of the exchange of goods and services across borders) will continue expanding considerably more rapidly than global output. With respect to the production factors, labor and capital, the thinking nowadays is less and less in terms of national borders, as the division of labor has become significantly more international. This means, that more efficient, globally available alternative ways of producing goods and services are being used more intensively.

Such a development certainly seems achievable. Long-term growth of the global economy is extremely desirable from the viewpoint of existing global economic problems—abject poverty of 20% of the world population and a lack of sustainability in development.[10] Such long-term growth will become possible when developing countries can take part in it or even become the actual driving force for global expansion. Therefore, the leadership position in global economic growth would have to alternate between different parts of the world so that ultimately the entire global economy profits from this momentum. A fallback into protectionism—particularly in Europe—cannot be excluded. However, it is likely that the Asian countries, under the leadership of China, Indonesia, the Philippines, Korea, and Vietnam, will initially remain the driving force—once they have thrown overboard the Japanese government-controlled economic model—and if they trigger the right kind of pressure on the encrusted European economies. Additional driving forces for the global economy include reaccelerating trends in Japan, an opening of the Russian market, and also actively pushing forward consolidation and expansion of the EU. The large number of cumulative trends and forces in the world that can be observed at present certainly make a long-lasting, sustainable upturn in the global economy a realistic scenario. (cf. Graf, H.G., *Global Scenarios*, 2002).

NOTES

1. Kusnets, S. (*Concepts*), 1954, p. 11.

2. Bleicher, K. (*Konzept*), 1996, p. 35, as well as Espejo, R. et al. (*Learning*), 1996, pp. 59ff., with reference to Ashby's Law of Recursive Variety (Ashby, W.R.: *An Introduction to Cybernetics*, London, 1964, pp. 206ff.), according to which only an increase in (internal) variety can absorb external variety.

3. Bleicher, K. (*Konzept*), p. 35. One of the central tasks of scenarios is to increase complexity depending on the situation, in order to be able to better understand the environment; cf. Part III.

4. In this sense the St. Gallen Management Model should be understood as an 'empty framework for meaningful things' (Ulrich/Krieg, (*Managementmodell*), 1974.)

5. Within the scope of marketing, the definition of markets and the determination of the then-realizable potentials play a central role; cf., among many others, Weinhold-Stünzi, H. (*Marketing*), 1988, pp. 65ff.

6. Cf. the chapter on business cycle forecasting in Part IV.

7. Negative utopias suggest the opposite route by showing what must not happen under any circumstances via their description of negative images of the future. Well-known examples are George Orwell's *1984* or Aldous Huxley's *Brave New World*.

8. Cf., among others, Kant, I., *Der Ewige Frieden*, (1795), in: Kant's gesammelte Schriften, Berlin, 1910; Angell, N., *The Great Illusion*, London, 1910; as well as Rosecrane, R., *The Rise of the Trading State*, New York, 1986.

9. A particularly clear example of the exceptionally explosive force of deregulatory measures is the financial markets, a sector that was completely transformed from individual job profiles through to the sector's structures.

10. Cf. United Nations Development Program (UNDP): *Human Development Report 2001*, New York, 2001.

3

EVALUATION CRITERIA

FORECASTING OBJECTIVES

Economic forecasts are very important in economic life. This is due to the frequently neglected circumstance that all decisions are oriented toward the future and still have to prove themselves with respect to developments that have open outcomes. The importance of economic forecasts can be illustrated by the following three objectives: create a basis for economic decisions that is as objective as possible by making these decisions intersubjectively retraceable, reduce areas of uncertainty by separating known from unknown developments, and decrease the danger of planning errors by disclosing economic forces and relationships.

DATABASE

The quality of the information on future developments collected for making a decision depends on two central factors: the database on which it is built and, adequate implementation with respect to the issue addressed.

Research institutes or individuals specializing in developing publicly accessible forecasts usually know the necessary empirical fundamentals or have at least sufficient knowledge of them. By contrast, this is rarely the case with many individual proposals for decision making because the necessary information is completely unavailable or available only partially or in insufficient form.

In such cases a data acquisition and adjustment phase has to precede the development of a forecast. Here, particular attention should also be paid to the quality of the data acquired, and it should also be ascertained that they address the issue adequately.[1] This is because a forecast can be only as good as the knowledge and understanding of past relationships and developments on which it is based. Even though past developments can only rarely be projected into the future, errors in perception of the past will, in any event, be transferred to an assessment of the future.

METHODOLOGY

Using a reliable database is far from being a guarantee of a reliable forecast. As a first step it is essential to structure the available data and information to prepare them in a comprehensible way. If the basic information consists mainly of qualitative data, then they should be ordered by means of heuristic procedures. For this purpose the scenario technique and Delphi method are particularly suitable. Empirical data have to be analyzed statistically.[2] The choice of a forecasting method must be guided, in any case, by the question addressed. For further details, see the dimensions of forecasts introduced in the preceding chapter. It is imperative in both cases that a methodically correct approach be used in order to obtain reliable forecasts. Only in this way can they ultimately meet the scientific criteria of reconstructability.

OBJECTIVITY OF STATEMENTS

Next it has to be checked if the objectivity criterion has been observed. The simple question that can be formulated here is: Who for whom? With respect to the question of 'who,' it needs to be resolved whether the person producing the forecast looks at a specific problem through 'special glasses,' so possibly distorting the analysis and/or forecast. This question is particularly relevant with forecasts prepared by lobbies, as their central mission is representing their specific interests, and a certain bias therefore seems possible. The accusation of biased opinions is often raised, especially in connection with basic policy discussions, which serves no purpose other than justifying already gridlocked positions.[3]

RECIPIENTS OF FORECASTS

The target audience addressed can cause the forecast producer to take a certain standpoint and also adversely affect the foundation for the viewpoint of his or her analysis (e.g., by making a one-sided selection while working out a topic scientifically). Such one-sided orientation of an analysis and forecast is, of course, highly pleasing to users of forecasts and worthy of their support, especially if the forecast meets their particular points of view. This example illustrates particularly well the problem of one-sidedness or the lack of a comprehensive deliberation. This problem can often be observed especially at the political level, because the focus is on creating an interest on the parts of voters for a specific issue and ultimately a politician's career. The issue of independence and objectivity of forecast producers is a central feature of assessment. A forecast is accepted only if it can be reconstructed (also by the opposing party), at least in terms of its structure.

IMPORTANCE OF ASSUMPTIONS

Nonetheless, distortions are still possible, even if it is assumed that a forecast meets these requirements. An informative and also authoritative assessment of forecasts is ultimately possible only on the basis of the underlying assumptions. Surely, it is also essential to check that a forecast's analytical approaches are complete; however, this can also be derived from the underlying set of assumptions. In an analysis the focus is on making apparent the structures describing the various problem areas and guiding their development. In contrast, the assumptions with respect to external ('exogenous') variables or structural changes of the system investigated determine forecasts of its future development; that is, for a 'good' forecast the assumptions also have to be stated clearly, so that the entire set of assumptions can be retraced intersubjectively and—as mentioned before—so that the issue of completeness of analysis can be checked.

The demand by forecast users to check assumptions is often confronted with the difficulty that these are rarely stated clearly, so that users are forced to dig into basic publications. This frequently creates problems for inexperienced nonprofessionals so that the most important issue of assessment, in particular, remains unfulfilled. Therefore, users frequently pick forecasts showing results that come closest to their own points of view. This method usually proves the worst, because one's own desires in particular are the least likely to occur. However, by deferring to some environmental forecast it is then possible to pass on all blame for a wrong decision; the forecast is reduced to being a mere alibi.

NOTES

1. As to the methods of empirical social research and their requirements, cf., among many others, Atteslander, P. (*Sozialforschung*), 1993, as well as Kromrey, H. (*Sozialforschung*), 1983.

2. For an overview of methods, cf. Bohley, P. (*Statistik*), 1989.

3. Often such reports are useful only as 'political ammunition' (Kirchgässner) [*Modelle*], 1997, and lack the all-so-important scientism.

4

THE DISCREPANCY BETWEEN REALITY AND FORECAST

PROBLEM WITH PERCEPTION

In principle it should be noted that assessing a forecast's quality on the basis of comparing deviations between actual and predicted developments is by no means always the appropriate or suitable inspection procedure. Such deviations can have two different causes: (1) the environmental forecast, from which corporate target figures were derived for turnover, cash flow, output, and so on, turns out to be 'wrong'; and (2) the environmental forecast was 'correct'; the deviations are due to one's own behavior or an incorrect estimate of the parameters connecting in-house figures with the environmental forecast. An example would be shifts in market share. Experience has shown that differences due to such deviation analyses—especially when the comparison is in someone's disfavor—are in most cases attributed to the 'always incorrect' environmental forecasts. This means that such comparative investigations show environmental forecasts to be effectively always wrong. Thus, a rather disturbing picture can be observed generally regarding the accuracy of forecasting that has been assigned to professional augurs. Essentially, they are accused of having produced only wrong forecasts, and should they by chance have scored a hit, this must surely have been, as with a notoriously bad shot, due more to accident than skill. This widely held belief amounts to making forecasters responsible for all of the differences between 'forecasts' and reality, while the very best that they can hope for is receiving credit for having scored a chance hit, should their forecasts have been correct. This belief is simply wrong. Not only does it misunderstand the sense and purpose of many forecasts, but it also masks two problems that users of environmental forecasts should consider more: self-destruction of a forecast and self-fulfillment.

THE PHENOMENON OF SELF-FULFILLMENT

The phenomenon of self-fulfillment applies particularly to short-term economic forecasting. Here, those inherent laws of market-oriented national economies come to light that play a dominating role in 'psychological cyclical theories' (cf. Chapter 19). Cyclical development is determined decisively by future expectations; these are based largely on subjective assessments of economic development, which in turn are strongly influenced by the prevalent economic climate at any particular time.[1] Generally known is the extent to which modern news media in particular can contribute to aggravating such waves of sentiment, especially by exaggerating negative reports. Such subjective portrayals of an economic situation are of such importance because they generate, by mass psychological means, the peculiar general agreement in terms of thinking, aspirations, feelings, and activities that drives cyclical fluctuations far beyond the scale of the disturbances that should have occurred on an objective basis. A well-known example is so-called bubbles that can develop in financial markets due to a general buildup of expectations (cf. Kindleberger, 1996).

The consequences are clear. If, for example, a setback in economic activity is forecast, and economic entities abide by this forecast, then it has every chance of being fulfilled, possibly even being 'overfulfilled.' With a forecast that predicts an acceleration in inflation, the situation is similar; if the economic entities believe in it and act accordingly, then there is the danger that the forecast will be fulfilled, even if such a development did not have to occur because of objective reasons. The anticipation of an event can generate its fulfillment. An 'inflation asked for' or a 'crisis asked for' is a long-known phenomenon in the economic history of Western industrialized countries. It should be noted, however, that conjuring up a 'good' economic situation has so far shown little success and that bringing about a 'bad' economic situation has been much more successful.

Knowledge of such phenomena has the effect that those public authorities responsible for a country's short-term economic policy always apply—depending on the situation—a bit of calculated optimism or pessimism when assessing future economic prospects in order to counter mass psychological reactions that could aggravate the situation. To a certain degree this is true even for statements made by official or pseudo-official experts. Should they be forced by irrefutable evidence to forecast a deterioration in the economic situation, their forecast still ends eventually on an optimistic and conciliatory note. After all, they do not want, and must not create, panic and so frighten away their own customers.

Of course, such a strategy can also be counterproductive, namely, in cases where companies that desperately need restructuring are driven by widespread calculated optimism to wait—full of hope but otherwise inactive—for the proclaimed better times, as if these were to arrive of their own accord and without any effort on their parts. This is a fatal fallacy that often has to be paid for with bankruptcy and that also creates problems for the lending banks according to the motto 'caught together-hanged together.' Finally, many governments already anticipate the effects of certain planned stability policy measures in their officially stated economic forecasts, which has been the case in Europe during the final half of the 1990s. This makes one understand completely the problem associated with a statistical comparison between forecast and actual development whose sole purpose is calling those forecasts deviating least from reality the best.

THE PHENOMENON OF SELF-DESTRUCTION

The phenomenon of self-destruction applies primarily to long-term forecasting, whose purpose is not so much predicting but rather showing up possible problem and danger areas. This is necessary so that those in business and politics making decisions do what is necessary to remedy or prevent such situations. The purpose of such long-term perspectives is precisely to trigger actions and plans that counteract a 'forecast' and ultimately cancel its validity. A good example are the 'educational forecasts' prepared after World War II. All of them predicted an intensifying shortage of qualified labor in the labor market; at the time there was talk of an imminent educational crisis or an increasing gap in education and training. Looking back into history, such forecasts contributed substantially to additional efforts on the part of government and private industry toward increasing the supply of qualified labor. For that reason it would be wrong to attempt assessing the quality of these forecasts on the basis of a comparison between 'predicted' and actual development.[2]

THEORY, EXPERIENCE, AND INTUITION

When assessing forecasts, the question as to whether or not they have a sufficiently theoretical foundation is considered very important. In this context it has to be emphasized that it is not compulsory that there be a connection between a theory's and a forecast's quality. Fundamentally, there are four possible cases: (1) the theory is correct and also leads to an accurate forecast; (2) the theory is correct, but the forecast based on it proves incorrect due to special influences that were not taken into account in the theory; (3) the theory is wrong, but the forecast built on it—again due to special influences—leads to the correct results; or (4) the theory is wrong and also leads to the wrong result.

It is generally assumed that by improving the theoretical foundation, the likelihood of a forecast's proving correct also increases. This agrees with both daily experiences and scientific theory, because via learning processes people are capable of constantly improving their perception of their environment and so can understand it better. Whether there is an accumulation of knowledge or whether knowledge develops in leaps is less relevant than the fact that it increases. At the same time, there is a constant increase in complexity in the environment investigated. This, in turn, puts knowledge in perspective, because additional influential factors and feedback mechanisms develop that have to be taken into account in forecasts.

However, these considerations are rooted too much in the traditional quantitative view. In particular, they are also oriented toward the idea of decimal-point accuracy of a forecast, which has to be compared with actual development. The theoretical foundation is undoubtedly a crucial prerequisite for correctly assessing the future; however, it is not the only one. In fact, a forecast's quality depends on three crucial influential factors: (1) the *theoretical* foundation, that is, the knowledge about mechanisms of effect, functional relationships, and laws of economics that influence decisively the development of the variable investigated; (2) *experience*, which determines a futures researcher's ability to apply theoretical knowledge to individual cases in hand, which will all be different; and (3) *intuition*, which again determines the forecaster's ability to recognize correctly, both intuitively and emotionally, the specific future relationships relevant to the forecast and to also shed light on alternatives. The quality of a forecast is characterized in each case by the least-represented feature. The use of only theoretical knowledge leads to sterile abstraction, which is of purely academic interest and surely does not represent a way of supporting effectively a specific forecast. Experience alone, on the other hand, leads to pragmatism (that is often smug but useless for tackling future problems because it is backward-looking), so opening the door to false interpretation. Intuition alone may make an artist's soul; however, it does not—on its own—constitute a sound basis of information for decisions. It is true that intuition plays an important part because every forecast contains judgments based on estimates, which necessarily have to be arrived at subjectively. Yet, intuitively composed judgments based on estimates alone lead to mere speculation. In combination, however, these three characteristic features trigger a synergistic effect, allowing creation of a comprehensive information base for decision making and also thinking in terms of alternatives relevant to a specific case.

NOTES

1. The economic climate isn't a product of thought, nor is it composed of views that have been thought up by individuals, although its creative process is at times accelerated by the public statement of someone who has thought or planned. It develops unconsciously in an individual or through a joint stimulus in many individuals and spreads persistently from one individual to the next, like a forest fire from tree to tree. However, it is that which is flammable in a tree that makes it possible for the fire to spread; and in the same way as green healthy trees can also die in a forest fire, the contagious effect of mass feelings also knocks over sober-minded people.

2. Numerous examples could be cited supporting this fact. A classic example was the forecast of the 'Jöhr commission'—in which a large number of today's well-known Swiss economists participated—that 'predicted' in 1965, for 1970, a massive deficit in the Swiss federal budget on the basis of specific, explicitly stated assumptions. This did not happen in 1970, and derisive laughter over the lack of accuracy of forecasts resounded throughout Switzerland. In so doing, it was overlooked in particular that—because of this forecast— measures were taken regarding the federal budget that led to an increase in income; also, spending was cut back rigorously so that such a development would not occur.

5

A COMMON LANGUAGE

FORECASTING AND PLANNING BELONG TOGETHER

We live and work in a world in which instability, insecurity, the constant danger of ever new crisislike setbacks, and the virtually boundless complexity of economic and political events have become a permanent feature of development. This requires, particularly with a long-term perspective—and the longer-term it is the less we can escape it—new methodological approaches for assessing the future. We have to depart from the idea that the economic future can—in the long term—be forecast like the weather or can at least be forecast within a certain range derivable via probability theory. It is essential, therefore, to give more thought to the future with its entire spectrum of possibilities and alternatives and to also invest more time in such a process.

To date, often not enough attention has been paid to this requirement in daily business situations. Frequently, this task is assigned to a large extent to external consultants or opinion leaders or internal staff.[1]

However, analysis of the general conditions and their future development from a structural and process point of view cannot simply be passed on to an outsider and be acquired 'ready-made,' so to speak. This is particularly so because the various scenarios to be checked ultimately have to be 'custom-made,' as the unique environment of a company (or national economy) has to be at the center. From this fact results the imperative necessity of developing such images of general conditions via a dialogue. Relevant and, in the long run, meaningful scenarios of the general conditions of a company or country can—and must—be developed in each case by including the user. In so doing, it is essential that at the same time a common language be developed between the producer and user of this information. Only through such a language can it be assured that such information is interpreted accurately and used in a targeted manner.

Even though we emphasized this fact years ago (Kneschaurek and Graf, 1986, p. 71), we continue experiencing a crisis in the conversion of future-oriented studies into economic and corporate policy decisions. Especially the integration of scenario thinking in the planning process and decision-making culture of companies proves a much greater challenge than most managers expect. This circumstance can, on one hand, be attributed to the fact that working with scenarios has to primarily fulfill efficiency criteria. On the other hand—and this is particularly significant—corporate culture has to be changed such that it is compatible with scenario thinking.

CLARIFICATION OF TERMINOLOGY

Probably the most important source of misunderstandings when working with and assessing information about the future is terminology. Usually such information is referred to as 'forecasts' without considering that there are all kinds of forecasts, each of which has a different intended message.[2]

Still to this day there is the belief in wide sections of business and public administration that it is a long-term forecast's job—in the same way as for a short-term forecast—to show the 'most probable' basic trend of the variables of interest. There is also the widely held belief that there must be such a thing as a long-term economic weather forecast, which only has to be supplemented and concretized with information as to its probability of occurring, and is therefore capable of generating 'knowledge' about the future.

However, it has to be emphasized very strongly that this prevalent conclusion is inadmissible. This is because probability theory can always be applied only to the development of a known area of experience that lies in the past. Therefore, it is not possible to transfer knowledge that was obtained through analysis of the past to an unknown future. Reality has shown that potentially exactly that function that best records past development of the variables of interest to us is the least capable of predicting the future. This case occurs particularly when the general conditions relevant to the development of forecast values change fundamentally, as in the case of 'structural setbacks' or 'wild cards,' for example.

It is obvious that an economy's development is determined decisively by the behavior of people and their underlying values. It is, at least in part, problematic even in the short term to assume constant patterns of behavior, as well as constant general structural and institutional conditions. Such a fundamental assumption can certainly not be upheld for a long-term perspective. With respect to this aspect, there is not one future that could be forecast as the most probable, but rather there are always several possible futures. Which one of them actually occurs depends essentially on the decisions made in industry and government (i.e., always on decisions that will not be made until sometime in the future).

Basically, the point about long-term forecasting is not making a prediction. Rather, it is giving thought to possible future situations and developments, partic-

ularly with a view to their economic and social consequences in order that decisions can be made that allow optimal adjustment to expected changes. It is pivotal,
therefore, that future problem areas are recognized, in order to develop in time
strategies for overcoming them and to preserve one's own chances. Consequently,
thinking in terms of alternatives (scenarios) becomes much more important over
the long term. Only in the short term can the relevant information base for such a
(short) time horizon be developed, on the basis of forecasts and traditional methodological approaches.

Another reason for misunderstandings and confusion arises from the fact that
with a long-term view short-term cyclical fluctuations have to be disregarded. In
contrast, exactly the opposite has to be done in a short-term economic study,
namely, factoring out long-term trends. These methodological principles are a
constant source of misunderstanding and misinterpretation in business applications. Consequently, with a short-term view, trend statements always appear
wrong, because it is exactly deviations from a trend that an economic forecast
wants to show. This clearly demonstrates the necessity of distinguishing unequivocally between short- and long-term forecasts.

From a short-term point of view, it is often also not possible to call into question
the issue of usefulness of other long-term trend values, determined by the confusion of changeable economic circumstances. Therefore, a growth market remains a
growth market because there is unsatisfied demand, even if a decline in sales is to
be expected in the short term due to cyclical underutilization. Depending on the
nature of an issue, it is important to use the right forecast from the vast range of
forecasting terminology in order to obtain an appropriate and targeted information base for making a decision (cf. Figure 5.1). In this context it should be noted
that there cannot be 'either/or,' only 'both/and.' Decisions, which have to be made
constantly in the short term, must not contradict the longer-term system of objectives and priorities. Therefore, the point about a decision making process always is
combining both bases of information.

Traditionally, economic forecasts and long-term developmental scenarios have
been worked on separately and published accordingly. Therefore, users of forecasts are faced with the additional problem that often even the foundations of the
two forecasts do not coincide. This means that the short-term forecast is not em-
bedded in a longer-term basic trend, making interpretation of the various forecasts
exceptionally difficult.[3] Ultimately, the question also arises at the corporate level as
to the extent that the economic environment brings in its wake medium-term repercussions, so that for this reason alone planned or budgeted figures for the short
term have to be combined with the corresponding longer term objectives of the
strategic/normative view.

Particularly at the macroeconomic level this demand should be taken into account to a large extent. It should be noted, however, that also in economic policy
either that the repercussions of long-term projects are forgotten in the short-term
view or that longer-term projects, which, for example, serve to improve an economy's infrastructure, are put into the service of economic policy. In so doing, the

Figure 5.1
The Broad Field of Prospectives

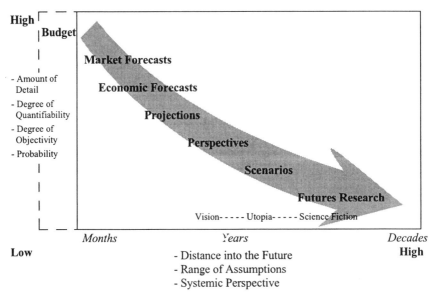

effect of improving a location's appeal in the long term is sacrificed for a short-term view. The prevalence of a short-term view can be explained, particularly at the macroeconomic level, not least by the relatively short terms of politicians in office. To them their reelection is no doubt, and understandably so, one of the most important aspects of their political activities. However, this usually gives too much weight to the short-term view.

The choice of words in association with developing information bases for future decisions is central to avoiding misunderstandings. Figure 5.1 shows the different kinds of forecasts. They result from the different assessment criteria shown alongside the graph's axes. Of particular significance is that—be it at the corporate level or in economic policy making—the persons participating in a decision-making process are aware of the kind of forecast with which they are dealing (i.e., a common language is developed initially, also with respect to terminology). It forms the basis for a common understanding in a joint decision-making situation.

INTERNAL/EXTERNAL VIEW OF A PROBLEM

In addition to the necessity of coming to an agreement on terminology, it is important to describe a viewer's location in each problem situation. We already pointed out in connection with Figures 2.7 and 2.8 that the point of view is different from a microeconomic compared to a macroeconomic perspective when studying future-oriented issues. The main difference is the direction of view, which in the case of the microeconomic perspective is from the inside out and which from the macroeconomic perspective is from the outside in. This differentiation is particularly significant because different questions result depending on the chosen visual angle, and there also has to be an entirely different focus for the 'photograph' taken. The microeconomic view uses a telescope with a narrow focus, while the macroeconomic one, by contrast, uses a wide-angle lens.

Also entirely different are the questions that need to be asked for the problem investigated. This circumstance is illustrated schematically in Table 5.1.

In the first case—the traditional perspective—we are trapped, as it were, in the system, and our interest focuses on a narrow section that is directly connected to each problem. By contrast, in the second case we jump out of our (mental) prison, so to speak, and try gaining an overview of relationships, rather than just thinking along the lines of familiar relationships. In particular, questions arising from a traditional point of view cannot be answered in a future-oriented way in the longer

Table 5.1
Internal and External View

Traditional Perspective (from inside out)	Systematic View (from outside in)
Analytical, linear, and isolating way of thinking:	Holistic, circular, and integrating way of thinking:
• More details and more precise information (market analyses, development of databases)	• What kind of a system is it? (relationships, mechanisms of effect, critical and buffering variables)
• Change in social values (lobbies, new rules and regulations, image, hedonism)	• Innovative ability (flexibility, diversity, controllability)
• What do others do? (competitive analysis, lobbyism)	• Scenarios (flows of information, dynamics of change, turnaround effects, simulations)
Modeling:	Modeling:
• Large (econometric) models	• How does the system work: relationships, feedforwards and feedbacks? (players, driving forces, active and reactive elements, self-regulation); scenarios
• Forecasts and trends (development of demand and the economy; consumer behavior)	
• Bottom up	• Top down
Type: trivial system Analogy: machine	Type: nontrivial system Analogy: ecosystem

Source: Following Ulrich, H. and Probst, G. (*Anleitung*), 1988.

term and with a view to strategic decisions. In contrast, with systemic approaches additional information is already available via the information on the effects of the relationships investigated, and so the basis for decision making is improved.

Focusing usually becomes less precise with a systemic approach; however, this does not make the entire picture less clear. The usual approach, from a traditional point of view, can certainly still be promising for areas of investigation with little dynamics or fixed structures (cf. Chapter 2). If, however, a structural change is the focus of investigation, or if—in an economy's dynamic developmental process— increased structural change has to be assumed with increasing distance into the future, then the traditional approach can no longer be promising. In such a case only a view that gains an overview from the outside can help. In this context, it has to be emphasized that the definition of the direction of view and a joint understanding between forecast producer and user regarding such issues form the imperative prerequisite for adequate interpretation of the obtained results and assurance that interpretation is not overburdened by the required decisions.

THE ISSUE OF IMPLEMENTATION

The issue of a common language (i.e., understanding the information base made available for each question to be addressed) plays a central role in the conversion of future-oriented views into economic and corporate policy decisions. The term 'implementation crisis' continues to be appropriate. We continue observing frequently an inability and, in part, a lack of willingness on the part of decision makers to include also the insights of futures research when making their own decisions. Political opportunism and reelection considerations, as well as shying away from unpopular measures, seem to make this attitude understandable, but this is not why politicians were elected, nor is it an omission on the part of managers that can be forgiven.

In an effort to solve this problem, it was attempted initially to structure problems to be solved more clearly and to so develop procedures ensuring that relevant data (i.e., the information base for imminent decisions) would constantly be tracked and available in their entirety. This idea failed exceptionally quickly due to the ultimately unmanageable degree of complexity, which is inevitable with such an endeavor. The information required for a short-term decision at a certain time may be relevant and sufficient. However, if two years later the 'same' decision had to be made, entirely different information could possibly be required for coming to a targeted decision.

The dynamics of national economic processes plays a double trick on the idea that an environmental information system can be drawn up once and for all. First, the necessary information changes by itself, and second, the relevant information for answering specific questions differs depending on the time. Therefore, a corporate information system can, in its basic structure, ultimately be understood only as a model (Schlange, 1992, pp. 206ff.). First, such a lattice must have a simple structure and be easy to communicate. Second, it must be clear and very transpar-

ent. Third, it must also be capable, via its degree of abstraction, of supporting varying situations and scientific disciplines. This means that a successful information
system can essentially 'only' give clues for structuring a problem and for organiz-
ing a process. However, its content has to be filled in differently for each particular
question. In this respect, it also sets forth the basic rules for a common language for
the problem area investigated. At the same time, this basic structure includes a di-
agnostic function that allows detailed inclusion of the latest technological advances when making available information for decision-making processes in real
life situations. These issues are discussed in detail in Part III.

NOTES

1. This would by no means be wrong if only those entrusted were not so often received,
on completion of their work, with the sentence: 'What, such an extensive expert opinion?
You must know how little time we have. Why don't you prepare a summary of the essentials,
but please no more than one to two pages!' It is self-evident that in this way the most pre-
cious parts of such studies of the future will be lost—namely the entire foundation of
thought, including all assumptions and considerations, which often cannot be expressed in
terms of numbers. What remains is, in the majority of cases, a miserable, not even complete,
skeleton of quantitative information, which as such could lead to entirely the wrong
ideas—and as a rule does exactly that.

2. Kneschaurek, F. and Graf, H.G. (*Entwicklungsperspektiven*); see also Chapter 2.

3. The demand for combining short- and long-term environmental forecasts has been
taken into account for years, for example, in the SGZZ publication 'Konjunktur &
Perspektiven' (K & P). It has also been pointed out how assumptions are connected from
short- and long-term points of view; Graf, H.G. (*Konjunktur & Perspektiven*), 1998. Most
recently, the OECD has followed this example with its publication '*Economic Outlook*,'
1999.

Part II

Long-Term Economic Forecasting

6

INVESTIGATION SUBJECT
AND AIM OF PERCEPTION

SHAPING FUTURE DEVELOPMENTS

While with a relatively short-term view—as described in part I of this book—decisions are made essentially in order to adjust to expected events, with issues having a long-term perspective the focus is much more on shaping future developments. This is facilitated by a wider margin for action—especially with a view to structural characteristics. The substantially wider field of possible changes associated with increasing distance into the future is a specific characteristic of the great complexity of such general conditions. With increasing distance into the future, they are subject, to an ever greater degree, to influences and decisions that accelerate the system's dynamics and can, at the same time, guide it into new directions.

Therefore, in the long term, an entirely different phenomenon of national economic dynamics is addressed compared to the phenomenon of changes in cyclical trends, namely, an economy's growth or longer-term development. Rather, an abstraction is made deliberately from cyclical fluctuations in the utilization of production factors, and the focus is only on the basic longer-term trends of the variables of interest. From a microeconomic point of view, normative and strategic management, on one hand, and operative management, on the other, represent two sides of the same coin. The former is oriented toward shaping a company's general conditions. Within this scope occurs the operative implementation of short-term managerial decisions 'in day-to-day business.' 'While normative and strategic management have more of a formative function, the task of operative management is to intervene in corporate development in a guiding manner' (Bleicher, 1996, p. 73). Accordingly, the term 'St. Gallen Management Model' was basically intended by Ulrich and his students only for corporate policy (i.e., for the normative and strategic dimensions). For that purpose, concept-guided implementation within the scope of operational management represents a necessary additional step of 'integrated management' (Bleicher, 1996, p. 74). However, its focus is essentially short term so that it has to be addressed within the environment of forecasting.

INFORMATION REQUIRED FOR LONG-TERM DECISIONS

As has been demonstrated, the required information inevitably differs greatly depending on the level of decision making. It is, in any case, determined by a company's attitude toward its role and behavior in society. In addition, the three levels of management are also not independent with respect to the information used: between them various feedforward and feedback processes are at play. On one hand, planning targets of a normative and strategic nature show the way for operative management. On the other, knowledge gained in the market or production, in turn, has retroactive effects on the strategic and normative levels.

These interactions also apply to economic policy, even politics in general. At the government level, analogous basic decisions have to be made relating mostly to long-term provision of infrastructure in the most general sense. The focus is on transportation and energy industries, defense, public health and education, social welfare and similar areas. Frequently, such decisions have an impact horizon of one or more generations. Therefore, due to the responsibility toward future generations, it is imperative to become clear about the consequences of such long-term decisions.

As shown in Figure 1.3, this also touches upon—both at the corporate and government levels—the space dimensions of the required information. The areas of information that need to be considered become progressively larger and wider, in both their space and subject dimensions. This means that information on the development of a company's relevant markets can be compiled meaningfully only from the much wider viewpoint of national and global economic developmental trends and perspectives.

However, good images of the future require more than just externally available information. In a company, future-oriented knowledge in the heads of employees and major contacts (especially customers) also has to be gathered via such a process and be included in the assessment of a situation. In this way, scenario thinking provides a critical mirror image of the predominant future expectations in an organization, as well as assessments deviating from it, and permits a differentiated analysis of the external areas of influence in a company's environment. In this manner, specific bases for decision making are created that are relevant for each of a company's specific issues.

Naturally, these considerations also apply to the economic policy level. Democracy has developed a host of mechanisms for including citizens in the assessment of political decisions.[1] Sound decisions require that future expectations and scenarios of possible futures are also discussed initially at the political level. That way citizens are ultimately put in a position of making, on the basis of comprehensive information, sound, long-term decisions.

THE GROWTH PHENOMENON

The term 'growth' is used to describe the longer-term economic development of an economy. When considering information on future development, the main focus is on issues related to its growth potential. It should be noted that the term 'economic growth' had basically not developed until after World War II. This is because reestablishing potential output as quickly as possible became an issue in many countries in light of the damage left behind after armed conflict. For this purpose, wartime economic production structures had to be scaled back again to 'normal' times. In the OECD region this was accompanied by a significant acceleration in industrial output. After World War II, the promotion of economic growth was also often included for the first time as an economic policy goal in national political and legal systems. In some cases it was also embodied explicitly in economic constitutions. Reconstructing the economies of Western and Eastern Europe, Japan, and East Asia, damaged severely during war, was a challenge for these countries' governments. This led to the mobilization of all their productive capacities and the greatest possible utilization of existing growth potentials. The effort toward faster growth was intensified further by the tension between East and West. It culminated in Khrushchev's 'outstripping thesis' (1958), in which he announced that by 1970 the Soviet Union would reach, and partially exceed, the economic potential of the United States. This challenge was accepted by the American president, John F. Kennedy.

FROM QUANTITATIVE GROWTH TO QUALITATIVE DEVELOPMENT

This one-sided, growth-oriented view was criticized relatively soon. With the first report to the Club of Rome on the 'Limits to Growth'[2] a virtual avalanche of books was triggered. They contained horror stories regarding the effects of economic growth on the survival of earth and humankind. Whole libraries have been filled with the threats resulting from a population explosion, excessive use of resources, and environmental problems due to climate changes and pollution, from lack of water and soil erosion all the way to dangers arising from genetic manipulations. This brought about the realization that associated with human activity is also responsibility for future generations. Therefore, decisions with long-term effects have to be made from a comprehensive perspective and cannot include only the economic dimension—which is addressed by the term 'growth.'

However, the predominance of descriptions of potential dangers made a sober discussion of the growth phenomenon more difficult. As can be observed again and again, growth-related issues definitely receive more attention in the population in bad economic and employment situations. This is because ultimately income and employment are characterized to a substantial degree by an economy's long-term growth potentials. The predominant issue in the 1970s of the usefulness of further quantitative growth concealed the real, basic, existential issue of the never completed, but rather forever continuing, long-term development of national economies and societies. This is a problem that has been discussed for thousands of years, although without using the term 'growth,' but the terms 'development' or 'evolution.' They doubtlessly express much better than the reductionist term 'economic growth' the complexity of the long-term developmental processes of an economy, which far exceed the scope of the economic dimension. For the majority of people, 'economic growth' is to this day still dominated by the concept of a purely quantitative developmental process.

It should be noted in principle that quantitative growth ultimately represents an absolutely necessary requirement for human existence. This is in order that the fundamental requirements of a growing population can be met. Consequently, refusing quantitative growth to a poor country is an arrogant and even presumptuous attitude, because it must not be questioned in the light of the most original goals of human endeavor and activity. Nonetheless, the question arises as to how these goals can be achieved as sustainably as possible.

This problem was made known in an impressive way through the controversies at the population conference in Cairo. The more prosperous an economy, the more problematic is further quantitative growth, and the more necessary becomes *qualitative* development. Only the enhanced possibilities associated with an increase in prosperity allow a shift in emphasis to qualitative development, which includes more and more phenomena of social coexistence. Such possibilities include the application of knowledge and skill, the implementation of research and development studies, and the intensification and expansion of cultural values.

Such a development finds its expression in increasing demands on the quality of manufactured goods and services, increased use of immaterial services, and a more sophisticated organization of life and one's own leisure time and finally also in more attention being paid to problems resulting from the use of nonrenewable resources and environmental pollution due to industrial production and usage of resources. In striving for qualitative and sustainable growth, the main focus is on increasing substantially the efficiencies of technical methods and processes as well as social and political relationships (cf. Schmidheiny, 1992).

These questions are frequently discussed at the ethical level: what characterizes a valuable person is 'being rather than having!' However, this well-sounding phrase conceals the fact that it is possible to be only when one has. But, this having does not represent some ever-lasting capital asset; rather, it has to be provided constantly through (one's own) efforts. Accordingly, qualitative growth by no means implies renouncing output. Rather, it is another form of further development—also of the economy—however, one that is far more efficient.

NOTES

1. For an overview of the Swiss political system cf. Fleiner-Gerster, Th. (*Staatslehre*), pp. 351ff.

2. Meadows, D. et al. (*Limits*), 1972, as well as the sequel Meadows, D. et al. (*Beyond*), 1992. For Switzerland, cf. the results of the project Neue Analysen für Wachstum und Umwelt (NAWU): 'New Analyses for Growth and the Environment' (1976); Binswanger, H.C., Geissberger, W. and Ginsburg, T. (*Wohlstandsfalle*), 1979.

7

THE EVOLUTION OF ECONOMIES

GROWTH VERSUS EVOLUTIONARY THEORIES

When discussing the development of national economies, we have to differentiate between evolutionary and growth theories. Evolutionary theories comprise a much wider horizon compared to modern growth theories developed after World War II, in terms of both methods and the information that they provide. With regard to methods, evolutionary theories start directly from observing specific developmental processes in an economy and try to find regularities or laws that can be generalized, so allowing us to derive from them indications as to future courses of development. By contrast, growth theories are limited to the analysis of economic relationships.

From the start, evolutionary theories aim at recording the national economic developmental process in all its diversity and explaining it by taking into account noneconomic influential factors of a political, social, demographic, technological, and ecological nature. This clearly goes beyond the scope of national economics, because one becomes aware that a national economy's long-term development depends on such a variety of factors that it can be understood only from a comprehensive point of view.

This applies particularly when trying to prepare meaningful corporate and economic policy analyses and scenarios for the future development of individual countries or groups of countries. They aim precisely at determining and describing the most favorable conditions for a national economy's smooth growth.[1]

From a company's point of view, it is mostly evolutionary theories that determine to a large degree management philosophy (i.e., corporate culture and the normative managerial level). Considerations relating to growth theory have an influence mostly—not least in connection with questions related to the structural development of national economies—at the level of strategic management. The operative level, on the other hand, is essentially associated with the economic cycle.

FROM 'CLOSED' TO 'OPEN' EVOLUTIONARY THEORY

Evolutionary theories have a long tradition. Their common theme is that economic development is understood as a dynamic process occurring as a sequence of developmental phases. Each of these phases is characterized by specific features, and none of them can be skipped, except at the expense of serious social and political upset and disturbances in growth. Older theories—which can be traced back to antiquity—have visions of a development that has an initial phase, no matter how it is described, and moves irrevocably toward a final phase, in which, sooner or later, all national economies come together. Marx's thesis of an inevitable development of capitalism into communism is a typical example of such a 'closed' evolutionary theory that has a definite final phase.

It is not surprising, therefore, that these theories were accused of historical determinism ('have to'). For example, Marx with his theory of the demise of capitalism and global victory of communism says that none other than all events in the world are strictly predetermined throughout. Critics of this view rightfully point out that economic development is also determined to a large degree by human expressions of will and goals set by humans for economic and political activities. Humans—so argue critics—have the freedom to determine their own fate and to effect social changes; therefore, they are capable of disentangling the future from its 'objective historical confines.'

The determinism of the early evolutionary theorists was contrasted with voluntarism ('can do'). According to this theory, the course of history escapes any predetermined and determinable law, because it depends ultimately on the thinking, behavior, and will of societies, namely, their elites, who determine history. This battle of opinion has led to a fundamental change in evolutionary history. Although its supporters continue presenting historical developmental processes, which are generalized in terms of their basic trends, they note at the same time that the specific course depends, in each case, on the dominant economic and social policy objectives.[2]

In so doing, evolutionary theorists have rung in, so to speak, the 'age of developmental scenarios' by initiating the ever-expanding method of giving thought to the future. This method precisely starts from the basic idea that the future is not predetermined by some law of nature and is therefore 'predictable' but rather that there are several possible futures. Which one of them will occur depends essentially on the policies at all relevant levels of decision making in industry and government and the values and objectives on which they are based.

Hence, the criticism of the deterministic models has prompted modern developmental theorists to more intellectual 'subtlety.' The work of W.W. Rostow has been a breakthrough in this regard. To begin with, he dispenses with developing a universal evolutionary theory that is valid for all time and concentrates deliberately on the time after the beginning of the Industrial Revolution. He shows that since then all national economies can be 'positioned' in one of the following stages of growth (Rostow, 1962, pp. 4ff.) (cf. Figure 7.1).

1. The first stage represents the 'traditional, stationary society.' It is characterized by a dominant agricultural sector, a low level of education and prosperity, low productivity and primitive technology, a fatalistic attitude oriented toward a conservative level of expectations, and a social structure determined greatly by hierarchical, feudalistic, or caste-system elements.

2. The second stage is the 'preconditions for takeoff period.' Here the economic, social, and political preconditions are created for the transition from a stationary to a dynamic national economy.[3]

3. The third stage is the 'takeoff society.' Once the preconditions for the transition to a dynamic society are in place, it can take off like a jet from a runway toward rapid independent growth. This stage is characterized not only by ever-increasing numbers of dynamic entrepreneurs prepared to take risks, but also by an increasingly achievement-driven workforce. It is also characterized by the emergence of personalities in political life who are willing to acknowledge modernization of the economy as a major economic policy goal and to also implement it.

Figure 7.1
Possible Developmental Profiles of a National Economy

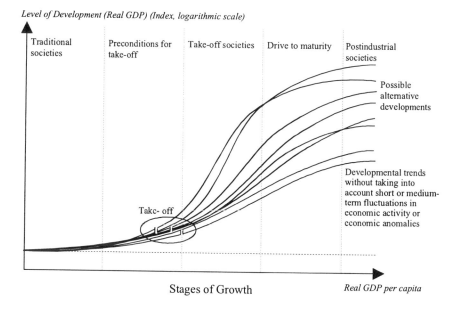

Level of Development (Real GDP) (Index, logarithmic scale)

Traditional societies | Preconditions for take-off | Take-off societies | Drive to maturity | Postindustrial societies

Possible alternative developments

Developmental trends without taking into account short or medium-term fluctuations in economic activity or economic anomalies

Take-off

Stages of Growth   *Real GDP per capita*

Source: Following Rostow, W.W. (*Stages*), 1962, p. 9.

4. The final stage is the 'drive to maturity.' Takeoff is followed by a longer phase of rapid, but not necessarily disturbance-free, growth. Yet, during this stage general prosperity will rise substantially, and wide sections of the population will have a better and ample supply of goods and services of all kinds. However, this economic growth will slow down again over time, namely, to the same degree as the economy approaches its stage of maturity. This stage is characterized by great and widespread prosperity, a population amply supplied with goods of all kinds, a relatively balanced spread of income, a high level of production efficiency, a high level of education and training, and a highly developed infrastructure, including social services. As has been mentioned previously, Rostow's theory of growth does not have a 'final stage,' that will be reached by all countries, in order to stay there forever. Rather, Rostow outlines three equally possible forms of development for a mature economy:

- Development into a mass-consumption society according to the U.S. pattern that strives for the greatest possible degree of satisfaction of individual need of a mostly material nature.

- Development into a welfare state, in which common social goals are given priority over the objective of the greatest possible satisfaction of the need of the individual (e.g., Sweden).

- Development toward increased stature and power of a nation, in which the ambitions of those in power for (world) political influence are the dominant feature (e.g., Germany under Hitler).

Which course of development an economy will take is, following Rostow, a matter of the prevailing social and economic priorities in each case. This means, at the same time, that with a change in such priorities (either through a democratic expression of will or via a totalitarian decision), a society can depart from its prior course and change over to another.

EVOLUTIONARY THEORIES IN A MORE RECENT ENVIRONMENT

Rostow's theory is also not fundamentally challenged by the fact that a certain mixing of elements of various stages of growth can presently be observed in a number of developing countries. It can claim to be generally applicable insofar as no country can accelerate its process of development at will, skip one or several stages of the described developmental sequences, or restrict itself to one-sided promotion of economic growth by neglecting sociopolitical requirements. In particular, experiences in developing countries have shown that too much mixing of elements from several stages of growth intensifies enormously social and domestic political tensions and counteracts organized economic growth.

It should be added that at present a development is taking place in the old industrialized countries, away from industrial societies to 'postindustrial societies,' in whatever way they may be defined, where the industrial sector is no longer dominant. We are presently in a phase in which society is being transformed fundamentally in terms of its view of the world, its values and social and political structures, its art and its central institutions. This transformation is in the process of forming a postcapitalist society.[4] During this process, the central factors of capitalist society, labor and capital, are increasingly being replaced by knowledge. This does not primarily consist of isolated individual knowledge but rather collective knowledge that relates to both thematic areas and the courses and handling of processes.[5]

Part of these forms of knowledge is also the methods and approaches of futures research. As has been demonstrated, neither is there one future, nor can it be forecast with certainty. Nonetheless, there are ways of creating images of 'futures.' In so doing, similar transitional problems arise as described by Rostow for the transition from primary to secondary societies. This is because ongoing development also requires not only economic structural change—although this is already associated with difficult problems of adjustment—but additionally a comprehensive change in the motivation for economic and social behavior. Furthermore, there needs to be a change in the political-institutional structures and particularly the relationships of the individual to society and government.

In addition to ecological challenges, the relationship between the industrial society and risk management makes imperative a more thorough analysis of the consequences of industrialization and possible approaches for handling them.[6] Of central importance to the development of humankind are dealing with the future in a targeted manner and the ability to make developmental expectations the basis for specific decisions.[7] Future developments are uncertain and consequently filled with risk with respect to their final form. These risks can be assessed only if we succeed in creating images of the future. The term 'risk,' which is closely associated with future developments, has its roots in the old Italian word risicare and means 'daring something.' In this sense, risk means making a selection, not fate (Bernstein, 1996, p. 8). Accordingly, dealing with the future correctly presupposes decisions in the light of one's own expectations.

WAVES OF GROWTH

As Rostow's theoretical considerations have shown, a secular trend is assumed for the evolution of national economies. For countries with market economies, this trend has an S-shape and characterizes at the same time the development from a predominantly agriculturally oriented primary society, via an industrial society, to a postindustrial (service) society. Empirical studies have shown, however, that this secular trend is not linear and also not continuous. Rather, the long-term development of an economy is characterized by a succession of phases of rapid, at times pronounced growth and phases of declining growth dynamics, sometimes even negative growth. These waves of growth extend over decades. Figure 7.2 shows that in Switzerland a slowdown in the speed of development has already been observed three times since the beginning of its industrialization. This phenomenon can also be observed in other countries and has led to the theory of waves of growth.

This theory is closely connected with the names N. Kondratieff and Josef Schumpeter.[8] So, economic growth is not a continuous process; rather it pro-

Figure 7.2
Developmental Phases of the Swiss Economy

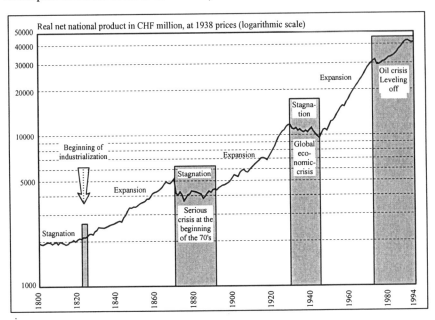

Source: Kneschaurek, F. and Graf, H.G. (*Wirtschafts- und Marktprognosen*), 1986, p. 129.

gresses in waves, as a succession of longer-term phases of rapid economic development. Empirical investigations of this phenomenon have shown that we are not
actually dealing with undulation and that a better term would be step-by-step development, in which several S-shaped growth curves are linked together. In addition, these investigations have shown clearly that there is no regularity with respect
to the duration and intensity of individual developmental phases. Furthermore,
considerable differences can be observed between countries due to the fact that the
process of industrialization started at different times.

The causes for these waves of growth have been investigated frequently.[9] The
main focus has been on an explanation based on surges of innovation, whereby innovation is understood not only as the introduction and commercial exploitation
of new products and manufacturing procedures but also as the development and
offering of new solutions to problems (for already known goods). In fact, introduction of innovations into the market can be observed to occur in concentrated
time periods. However, retroactive economic effects will not result until the actual
diffusion process (i.e., when these innovations are used increasingly widely in the
economic process). The fact that diffusion—with relatively continuous innovative
activities—ultimately occurs within a narrow time span is determined mostly by
the degree of freedom in an economic system.[10] Accordingly, surges in growth develop especially when there is a particularly wide scope of freedom for entrepre-

neurs to develop their initiatives. From this follows the question as to why times of especially liberal orientation are always succeeded by times of excessive government intervention. This circumstance has been explained by the fact that economic liberalism also makes possible undesirable developments (i.e., misuse of this freedom).[11] Microelectronics, genetic biology, and telecommunication technology all have a pronounced potential for development. However, freedom is evidently so limited in companies, particularly in Europe, that it presently does not lead to an actual qualitative surge in development (i.e., an increase in efficiency). This is in stark contrast to the United States, where virtual growth euphoria could be observed during the whole of the last decade, abating, however, in the new one.

NOTES

1. For an overview on growth models cf. Walter, H. (*Wachstums- und Entwicklungstheorie*), 1983, as well as Oppenländer, K. H. (*Wachstumspolitik*), 1988.

2. Cf. Kennedy, P. M. (*Rise and Fall*), 1987. He illustrates the importance of basic social attitudes to the developmental processes of countries and nations.

3. For this transition the following *economic preconditions* are mentioned: an increase in the rate of investment (initially by drawing on foreign capital), an expansion in infrastructure (transportation and energy industries, education and public health, etc.), and a rapid increase in the productivity of agriculture, in order to release the material means and human resources for industrialization. A general change in values is mentioned as the *social precondition*, where the belief in progress, striving for earnings, and motivation for achievement replace the previously dominant values determined by traditionalism and fatalism. As the *political precondition*, Rostow mentions establishment of a strong nation-state whose elite gives increasing priority to developmental policy objectives. Political power should no longer be used primarily for the enrichment of minorities in power or for implementing noneconomic, mostly political and military goals. Rather, it should be used for promoting economic development and general welfare (priority of economic policy goals).

4. Drucker, P.E. (*Post-Capitalist Society*), 1993, p. 1. Similar transformations took place in the 13th century with the development of cities and trade. In the 15th century the Renaissance was rung in by the invention of the printing press and the Reformation. In the 18th century Enlightenment and the American and French Revolutions gave rise to burgeois societies as well as their industrializations.

5. Cf., Graf, H.G. (Sektor), Frankfurt, 2002, pp. 31ff.

6. Cf., among others, Beck, U. (*Risikogesellschaft*), 1986, Königswieser, R. et al. (*Risiko-Dialog*), 1996.

7. Cf., Bernstein: 'The revolutionary idea that defines the boundary between modern times and the past is the mastery of risk: the notion that the future is more than a whim of the gods and that men and women are not passive before nature.' Bernstein, P. (*Risk*), 1996, p. 1.

8. Kondratieff, N. (*Lange Wellen*), 1926, Schumpeter, J.A. (*Entwicklung*), 1988.

9. For an overview, cf. Kneschaurek, F. (*Volkswirtschaft*), 1996, pp. 131ff.

10. Cf., Alesina, A., Roubini, N., and Cohen, G.D. (*Political Cycles*) 1997, Brunetti, A. (*Politics*), 1997.

11. Cf., Kramer, E.A. (Wirtschaftsrecht) 1997, Meier-Schatz, Ch. (Wirtschaftsrecht), 1982. For an overview on Swiss economic law, cf. Vallender, K.A. (*Wirtschaftsfreiheit*), 1995.

8

IMPOSSIBILITY OF
(LONG-TERM) FORECASTING

FUNDAMENTAL PROBLEMS WITH FORECASTING

With a view to the information bases required for making decisions that prevail in the long run, the term 'forecast' provides an inaccurate image of the problem to be solved. This is because in doing so, the focus cannot be on forecasting a probable event or development. Rather, it has to be on creating various possible images of the future, to each of which has to be assigned the same probability of occurrence. Therefore, when dealing with long-term future issues, we come across two problem areas: the phenomenon 'future' with all its uncertainties and a reality that is interconnected, to a high degree, both with the inside and outside and—due to the dynamics of change—shows a high degree of complexity. Future problems are always also burdened by a time factor (i.e., the uncertainty of the future and changes with time, including varying speeds of change). Therefore, the causes for the complexity of an issue or problem are cross-linking and the time factor.

The increase in complexity that a company's or government institution's management is presently faced with is not only limited to the issue of increasing internationalization of the division of labor and competition in increasingly global markets. In addition there are—as illustrated in Figure 2.7—social, technological, ecological, and political changes and circumstances that increase the difficulty of the decisions to be coped with. 'Topics such as large-scale technologies, environmental destruction, etc., become political issues and legal conditions' (Bleicher, 1996, p. 30).

Systems analysis presents itself for analyzing and understanding complex issues. With its help one tries to describe cross-linking as a systems relationship. Here the system is an entirety of elements that are interrelated. The more elements that relate to each other, the more complex the system. A system reaches its highest degree of complexity when it shows, at the same time, a great number of dynamic changes. The system itself has internal and external relationships. In part they are of a scientific causal nature and in part due to social reasons. In the first case they can be determined and proven and are given in the way that they occur in nature. By contrast, social conditions are difficult to describe, because they are not governed by natural laws. They exist in many forms and are in part even related to values.[1]

REDUCTION IN COMPLEXITY?

As the dynamics of such a system makes analysis more difficult, the system is often regarded as a given and then investigated. However, in order to make allowances for the system's dynamics, comprehensive systems analysis has to include a time axis. The attempt to disregard the system's dynamics leads to insufficient capacity when coping with a problem and the wrong orientation. In such a case, structures of the past, determined by a different set of values, would be used as a basis, which would be in conflict with the changes expected in the future. At the same time, systems dynamics results in dealing with highly complex problems, because the decisions that have to be made usually also show an effect in other system environments. The characteristic of highly complex systems is that they can assume a great number of different conditions during a certain time period, which can lead to various possible behaviors that are hard to predict (i.e., uncertain). This makes their control by humans exceptionally more difficult. Decision makers, who think and act in a purpose-oriented way, often have difficulties in dealing with such systems, because the assumption that a measure will certainly lead to a specific result does not apply.

The traditional idea regarding the control of complexity in social systems also becomes apparent in the approach to problem solving, which ultimately forms the basis for thinking in terms of forecasts for coping with the future. This approach includes seven steps for finding sense- and purpose-oriented solutions:

1. The problem is finally defined on the basis of the available specialized knowledge.
2. Problems that are too big are broken down into partial problems.
3. For each problem the specific determinants are looked for, and key factors are determined.
4. Precisely defined problems are solved one by one.
5. One problem is completed, including its solution.
6. Inadequate solutions are explained by insufficient data.
7. The acceptance of solutions is ensured on the basis of scientific standards.

Ultimately, such an approach is an attempt to reduce complexity by switching off the relationships between the system's individual elements and by screening out time dynamics. Ignored are changes in the influence of individual problems within the systemic context. Such a simplification strategy is rarely successful because we behave as though we are really dealing with a simple situation that can be controlled fully by logical thought. This is because reality cannot be influenced in such a way. As has been mentioned before, frequently only a single problem is being solved using such an approach, which never even existed originally in the form in which it was dealt with (Ulrich and Probst, 1988, p. 110).

Such reduction in complexity can be achieved within a company by systemic division of labor and individual/professional specialization. This way, the complexity induced by the outside will be reduced internally. In companies complexity buildup has led to analogous developments in their organizational structures and internal accounting. Both aspects demonstrate that it is necessary to adjust structures and information.[2] However, internally there is an additional complication that triggers additional coordination and integration-related tasks for management. 'It is not surprising that it is being attempted today in various ways to avoid the negative consequences of excessive division of labor and specialization. This is done by attempts to increase the scope of duties through expansion and enrichment of work, by dismantling hierarchies, and by programs that strengthen 'corporate identity' (Bleicher, 1996, p. 33).

PREREQUISITES FOR 'SURE' FORECASTS

Due to these reasons, it is ultimately impossible to make sound forecasts as to social and economic developmental processes. According to Fulda, Härter, and Lenk,[3] at least four prerequisites have to be fulfilled for reaching a sound perception of the future:

1. The observed events occur according to, and only to, deterministic laws.
2. These laws are fully known when preparing the forecast.
3. Individual data for describing the forecast subject are observable and can be compatibly assigned to the laws in question.
4. These data are known when preparing the forecast; they are in fact assigned correctly to these laws.

Therefore, the focus, on one hand, is on theoretical problems (points 1 and 3) and, on the other, problems associated with data, which relate both to the forecast subject and to its characteristics and the level of knowledge of the forecaster. In any event, fulfilling all four minimum requirements is impossible in reality—particularly with a view to longer-term forecasts. Therefore, 'sound forecasts' for the long term that reflect accurately and completely the information required for making a decision remain ultimately impossible. This fact cannot be doubted, first, because with long-term economic issues we are dealing with a dynamic and highly complex situation and, therefore, it is not possible in such an extensively cross-linked environment to develop theories that can meet the required great demand of both general applicability and provision of information, and second, because it has to be excluded that complete information can be acquired, in the sense of scientific evidence, for all system relationships and interdependent directions of effect and strength.

In addition to the problem with theory and data, it is important to take into account the indeterminateness of the processes in open systems. These will essentially always be encountered in economic and social areas. In such a context, causes and effects can hardly be determined definitively because the various feedforward and feedback processes cannot definitively be determined.[4] From this fact it follows simultaneously that developing systems show various instabilities, so that both abrupt changes in direction and actual tip-over effects of systems can be observed. They can also not be recognized on the basis of thorough analyses of prior developmental trends, as they have not occurred previously.

This means that cause-and-effect relationships can no longer be dealt with as linear phenomena that are limited to two dimensions. Rather, they have to be looked at as part of the causal structure of the overall view of the subject of investigation, in which each observable effect can be attributed to a great number of causes. This will, in turn, precipitate effects on an equally large number of other variables. According to Forrester (Forrester, 1971, p. 55), such networks can behave counterintuitively (i.e., they develop in a different way than would be expected from an intuitive assessment). The consequence are discontinuities, structural setbacks or erratic individual events that are exactly the ones that are not predictable.[5]

CHANGING STRUCTURES

There is also another circumstance. We have already pointed out that with a view to understanding future events, in the sense of a forecast, the focus always has to be on finding causal or key factors that determine decisively the system observed. Then, assumptions have to be made as to how these exogenous variables develop in order to be able to derive a forecast for the subject investigated. There are three fundamental prerequisites for being able to prepare a forecast for such a system: (1) The structure of the subject investigated remains the same or changes according to a predetermined, unchangeable pattern (structural identity), (i.e., the structures of the subject investigated are identical at the time of observation and in the future); (2) accordingly, this prerequisite implies that such a system is stable over time (i.e., demographic aging processes, for example, are not relevant); (3) the system is described conclusively (i.e., no third variables become effective that would be able to disturb the previously valid key relationships). Now it is obvious that these prerequisites can surely only be observed in social and economic systems in exceptional cases and at most for short periods of time.[6] Even in the short term, stable patterns of behavior, as well as stable structural and general institutional conditions, cannot always be assumed; such a fundamental assumption can definitely not be upheld with a long-term view. This means that with a long-term view there cannot be *one* future for social and economic systems that could be forecast as the most likely one. Rather, several possible futures have to always be expected because it can be excluded that the prerequisites listed in the previous section for a forecast could really be guaranteed entirely and conclusively.

FROM A SURE FUTURE TO CHOOSING BETWEEN ALTERNATIVES

This proves that it is exceptionally difficult to provide unequivocally information for shaping, for example, longer-term economic policy. This is because it is neither known exactly which specific subject-related information is required nor clear which parts of an economy's environment require elucidation, especially because such environments show great developmental dynamics. In the end this means none other than that the classic idea of providing a conclusive, complete set of information for long-term decisions will prove quite unfeasible, be it at the company or national economic level.

Rather, the focus should be on understanding the subject investigated as a system, with its various internal and external relationships, without ever being able to clarify all interactions. Therefore, the central issue is the fact that it is not important to know all the details. Rather a path should be followed that is as comprehensive as possible (i.e., excels in keeping track of the whole system in each case—cf. Senge, 1993). Such an image may be less sharp compared to conventional detailed investigations and quantification procedures. However, the mechanism can be visualized much more clearly this way than could ever be possible by trying one's hand at a useless analysis, no matter how detailed. As has been emphasized, a long-term forecast is not possible; what matters with a longer-term view is to think in alternatives. A decision always has to be understood as a 'choice' between such alternatives, not as the 'correct' decision on the basis of 'knowledge of the future,' which nobody can obtain.

NOTES

1. Within the scope of scientific theory this circumstance has led to the fundamental debate as to whether scientific methods and procedures can be applied to social science at all. This resulted in the central demand that value judgments and personal beliefs should be clearly defined as such and be separated from scientific statements. Cf. Riklin, A. (Wissenschaft), 1987, pp. 9ff., containing numerous references.

2. Cf. Walter-Busch, E. (*Organisationstheorien*), 1996, pp. 93ff., as well as Johnson, T.H. and Kaplan R.S. (*Relevance*), 1987. pp. 19ff.

3. Fulda, E., Härter, M. and Lenk, H. (Prognoseprobleme), 1989, p. 1639.

4. Such circumstances resemble the famous chicken-and-egg situation.

5. This applies both to individual events and to social development as a whole; cf. Galbraith, J.K. (*Uncertainty*), 1977.

6. An impressive example is the presently occurring upheavals both in the economic area and in society.

9

MACROECONOMIC PERSPECTIVES

PRELIMINARY REMARKS

As shown in the previous chapter, it is difficult in many cases, if not impossible, to make a forecast for longerterm developments in the classic sense (i.e., a statement like 'this is how it will be'). Very brief descriptions are given in the following section of the methods used for such developments, including their specific strengths and weaknesses. This is because longer-term scenarios cannot be created only in our minds; they also have to be quantified. At any rate, adequate methodological approaches are required for the development of qualified alternative futures that ensure the necessary consistency in these scenario images. We would like to concentrate on explaining the approaches for working out the potential development of general macroeconomic conditions. It is essential to make apparent the connecting points with the environment of the economic level in order to be able to show the influences of other areas (i.e., social, political, demographic, or ecological) on economic development.

PRODUCTIVITY AND TECHNOLOGICAL PROGRESS

The development of productivity as an expression of technological progress plays a key role when working out macroeconomic scenarios for the assessment of future economic development, structural change, or employment. It basically represents the relationship between output and input and shows how efficiently the production factors are being employed. While in the original theories land was the sole source of production, labor also gained importance in economic theory with industrialization. Not until later was the role of capital realized and included in explanations of economic development. Even later was it supplemented by the role of technological advances and knowledge. Thus, in the United States, widespread implementation of information and communication technologies is presently being used as an argument in the controversial discussion on increasing productivity. Proponents of this thesis argue that the increases in productivity are responsible for the great increase in stock market values and allow a more expansive monetary policy than has been exercised earlier.[1]

Today the discussion of productivity and its development focuses mainly on the competition between the production factors labor and capital, or how their relationship is determined by technological advances, on one hand, and increased training and education, on the other. However, it should not be overlooked that, in doing so, the general legal and social conditions play a central role. They also determine the attractiveness of a location in international competition. In this context it should be noted that capital still is a more mobile factor than labor.

PRODUCTIVITY AND ECONOMIC GROWTH

The following questions are at the forefront when discussing the 'growth' phenomenon and studying the evolution of a national economy:

- How large is the possible output of goods and services when utilizing fully the available factors of production (orientation on potential output)?
- How large is the actual demand for output of goods and services?
- Why is there no demand for the actually possible output and why is part of the production factors, particularly labor, not being utilized? What are the causes?
- What is growth of potential output itself based on?

The economic system as a social subsystem is determined decisively by the general social and legal conditions. These are supplemented by factors from economic, ecological, and technical areas. When deriving models and forecasts, an abstraction is made from these general conditions: and a narrowing down takes place in favor of quantifiable factors (Walter, 1983, pp. 3ff.).

The starting point for the following considerations is the potential output (P^*) of a national economy, that is, its total output when utilizing fully all available factors of production (= full employment). It is determined by the following basic factors: potentially deployable labor (L^*), potentially usable real capital (C^*) (infrastructure, production facilities), and state of knowledge (K^*), particularly in professional training, science, and research as well as applied technologies.

$$P^* = f(L^*, C^*, K^*)$$

Potential output is the product of a supply-oriented view of growth. It orients itself on an operational production function, which forms the basis for numerous (neo-classical) growth models. At the center of these considerations are balanced ('steady state') growth and its preconditions (cf. Walter, 1983, pp. 32ff.).

However, usually there is not sufficient demand for the entire potential output, only for part of it. Actual output (O) depends on actual demand (D), which, in turn, is determined greatly by individual assessments (A). The latter, on the other hand, depend greatly on individual (future) expectations.

$$O = f(D, A)$$

The difference between potential and actual output is the so-called output gap (OG) (cf. Part I, Chapter 2). The more agreement there is between supply and demand, the smaller the gap. While with a short-term view future expectations are mostly the determining factor (business cycle), with a longer-term view it is mostly the structure of the economic system (S*) and its general conditions. The latter determine the operative regulatory environment for the ongoing adjustment processes (structural change) and are responsible for more or less severe frictions. The following equation presents this relationship schematically:

$$OG = P^* - O = f(E, SP^*, S^*)$$

The sociopolitical system (SP*) sets the general economic, social, and political conditions for the growth process. It is determined, in relation to growth, by the prevalent economic and social structures, the target system, and the priorities during economic and social governmental interventions, as well as economic points of view (performance orientation, work motivation, etc.). Finally, the environmental system (E) has to be considered, which also includes an economy's supply system with the necessary resources.

In the long term, economic growth is determined by the development of potential output. This, in turn, depends on the production factors employed and their optimum combination. In this context, changes in production structure are caused by changes in the structure of demand (e.g., consumption habits) and by competition between suppliers. In accordance with its open definition, the concept of productivity can also be applied to the individual factors of production: land, labor, and capital.

In modern industrial societies labor and capital are mostly the decisive factors. Both are continuously expanded and changed by technical progress and the availability of new knowledge. Productivity in its entirety can be regarded as a reservoir for the various influences on the production process, that is, as an interconnected system of effect (Sombart, 1960, pp. 148ff.). While in the short term, input of individual factors can be increased, it is the development of productivity that counts in the long term.[2]

PRODUCTIVITY OF LABOR

Due to the limited comparability and availability of statistical data, the study of productivity is usually limited to labor as the only factor of production. Productivity of labor is defined in national income accounting as 'output per unit of labor input at prices of a specific base year.'[3] Output is the balance of a sector's production account and is, in the case of an entire economy, equivalent to the gross domestic product (GDP). Output is related to the volume of labor deployed, whereby various reference figures are possible.[4]

Applied to the production factor labor, the general production function is

$$P^* = L^* * P^*/L^*$$

where P^* stands for potential output, L^* for volume of labor and P^*/L^* for productivity of labor (cf. Kneschaurek, 1996, pp. 121f.).

Productivity of labor reflects the qualitative characteristics of labor and depends on the conditions of production. In particular, an increase/decrease in productivity of labor can be attributed to the following changes, whereby it is important to take into account the close connection between several of these factors (Figure 9.1).

From a business administration point of view, productivity of labor can also be applied to the productivity of an individual employee or position. This is of interest particularly when observing investments and optimizing operational processes. Usually, it can be assumed that productivity of labor can be accelerated significantly only through longer-term investments.

PRODUCTIVITY OF CAPITAL

Productivity of capital means—analogously to productivity of labor—how much output can be generated with a certain input of capital. The amount and type

Figure 9.1
Factors Determining Productivity of Labor (Output per Employed Person)

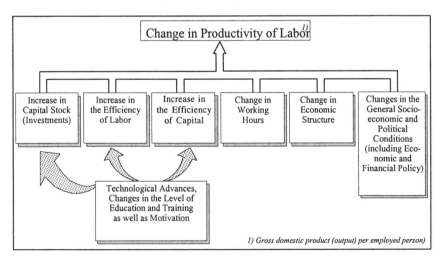

of capital input depend heavily on the corporate structure in each case. From this point of view, capital is understood in a comprehensive sense as the sum of all assets (buildings, machinery and equipment, patents and licenses) used for production. The factors determining productivity of capital are: degree of utilization and useful life of machinery and equipment; composition of capital; average age of equipment; degree of specialization of machinery; efficiency of processing resources and operations; and degree of integration and connecting points in the output chain. On the financial side the question arises as to the origin of the funds employed. Productivity is then reflected in the return on capital employed and can be divided into return on equity and return on outside capital. This point of view corresponds to the finance perspective of equity providers in the capital market.

Real capital return is a measure of the income earned by a company relative to real capital invested. In the same way as total equity return, real capital return depends mostly on the development of income (Görzig et al., 1988, pp. 52ff.). Compared with wage rate development, real capital returns permit indications as to the relative importance of the production factors labor and capital (Görzig et al., 1988, p. 64).

KNOWLEDGE AND TECHNICAL PROGRESS AS FACTORS OF PRODUCTION?

When discussing new information and communication technologies, knowledge is often mentioned as another factor of production. New knowledge and technical advances have always had a crucial influence on products and manufacturing processes. Product innovations can lead to an increase in the range of products (diversification), an improvement of existing products, or introduction of entirely new products. Most of all, product innovations lead to cost-reducing rationalization measures, reflected in decreased factor input and so increased productivity.

However, it is practically impossible to consider knowledge and technical progress in an isolated manner as production factors in their own right. Rather, they are part of the factors of labor and capital. Knowledge is the general state of knowledge of employees (education and training) or specialized corporate knowledge. Technical advances can become apparent in new means of production (machinery and equipment, computers, software) and in the form of patents, copyrights, and licenses. Intangible asset rights become capital through legal protection, so that their value can be recognized as a production factor.

Knowledge has to be differentiated into company-specific, organizational knowledge, which is stored in operational processes, and knowledge that is taken home with employees in the evenings. The first case is a specialized form of capital, while in the second case employees offer particularly skilled labor. Both forms of knowledge lead to improved productivity of the factors engaged.

Technical progress becomes apparent in better quality and more economical or ecologically justifiable forms of production. Such innovations can be related either to specific processes or to operations in general. In the former case a new process can be protected by means of patents and so becomes capital that can be either exploited directly or passed on via licenses. That way technological progress congeals to real capital and can be sold and acquired. Process improvements ultimately become evident in increased organizational efficiency.

INTERACTIONS BETWEEN LABOR AND CAPITAL

In addition to the qualitative characteristics of labor and capital their productivities are closely connected. For example, productivity of labor is determined decisively by the investments associated with the employment of capital as well as substitution of the factor labor, which becomes relatively more expensive (cf. DIW, 1997, pp. 115, 127f.). If the proportion of capital is increased at the expense of labor, then, inevitably, increased factor productivity of labor follows. However, an economy's total productivity does not increase until labor released in this way can be employed more efficiently elsewhere.

With respect to investments, they usually represent a substitute for an existing facility and, at the same time, also allow a decrease in factor input (particularly labor) and cost due to new technological features. This rationalization effect is usually enhanced by the possible complementarity of process innovations and real capital investments in that investments in machinery and equipment create incentives for companies to replace labor with capital (substitution effect). On the other hand, this effect of process innovations can be compensated by new jobs created due to product innovations and new services.

Depending on sector and labor intensity, the development of jobs is connected more or less tightly to the investment process. For example, in the service sector new jobs can be created with relatively small amounts of capital (e.g., personal services, consulting), while in industry even high investments usually create only a few jobs (e.g., automated manufacturing processes). It should also be noted that many of the jobs created in industry are, from a functional point of view, part of services (tertiarization of the secondary sector).

In addition to providing jobs, new technologies have important effects on the employment and requirements of employees. Here, both direct and indirect influences are important; technology creates and destroys jobs at the same time; however, not all fields are affected equally. While in industry mostly highly skilled (office) jobs ('high-skill white-collar jobs') were created in response to the reduction in classic industrial jobs ('blue-collar jobs'), in the services sector jobs were created in both areas ('high-skill' and 'low-skill').[5] However, due to new information and communication technologies a shift toward high-skill jobs can also be expected in the services sector. Within the scope of this so-called up-skilling a revaluation of human capital is taking place with increased importance of technologies.

Progressing rationalization has in part raised the question whether technical progress could in the end lead to extensive displacement of the production factor labor. Related catchphrases are 'jobless growth' or 'decoupling of growth and employment'; also the existence of a 'productivity-production-gap' has been postulated.[6] As has been shown, new technologies and their applications have different effects depending on sector. Growth without additional employment could be reached only if rationalization took place only in production of existing products and services. However, there also is a continuing change in demand that becomes apparent in new requirements for higher quality and in turn, in more labor-intensive products and services. In order to meet this demand, supply structures also have to adjust themselves continuously (structural change). Economic development and competition have to be understood as 'creative destruction' (Schumpeter); that is., 'old things' are destroyed, and, at the same time, 'new things' are reconstructed (Schumpeter, 1975, pp. 134ff.).

NOTES

1. Cf. the discussions on increasing productivity of labor in the United States and its implications for monetary policy. The wildly erratic price swings following these discussions demonstrate the misjudgments that can result from such a one-sided view with apparently clear causalities.

2. 'Productivity isn't everything, but in the long run it is almost everything. A country's ability to improve its standard of living over time depends almost entirely on its ability to raise its output per worker.' Krugmann, P. (*Expectations*), 1996, p. 13.

3. Swiss Federal Statistics Office (*National Income Accounts*), p. 27.

4. For example, productivity can be applied either to individual hours worked or to the number of wage/salary earners or persons employed. There are also differences among the persons employed. For instance, the number of part-time employees can be included or not or converted into full-time employees via full-time equivalents; cf. Swiss Federal Statistics Office (*National Income Accounts*), p. 27.

5. Cf. OECD (*Technology*), 1996.

6. Cf. for an overview on this discussion by Oppenländer, K.H. (*Wachstumspolitik*), 1988, pp. 240f.

10

Methods for
Long-Term Forecasting

NATIONAL INCOME ACCOUNTING APPROACHES

The Causal Theoretical Approach

It should be a basic principle that approaches based on the theory of cause and effect should be used when preparing long-term macroeconomic projections. It is obvious that time (as a variable) is inadequate for explaining the development of a national economy. Therefore, pure extrapolation of developments over time will not provide sufficient information as a basis for planning, for either economic or corporate policy. Nonetheless, such extrapolations are used relatively frequently in government and industry.

The term 'causal theoretical forecast' is used when investigated variables are put in a dependent relationship with their relevant determinants and are then predicted on the basis of this knowledge. This is done step by step: first the factors determining the development of the variable investigated are established; second, the influence in terms of degree and direction of these determinants on the variable investigated is registered and recorded as quantitative behavioral and reaction coefficients, and third, a forecast is derived on the basis of the presumed (estimated) development of the determinants (exogenous variables) of the variable to be predicted, using the reaction coefficients found in step 2. Procedures based on this basic concept—shown in Figure 10.1—range from simple behavioral equations to comprehensive econometric models. In behavioral equations the development of the variable to be predicted is attributed to the influence of a single dominant determinant, while with econometric models the variables to be predicted are seen as variables of an integrated system of mathematical equations. In so doing, the interdependencies between the relevant variables are recorded as behavioral and definition equations.

Figure 10.1
Structure of a Forecast Based on the Theory of Cause and Effect

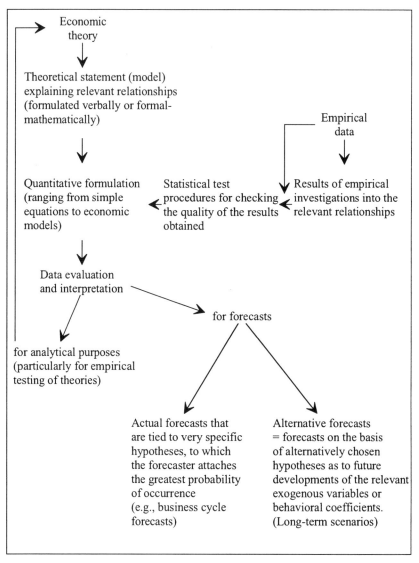

Source: Kneschaurek, F. (*Volkswirtschaft*), 1996, p. 322.

Procedures for forecasting individual variables are of interest primarily when directly deriving individual pieces of economic information. Nevertheless, other forecasts can also be developed, for example, the propensity of private households to spend or the development of capital market rates. However, as a ready-to-go car is more than a heap of undoubtedly useful parts, a macroeconomic developments forecast consisting of a self-contained system projection is qualitatively very different from a collection of isolated, individually forecast variables. There are virtually no one-sided causal dependent relationships between macroeconomic variables, rather, only interdependencies.[1] For example consumption depends on income; however, income, in turn, also depends on the amount of consumer spending. Only when a self-contained system is predicted can these interdependencies be taken meaningfully into account. Many structural data can be determined on the basis of the fixed relationships of the System of National Accounts (SNA),[2] which permits testing of individual forecasts for their significance. However, predicting an entire data system is a considerably more elaborate process than forecasting individual variables.

The approaches used in the SNA system can be structured either in the form of closed models (see also section entitled Eeconometric Simulation Models) or as single equations for individual components. In the latter case the approach's consistency has to be ensured via the theoretical parameters set for the system of national accounts.[3]

Iteration Methods

In most cases iteration methods are based on the quantitative structure of national accounts. Production functions are frequently used for determining an economy's growth potential. The development of a country's potential output is made a function of the availability of production factors, so allowing estimation of the quantitative growth potential of the national economy being investigated.

In so doing, it is usually possible to determine, also for the long term, quite accurately the potentially deployable workforce on the basis of demographic models. In most countries productivity of labor also follows—in retrospect—a certain trend determined by the basic social attitudes of the respective populations. A country's changing attractiveness of location can considerably accelerate or slow down the inflow of capital and so also an economy's growth potential.

When calculating an economy's demand components, the focus is typically on the utilization side of SNA, as shown in Figure 10.2. We are dealing with—figuratively speaking—a set of equations that includes the system's structure (left-hand column), that is, the so-called definition equations of the system. It also reflects the behavior of players in this system in the form of behavioral equations for individual utilization components.

The more loosely structured way of working with single equations opens up a relatively large amount of freedom to the person handling this matter, in terms of both the development of individual exogenous variables and the issue of changes in behavioral parameters. However, this makes intersubjective reconstructability more difficult, because in the end, the choice of parameters is based on subjective assumptions. Nevertheless, this problem is defused by the fact that the assumptions of the entire system have to fulfill the consistency requirement. Here we are

Figure 10.2
Use of Income Side of SNA and Its Determinants

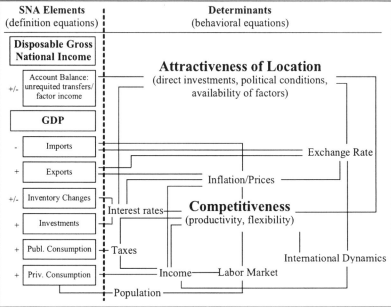

dealing with a considerably more open procedure than is used, for example, with closed simulation models or other methods, which are described later.

With such iteration methods all variables are predicted independently of each other, which means that a large number of different forecasting procedures are used. Results obtained in this manner are reconciled with one another on the basis of further (alternatively calculated) dependent relationships and by taking into consideration the fixed relationships of national accounts. As a rule, this reconciliation process has to be repeated several times in order to take into account the various relationships; therefore, this process is referred to as iteration or successive approximation method. At least, this procedure ensures that the individual forecasts contained in the system are not in logical disagreement with each other. That is, such logical disagreement of individual forecasts would be the norm, if variables having a logical connection were predicted independently of each other.[4] In the vast majority of politically relevant forecasts at the macroeconomic level, individual forecasts are reconciled with each other by means of such iteration methods.

The more complicated the approach chosen, the greater the number of not only exogenous variables but also behavioral parameters that influence the individual elements of the utilization side of SNA. Their sum total has to reflect the demanded gross domestic product. Ultimately, this GDP makes possible, when compared, for example, with the predicted development of growth potential (based on a production function), a statement as to whether the factors of production can be fully exploited or whether so-called structural unemployment has to be expected in the long term.

Econometric Simulation Models

The general understanding of the term 'econometric simulation models' is that of a multiple equation system, which is used, for example, when predicting simultaneously all components of the utilization side of the SNA on the basis of a model structure that has been calibrated on the past. It should be pointed out that a simple, linear regression model for a consumption function also constitutes basically an econometric model. This is because, on one hand, it represents a simplified depiction of a section of economic reality, and, on the other, it is being filled with empirical data.

In economics, as in natural science, a model is a simplified image of reality. These are images of sections of the real economic environment, as it is being shaped by the various players (consumers, manufacturers, government). The purpose of an econometric model is to explain, as precisely as possible, changes in an (economic) variable due to one or more other variables (single-equation model). The model's purpose is determined in each case by the respective section of economic reality as well as the type of simplification chosen. Consequently, hypotheses are postulated in association with a model that reflect the presumed relationship between these variables. Economic theory means thinking in terms of models insofar as a theoretically presumed relationship is described by a single equation or a system of several interdependent equations (multiple-equation model). It should always be kept in mind when working with models that they approximate reality only with varying degrees of success. Simplification allows analyses that would otherwise not be possible within the scope of a highly complex reality.[5] It should also be kept in mind that the focus should be on registering the major characteristics and relationships in the examined section of reality. Consequently, a model can never be suitable for all conceivable questions.

Therefore, a central feature of econometric models is that they are filled with empirical data. However, the use of observational data during empirical testing of economic hypotheses creates numerous problems, which have been described, for example by Morgenstern, Holub, and Schips.[6] One of the main issues in this regard is the degree to which the effects of possible observational and measurement errors have feedback on the results of empirical studies so influencing the results of econometric estimates and conclusions derived from them. Because survey concepts of economic statistics are also rooted in basic theoretical ideas, they are often confirmed by these analyses as well.[7] Nonetheless, economics, which claims to be a science, has to test theoretical economic models in the real world. In this respect, it is insufficient to look at the world as a passive observer. Especially when shaping economic policy such decisions have to be examined closely as to their effects in each case. Methods of empirical economic research and econometric models are indispensable aids particularly when solving these problems (Kirchgässner, 1997).

Thus, by means of econometric simulation models the interdependencies between the individual variables in the system are recorded. While one-sided, causal dependent relationships are (erroneously) assumed for isolated estimates of individual variables, it is attempted by means of simulation models to record these interdependencies simultaneously. Following calibration of the model, one (and only one) solution is calculated for the entire system without having to carry out further adjustments.

When developing a simulation model, the relationships between the individual variables are specified precisely. In so doing, distinction is made between definition relationships and behavioral equations. The model is described by a system of equations, in which the number of equations and variables has to be the same. For some variables (so-called exogenous variables) in all models, certain future target values (assumptions) are usually specified. The entire system is then solved simultaneously by taking into account these assumptions and the model's definition and functional relationships expressed via the equations.

Should the results of the calculations not be plausible for some data, alterations have to be made, either to the assumptions for functional relationships (behavioral equations) or to the forecasts for exogenous variables. Such an approach is particularly suitable for making quick changes to the assumptions for exogenous variables and to so simulate different general conditions for the macroeconomic system under investigation.

The advantage of simulation models over the previously mentioned SNA methods (iteration methods) is that interdependencies are specified precisely and so are intersubjectively retraceable. This means that nothing can be forgotten or vastly under/overestimated so that the causes for wrong forecasts can be easily exposed and eliminated, if necessary. As experiences are gained with the model, they are expressed as changes in the structure of the model. Consequently, successive improvement of such a model means in practical terms that it is adaptive, whereas with iteration methods the acquired knowledge depends very strongly on the forecaster as a person, and the transfer of experience can only rarely be fully guaranteed.

At the same time, simulation models have the disadvantage that only one set of information can be processed with each relationship. Furthermore, this set must be precisely quantified and described by a (relatively simple) mathematical equation. Processing nonlinear equations, which is the rule in the business world, often creates a lot of problems in simulation models. It should be pointed out in particular that calibrating such a simulation model on the past means, at the same time, that the parameters acquired in so doing (the model structure) remain unchanged for the forecast period. The future is drawn via a model structure that represents the average of the calibration period.

However, a model used for forecasting should not be understood as an independent forecaster but as an instrument among many others, in the hands of the person dealing with this matter. When used correctly, the advantages of a model forecast (clarity, speed, completeness) can be combined with those of the iteration method (qualitative and plausibility considerations). This way, the serious disadvantages of parameter constancy can, at least partially, be overcome. However, this leads again to the problem that such combined models become dependent to a large extent on the forecaster as a person (cf. earlier).

It should be noted that using econometric simulation models for long-term issues is extremely problematic overall when the parameters of the model's behavioral functions are kept the same over a long period of time. The behavioral functions' parameters are based on technologies and behaviors that are subject to constant change. With normal econometric models the time span of applicability—as the past has shown—is constantly being shortened. This is because the structure of the economic system was very different 15 years ago, and a model still taking this structure very much into account cannot describe even the present adequately, let alone the future.

The method for constructing an econometric simulation model is largely the same as that described in the previous diagram for analyses and forecasts that are based on the theory of cause and effect (see Figure 10.3).[8]

Starting from economic theory, the relationships to be investigated are first specified in the form of single equations and filled with empirical data; then they are tested as to their usefulness for describing development during the basic period; after that, the single equations used, whose endogenous variables in turn influence other parts of the entire system as exogenous variables, are estimated at the same time (simultaneously); and finally, on the basis of the past, the model is examined for the greatest possible adjustment. Statistical methods are used in such a procedure in an effort to draw an image of the true structure of economic events. The central task of econometrics is establishing for a specified economic theory, with the data derived from economic statistics, a model structure that reflects the manifestation of reality as accurately as possible. Based on these facts, possible sources of error in such an approach can also be derived. These could be due to the following: (1) theoretical reasoning, which can be inconsistent, irrelevant, or unrealistic; (2) insufficient quantification of theoretical statements. This can be due to inadequate registration of individual variables (observation or measurement errors in the data), because the theoretical model reflects reality only to a limited degree. Another possibility is that there is a high degree of uncertainty in the decisions recorded by the parameters; (3) false estimates of exogenous variables or parameters. The greater the number of variables and considered interdependencies between them (i.e., the more complex the system), the greater the danger of such false estimates.

Input-Output Tables. The input-output table is the most comprehensive way of recording the interrelationships within a national economy. It is based on W. Leontief's pioneering work.[9] The original input-output matrix for the United States included around 550 sectors and was therefore an extremely productive instrument of economic analysis, particularly for describing the functional mechanisms of a highly specialized economy with a high degree of labor division. However, this instrument is totally unsuitable for forecasting, because, first of all the database is relatively uncertain.[10] Second, final demand would have to be pre-

Figure 10.3
Structure of an Econometric Model

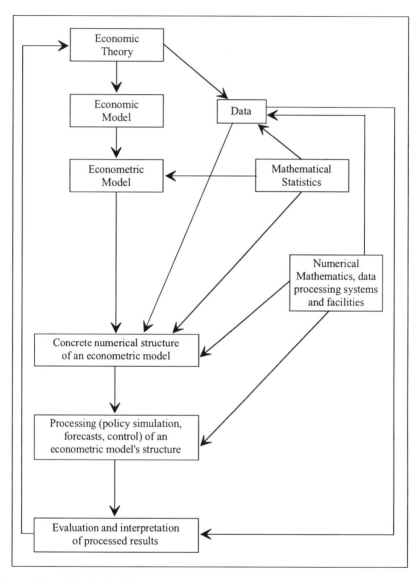

Source: Schips, B. (*Aufbau*), 1979, p. 4.

dicted for products and services in all 550 sectors, as well as for the categories of personal consumption, public consumption, investments, and exports and imports. This means that a large number of exogenous variables would have to be taken into account. Such a forecast would fail chiefly because the parameters connecting the 550 sectors and showing mutual supply relationships are subject to constant change and so cannot be assumed to remain unchanged in the future.[11] For example, changes result from technical advances or changed decisions on the parts of decision makers in business.

However, analyzing an economy's future structure on the basis of an approach that assumes an unchanging structure—as would be the case with constant parameters—is a contradiction in terms. This fundamental problem, which can be easily illustrated with input-output analysis,[12] basically applies to all econometric simulation models using constant behavioral parameters, no matter how complicated. Therefore, forecasts made on the basis of such approaches are limited to a (short) period of time, for which largely unchanged structures can be assumed. Consequently, if serious difficulties are already created by methodological, technical, and scientific problems during empirical testing of econometric hypotheses, then considerable restraint is called for with a view to using such approaches for forecasting. A lot of attention has to be paid to the limited amount of information provided by such a forecast and especially its short distance into the future.

Model Assumptions

We would like to point out again that the development of future-oriented statements is always based on assumptions and judgments based on estimates in the following two ways: first, all determinant (exogenous) variables have to be predicted in an equation, unless they are determined endogenously in a closed model (i.e., from within the model). Nevertheless, a relatively large number of determinant (exogenous) variables always remains in each statement or model that have to be predicted on the basis of assumptions so that the equations can be solved.[13] Second, it has to be decided in a forecast model the extent to which the reaction and behavioral coefficients, determined via empirical analysis of the past, will also be valid in the future, or whether they have to be revised. Such decisions also amount to judgments based on estimates.[14]

EQUILIBRIUM MODELS

Specialized forms of simulation models are calculable, general equilibrium models. Their function is to allow the analysis in a systematic, complete, and a logically consistent way, of the effects of interferences (changes in exogenous variables) in an economic system. In so doing, analysis is not limited only to direct and indirect allocation effects. In addition, the effects of (economic) policy measures on the creation and distribution side of national income accounts—apart from all feedback effects—have also to be determined. This again demonstrates that the SNA plays an essential part as a statistical basis for forecasts.

In terms of methods, all general equilibrium models are based on three central principles of economic theory: (1) individuals in economies act rationally and therefore try utilizing the information and possibilities available to them in the best possible way; (2) small changes in exogenous variables have only relatively minor effects in a model. This is an essential prerequisite for (economic) policy recommendations. That is, if minor interferences in a national economy caused massive and non-predictable effects, then economic policy would be a complete gamble; (3) individuals in economies react to price signals and try to compensate for the effects of changed relative prices via substitution. This means that with a constant standard of living, an increase in price of one product relative to another leads to decreased demand for this product and increased demand for the other. The kind of effect that (economic) policy measures have on the development of a national economy or its innovative capability depends, from a national economic point of view, on the information available or how the individuals in the economy form their expectations and are capable of reacting to changes. Their capability in adjusting and substitution possibilities are determined not only by technological conditions and individual behaviors but also by general institutional conditions. The tighter the regulatory framework of a national economy, the smaller its flexibility and so its innovative capability.

Calculable general equilibrium models are based on the theoretical concept of a perfectly functioning market economy. This means, most of all, that all prices are completely flexible and that no economic entity has power over the market or can influence crucially market outcome (i.e., there are neither monopolies nor cartels nor price fixing). Obviously, these prerequisites are not met in most national economies; however, some individual markets and sectors meet these requirements more successfully than others.

The general conditions of an economy and the decisions of the various players determine not only present allocation of goods and services to the individuals in an economy but also future margins for action, both for individuals and for (economic) policy. Many decisions made today determine capital goods stocks and, at the same time, the infrastructures that will be used in the economic process of the future. The development of national economies would be optimal if economic entities had rational expectations in the sense of correct and consistent ideas. They would be capable of predicting future developments correctly and could adjust their economic decisions to them accurately. At issue are whether the economic entities have the correct information and what they use as a basis for making their decisions.

An essential feature of calculable dynamic equilibrium models is the central function of markets for transmitting information, that is, the central role of prices, which not only coordinate supply and demand but also signal (relative) shortages and needs.[15] Therefore, the assumption that individuals in economies have rational expectations is equivalent to the requirement that an economy is organized such that all goods are traded in future markets. In future markets, negotiation of a contract that fixes prices and quantities is separated in time from its implementation. If all goods consumed in the future were traded in such markets, prices fixed in this manner would convey future shortages and needs.[16]

Consequently, in equilibrium models, prices convey economically relevant information about the future to economic entities. However, a market system organized in this way cannot be expected in reality. Economic entities cannot fully coordinate future plans, because the system of future markets is incomplete. Without intervention in the behavior of prices, calculable equilibrium models always show a trend toward complete market clearance.[17]

A way of overcoming these methodological weaknesses in equilibrium models is intervening in model structure by limiting the setting of prices or restricting needs and supply. These limits are set on the basis of past experiences. This procedure makes working with equilibrium models very similar to working with classic econometric simulation models, which capture such behavior as a result of past experiences in their system of equations and parameters. In addition, it should be noted that all the information on the behavior of economic players investigated is hardly ever available, as is required from the theoretical point of view of an equilibrium approach. Therefore, working with equilibrium models frequently requires a number of assumptions for which there is no experience available whatsoever.

FORECASTS ON THE BASIS OF SYSTEM DYNAMICS (CYBERNETIC) MODELS

Some people are of the opinion that system dynamics models are superior to conventional econometric models as instruments for economic analysis and forecasting. These models have, in fact, become more popular since the first Club of Rome report on the 'Limits to Growth' was published. These are always cybernetic feedback control systems that look at the relationships between variables not in a causal, but rather a functional (and therefore interdependent), manner. Particular attention is paid to feedback effects and disturbances in the system (cf. Ruth, Hannon, and Forrester, 1997).

It is true that feedback processes are taken into account in conventional econometric models. A classic example for this is the multiplier and accelerator processes developed via cyclical and growth theory, which describe the feedback effects of a change in investment or private consumption on economic development. Nonetheless, there are some important differences between the two models:

1. Due to their inherently unchangeable structures, conventional econometric models can essentially be used only for short-term (economic) forecasts (1–1 ½ years). By contrast, system dynamics models are used mainly for long-term forecasts with distances into the future of more than 10 years.

2. If feedback effects are taken into account in conventional models at all, then it is exclusively between flow variables (e.g., the effect of a change in private consumption on income, which in turn triggers another change in private consumption, etc.). By contrast, system dynamics models pay particular attention to interdependencies (and so to feedback processes) between flow and inventory variables (population, capital stock, natural resources, environmental pollution, etc.).

3. As econometric models focus on the short term, it is realistic to assume that the influences of important general conditions on the course of an economy will remain

constant, at least on balance. Cybernetic models, by contrast, depart from the assumption of unchangeable general conditions and include in the model mainly the changes in inventory variables. In addition, important structural data as well as behavioral coefficients are made dynamic in such models by means of so-called look-up tables, as shown schematically in Figure 10.4. However, such functions are, in part, empirically secured in a totally inadequate way and so ultimately represent judgments based on estimates on the part of those producing them.[18]

When trying to include such changes in a cybernetic model for forecasting purposes, the same difficulties are encountered as with the econometric model. The

Figure 10.4
Example of a 'Look-up Table' as Found in the 'Limits to Growth' Study

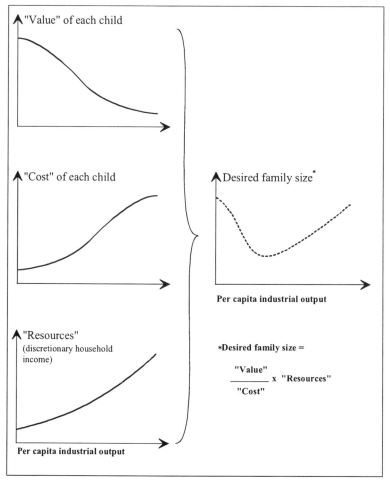

Source: Meadows, D. et al., Limits to Growth, Technical Report (unpublished), 1972, p. 30.

reason for these difficulties is that such changes have to be predicted via judgments based on estimates before the forecast can actually be formulated. The problems associated with doing so are even more pronounced with cybernetic models, because numerous interdependencies between variables and inventories have to be considered whose past impact is practically unknown or that cannot be put whatsoever in concrete terms.

AN INTERIM SUMMARY

Models are important instruments of economic analysis. Particularly computer-aided simulation models, as well as cybernetic models, can give an exceedingly valuable insight into the relationships of effect and functional mechanisms of an economy. In addition, they can make evident the 'strategic' variables and interdependencies that determine an economy's development in the short and long term. They also serve as (important) aids for economic forecasting. A national economy's future development is linked to past experiences only to a limited degree (i.e., can undergo important structural changes). This demonstrates that models cannot be independent instruments of economic forecasting in the sense that they vouch automatically, as it were, for a good forecast, just because they were able to reflect development well in the past. That is, if judgments based on estimates, which are inevitably part of every forecast, prove wrong, then even the most ingenious and most analytically sound model will fail in terms of its forecasting function. Therefore, the following statement by Henschel is justified: 'Models used in forecasting should not be understood as independent forecasters, but rather as instruments among many others in the forecaster's hands' (Henschel, 1979, p. 39).

NOTES

1. It is the numerous relationships and their feedback that transform the subject of investigation into a system.

2. The SNA provides the basis for empirical economic research. Concepts and methods are described in Brümmerhoff, D., *Volkswirtschaftliche Gesamtrechnung*, 1995. See also: UNO et al. (*National Accounts*), *System of National Accounts*, 1993.

3. We are not attempting to go into the details of the different approaches at this point. They are characterized very briefly for guidance purposes as to their usefulness. Cf. Swiss Federal Statistics Office (*National Income Accounts*).

4. It can only be assumed in rare exceptional situations that the predicted parts of components, of whatever sum total, add up to exactly 100%.

5. In contrast to natural science, experiments are possible only to a limited degree in economics and social science because the experiment, as such, influences reality.

6. Morgenstern, O. (*Genauigkeit*), 1965, Holub, H.-W. (*Wirtschaftsforschung*) 1996, Schips, B., 1990.

7. Holub, H.-W. (*Wirtschaftsforschung*) as well as (*Replik*), 1997.

8. Here we would like to refer to the literature for further details on these procedures: Cf. Greene, W.H. (*Econometric Analysis*), 1997; Theil, H. (*Econometrics*); 1971.

9. Leontief, W. (*Input-Output*), 1951. For an introduction cf. Holub, H.-W. and Schnabel, W. (*Input-Output*).

10. For Switzerland, there is presently 'only' one Input/Output (I/O)table available for the year 1990.

11. Admittedly, a supplier-buyer relationship cannot be assumed between all sectors. Nevertheless, the number of connecting parameters between sectors is likely to exceed 100,000, so that it can be excluded that meaningful assumptions are possible as to the future development of these parameters.

12. Leontief, W. (*Input-Output*). For an introduction cf. Holub, H.-W. and Schnabel, W. (*Input-Output*).

13. This is what makes a forecasting model fundamentally different from an analytical model. Although with the latter all descriptive variables are known and can be used in the model for empirical testing of theoretical considerations, their future development is unknown and so has to be predicted.

14. For example, the development of personal consumer spending can be explained via a simple model as a function of disposable income. In addition to the question as to the development of the (exogenous) variable 'disposable income' the question also arises as to whether consumer behavior remains unchanged (i.e., continues in the same way in the future as has been observed in the past).

15. The central importance of information for the functioning of markets is particularly evident in financial markets, which have a fundamental orientation toward the future.

16. This is obviously a very unrealistic idea. However, within the scope of the model it serves as an ideal that represents the starting point for the necessary adjustment.

17. This means, for instance, that the labor market would be cleared completely, even if wages had to be decreased to zero. By contrast, tight restrictions lead to an increase in price, which would also lead to market clearance, however, in that case, possibly at prices that use up people's incomes completely such that other needs could no longer be satisfied.

18. This is the reason for the pronounced weakness of the Club of Rome study on the limits to growth, particularly concerning the forecasting conclusions derived from it. As has been mentioned, the behaviors of economic entities change frequently in ways not observed so far, due to the influence of changing environmental conditions. Such changes also cannot be recorded with this procedure.

11

WORKING WITH GLOBAL
MODELS—LEARNING AND PREDICTING

INTRODUCTION

So-called global models are considered special forms of simulation models. They are analytical tools for studying global economic and social relationships. Global models are a reflection of the increased need for information at the beginning of the 1960s with the emergence of internationalization, combined with the first opportunities for computer-aided simulation.

After more than 20 years' experience, it is clear, however, that the generation of generally applicable forecasts and solutions via models by pushing a few buttons does not provide adequate information for shaping the future. The use of models supports the creation of scenarios for examining not one but several alternative futures. As early as the end of the 1960s first doubts were raised during a long-lasting global economic upswing as to its persistence. Both knowledge about global processes and awareness of the speed of change grew at the same time. Since 1968 global modeling has developed in two directions, which can still be used to distinguish the about 100 different global models in existence by now:

- *Modeling to predict.* When predicting global economic development, the main focus is on anticipating developments as precisely as possible for the following year as well as for the next two to five years. Core components are national income accounting variables and the international interdependence of trade flows.

- *Modeling to learn.* These models aim at an increased understanding of the concurrence of demographic, economic, social, technological, and ecological factors, in order to provide 'if, . . . then' predictions.

After more than 25 years' development, the diversity in objectives of the two fields equals that of their many representatives. Just as varied is their accessibility for 'working with global models.'

MODELING TO PREDICT

As representatives of this field, we would like to mention the 'LINK' model, which goes back to seven national models that were integrated by 11 econo-metricists in 1968. The search for coherent predictions of global economic development is today being carried out by more than 100 participants on the basis of a large model consisting of 79 national models. The calculation results of this model, inclusive of about 20,000 equations (Bodkin, 1991, p. 501) and assumptions shared explicitly by the participants, have been communicated regularly to the world public in the form of United Nations reports.[1]

Without getting into the discussion as to whether approaches like those used in the LINK model are useful, it should be pointed out that working with large econometric global models for predicting economic development is simply not within the possibilities (and means) of individual users.

MODELING TO LEARN

The inaccessibility of global forecasting models therefore leads, in the context of 'working with global models,' to a more intensive concentration on global models, in which aspects of 'learning' are the focus of developers and users. The model school, to which this approach is attributed, was also created in 1968, supported mainly via the Club of Rome.[2] This work is based primarily on J. Forrester's 'system dynamics' method as a means of formalization.[3] Probably the best-known report is the study *Limits to Growth—A Report to the Club of Rome*, published in 1972.[4]

Approaches that emerged from this school have the following characteristics, allowing to group them with the 'modeling to learn' category: first, that the underlying assumptions of the statements or forecasts be explicitly described ('If, . . . then') and second, that these models describing behavior have a functional foundation.

Following is a roughly outlined, idealized description of how such models are developed by using Meadow's 'World3' model as an example.

MODEL DEVELOPMENT

The starting point is the model's purpose and the problem to be solved. In the case of the World3 model, what happens if the world's population keeps growing unhindered? What will be the ecological consequences if economic growth continues at the present rate? The examined system consists of the world as a whole, without breakdown into regions or countries. The state of the entire global system was described by means of 18 variables of state. The model developers' points of view—their world-views and assumptions as to chains of effect in reality—were summarized initially as verbal chains of argument via the dominant relationships of effect. The interconnected chains of argument in their entirety can also be depicted graphically as a network of effects.

Mathematical formulation of relational equations and behavioral equations as well as initial values, parameters, and table functions means fixing relationships in the model system according to the worldviews, assumptions, and information available to model developers. That way the points of view and worldviews are 'cast' (so to speak) in the mold of the fixed mathematical formulas of the model structure. In addition, an algorithm has to be established to provide processing rules for the coupling process of the dynamic model system. The model's structure—18 differential equations in case of the World3 model—determines calculability.[5]

As for the presentation of results, it has to be decided which variables or aggregate variables have to be shown as observable behavioral variables. If a model is also to reveal past developments, the parameters have to be set such that the output variables match the observed past as well as possible. For the creation of scenarios, some global models provide adjustment possibilities that allow various arrangements of connections and equations, and so of worldviews or assumptions.

KNOWLEDGE GAINED FROM VARIOUS MODELS

Several models are now introduced here that are central to 'learning' and focus on global development. The basic knowledge gained from the World3 model resulting from a learning process is, in simple terms, that the world is a limited environment or system of renewable and nonrenewable resources. In this system lives a population that grows exponentially. Maintenance of the respective populations requires the use (production for consumption) of resources, which, in turn, produces waste products (environmental pollution). If the population does not stop growing, nonrenewable resources will be used up ever faster, while the increase in waste products exceeds the ability of renewable resources to regenerate themselves. From this the model's authors concluded that either the population has to stop growing, or there has to be a fundamental change in the way that we deal with resources in order to prevent the population from collapsing in a limited global system. In addition they concluded that it was high time for action: the later that humankind reacted, the worse would be the achievable and sustainable result.

These statements made in 1972 drew a lot of attention and triggered a discussion that is still ongoing. The basic message is now no longer being questioned. What remains open is the validity of the conclusions drawn on the basis of the methodology used. That model was relatively simple compared to its successors. It takes up only 150 kb in disk space these days (Bossel, 1992). However, some hair-raising modeling mistakes occurred at the time.[6] For example, assumptions made as to the amount of available nonrenewable resources, as well as technical efficiency of production, have since been frequent subjects of further investigation. These discussions also resulted in inverted assumptions, such as 'growth of limits' due to technological and organizational sociopolitical progress,[7] instead of the limits to growth postulated in the model. Finally, the 'global modeling movement' developed, leading to expanded models and requirements as to their 'validity,' as well as new methodological approaches.

The next report to the Club of Rome was based on a model led by Mesarovic and Pestel[8] that depicts the world as a system of 10 regions. Per region, it describes an individual, a sociopolitical, a demoeconomic, a technological, and an environmental level. The report draws the conclusion that measures taken to cope with global crises when the symptoms are already evident come too late and it demands long-term, global cooperation between regions. The populations of some world regions would 'collapse' sooner than others; however, such events would show noticeable effects worldwide. A call is made on 'developed regions' to make coordinated contributions to less well developed regions for the benefit of the entire global population and to also strive for organic growth. This extensive model was developed by 46 scientists for the subject areas of population, economy, energy, and nutrition.

A common feature of the first two models is that future development on the basis of assumptions is described only when present developments continue. Another model (BARILOCHE [Herrera, Skolnik et al., 1976]) tried to find out whether disadvantaged, less developed regions could achieve of their own accord an adequate standard of living. Various sets of assumptions were created as to the behavior of developed regions. Different sociopolitical, normatively guided developments in less developed regions were modeled. According to this model, Latin America and Africa could reach an adequate standard of living of their own accord only with exceptionally favorable sociopolitical conditions, such as socialistically inspired redistribution of land. Asia would depend on a lot of continued aid under any circumstances.

In 1976 a global—even though nondigitized—model[9] was designed by the Hudson Institute that also builds on the interdependence between global sectors, such as agriculture, resources, population, and production. The entirely different assumptions made as to the limiting conditions for the availability of resources as well as technological advances certainly are in great contrast to those of previously discussed models. According to this model, growth is definitely possible over the next 200 years.

The report 'The Future of the World Economy,'[10] which was supported by the UN and published in 1979, is based on a model inspired by W. Leontief that uses input-output matrices (cf. Chapter 10). It describes the preconditions for developing countries to be able to catch up in terms of per capita income: a high degree of debt, massive investments in their capital stock, and further increases in foreign aid, as well as the required agricultural land, increases in yield, and so on. The first specialized model (MOIRA[11]) had the function of working out the possibilities for combating world hunger. This model's results pointed out, on one hand, politically unfulfillable levers, such as sociopolitical reforms in countries suffering from hunger or the creation of a global food fund. On the other hand, a damper was put on other levers for combating hunger.[12]

Global models kept growing constantly in size and complexity, while they could not yet be accessed by wide circles due to still-inefficient hardware and software. The GLOBUS model,[13] developed in the 1980s, already represents 26 countries (and the rest of the world) and uses input-output models from the field of econometric research for the by now six sectors of goods. It took even a supercomputer several minutes to process the about 8,000 equations. However, this led to reconsideration such that the model was adapted for microcomputers.[14] Yet another dimension to learning with model simulations is opened up by integrating political behavior patterns and parameters.

WHAT HAS BEEN LEARNED?

Suggestions for shaping behavior patterns and interventions that take into account a global future will continue to be ruled by the different points of view and worldviews of model developers and those commissioning them. This makes any further agreement unachievable. Having said that, global models could have fulfilled their service as a temporary phenomenon and so disappear from the scientific and political stage. A number of issues related to global problems, which were raised by the Club of Rome in 1968, are considered resolved. However, suggested solutions failed during implementation or due to the otherwise prevalent differences of opinion. Tangible solutions cannot be expected at this time.

The addressees or parties commissioning reports who, due to their technocratic attitudes, expect solutions by pushing a few buttons are, and will remain, disappointed. Working with global models will be of greater benefit to users wanting to discover, via models adjusted to *their* worldviews, future problems before they are manifested via global developments. With scenarios developed in such a way, the effects of possible alternative behaviors can be simulated beforehand.

The models previously given as examples prove that there are great differences. First of all, each model is based on a dominant doctrine, and each doctrine 'experiences' reality differently. Furthermore, the various models examine political, economic, and ecological-technical issues at varying depths, depending on a model's primary purpose and the field of study. After more than 20 years, some generally supported points of view have crystallized within the field of global modeling: (1) global population growth will not be reduced by force or become negative in the *near future* due to physical or technical limits; (2) the unsatisfactory fulfillment of needs, if only material ones, of the vast majority of the world's population cannot be attributed to physical/technical causes but rather to sociopolitical and economic ones; (3) *continuous* growth in material consumption and world population is impossible; (4) the known patterns of behavior as well as global policy interventions used do not seem to lead to globally noticeable changes 'for the better,' with respect to either north-south or environmental problems—irrespective of the view held regarding the definition of 'good'; and (5) the more time passes without finding any solutions, the more drastic become the effects of such neglect or of measures necessary in the future—be they simple repairs or comprehensively designed changes in behavior. System dynamics (cybernetic) approaches are superior to econometric ones as learning models, while other modeling methods are very poor by comparison. The reasons for this are, first, the functional connections between variables and the possibility of taking feedback effects into account. Second, exogenous variables do not have to be predicted constantly by the user, as with econometric models. Third, the behavioral and reaction coefficients used in econometric models do not make a contribution to the functional structure of a model's assumed chains of effect, constituting a simplified image of reality.

All global models—irrespective of the approach—show certain weaknesses when used as instruments of forecasting. Time-series analyses, indicator systems, causal theoretical forecasts (econometric models), and system dynamics (cybernetic) approaches all have their own sources of error. The choice of assumptions determines in particular the predicted results, as has been indicated by the short excursion into models discussed so far. Although preparation of a forecast is made easier or more difficult according to the choice of method and problem to be solved in each case, a forecast's quality continues to depend on the *human* factor. The anticipation of structural setbacks, such as the past oil crisis or future ecological limitations, remains within the domain of human capability. Models are still tools, no matter how powerful they may have become.

INTERNATIONAL FUTURES—A WORKING MODEL

The International Futures model (IFs[15]) published in 1993, is the furthest advanced model among those available under the premise 'modeling to learn.' It is the first attempt to provide those willing to learn with the opportunity of working individually with global models. Its teaching concept is directed explicitly at individuals. Two features deserve particular mention: (1) all previously constructed models are accused of being influenced significantly, in terms of their behavior and results derived, by the developers' worldviews, through assumptions expressed as equations. Working with the IFs global model leads the user to developing his or her own view of the world by comparing dialectically a variety of views; and (2) in previously developed models political, economic, and ecological-technical topics have rarely been represented in balanced proportions. The IFs model's approach takes into account politically, economically, and ecologically dominated worldviews. On one hand, the view of *real*-politicians striving for security and peace becomes accessible by modeling their respective patterns of behavior. This view emphasizes the security dilemma and resulting action-reaction logic of zero-sum games, in a world consisting of anarchical countries looking only for their own advantage. On the other hand, the premises of 'globalists' can also be accommodated. They aim at 'win-win-situations' for cooperating members of the world community, which—driven by trade and increasingly widespread appreciation of democracy—grows ever closer together.

Economic objectives aiming at increased prosperity for as many people as possible assume adequate distribution. However, *liberalists* put efficiency criteria before the idea of (equal) distribution. It is possible to incorporate in such objectives more than just an emphasis on comparative competitive advantages, division of labor, and free trade. It is also possible to accommodate via parameters the views of *structuralists*, who focus on equal distribution of economic and political power, as demonstrated in the debate on terms of trade. Even for the patterns of behavior typical of *mercantilists*, this model offers levers for accommodating their 'behavior' in each of the 10 world regions. In their view, governments as central players on the world stage pursue today and in the future selfish economic policy objectives.

The two poles of the ecological-technical dimension also receive attention. The value system of *ecologists* conflicts with the *modernists'* point of view. Ecologists demand 'sustainability' within the earth's ecosystem, which has limited absorption capacity, as well as the limitation of consumption and consumers. Modernists ascribe—without ignoring the human environment connection—to humankind a great potential for finding technical and organizational solutions. Therefore, they prefer promoting such efforts to ecologically motivated self-restriction.

The open character of learning models, such as 'International Futures,' also makes using them as means for spreading political views impossible, as can be observed frequently. At the same time, working with such models destroys outdated *'board' mentalities*: (1) the switchboard mentality becomes untenable, because not even in models (i.e., simplified representations of reality) can simplified approaches generate desired behaviors or constellations. Knowledge gained from chaos research has in the meantime explicitly pilloried the switchboard mentality; and (2) the chessboard mentality has seen its day. In contrast to the royal game, it is possible neither in reality nor in models to make a move while other 'pieces' simply stay put. However, when dealing with such models, one has to always consider the assumptions *cast* in equations or the parameters set according to one's wishes. Also, dealing with models playfully helps toward appreciating the complexity and interdependence of the real world. Models are widely accepted as instruments of learning. Management games at university colleges of business and economics are by now part of the standard course repertoire. Interactive models find a wide selection of participants, not least through games like SIM-City and Railroad-Tycoon.

Due to their political nature to date, global models are only slowly becoming generally accepted as forecasting instruments and also for scenario development. Initially, econometric models were valued very highly, because their objectives are restricted exclusively to economic variables and because experience also makes all the difference in the field of modeling. Learning models are exceptionally suitable for preparing scenarios for comparative, conditional forecasts, as well as learning stages when assessing global developmental processes. They also take into account noneconomic general conditions, which cannot be included in econometric models due to their modeling method. The following overview shows a sample of a set of assumptions, which could be simulated by such a global model:

- Spending cuts of 15% in the U.S. health sector in 2002, and of 8% in the military sector in 2005.

- Cutback in foreign aid by approximately 50% on the parts of the United States and Community of Independent States (CIS) between 2002 and 2005.

- In 2004, a protectionist EU will introduce taxes on energy consumed during manufacturing of not only domestic but also imported products, even though 'large' companies have most of their manufacturing already done in 'other' regions (Southeast Asia, CIS successors).

- Rearmament of Japan in 2005.

- Decrease in global forestland by an additional 12% between 2002 and 2005.

- In North America, Japan, and the EU the efficiency of human labor as a production factor increases by another 12% due to technological advances.

- Increase (due to genetic engineering) in agricultural efficiency in Southeast Asia by 7% between 2002 and 2005.

- Decrease in agricultural yield by 4% in Africa between 2001 and 2003 due to overutilization of soil and increased mortality due to AIDS in the 20–30 age group.

Examination of individual trends or policies, particularly in giving up the *ceteris paribus* condition, leads to fast and cheap information on a system's possible behavior. However, a particular strength of some of the models is that they allow simulation of a whole bundle of measures and developments by taking into account various worldviews, as described earlier. In so doing, what is of interest is not the absolute amount of change in variables of interest—such as per capita GDP or otherwise determined indicators of the quality of life—for example in Europe. What counts are the degree and direction of change, compared with other scenarios.

OLD AND NEW ADDRESSEES OF GLOBAL MODELS

So far, nation-states and regions have been at the forefront, that is, mainly individual political entities or supranational alliances. Therefore, studies concentrated on modeling developments from their points of view. As the addressees of these models were, for a long time, considered to be only economists and political scientists, functioning as interpreters for those directly involved in the political process. Intermittently, political as well as nongovernment, politically oriented organizations (NGOs) were also among the recipients. However, it appears that what is achieved via politically motivated scenarios is welcomed only, when such use of global models also provides results and lines of argument that *suit* clients. The search for knowledge and ideas—in short, their use as instruments of learning—is rarely desired or honored. However, the real strength of global models lies in dealing with interconnected systems, acknowledging real complexity, and including mentally feedback effects of individual (or an entire bundle of) measures on a whole system. However, representatives of political entities *appear* to be looking more for simple linear lines of argument that are easy to communicate. A comprehensive view is not often introduced in political work.

Companies can use images of their greater environments *without* the *compulsion* to simplify. The environment to which companies are exposed is characterized by increasing complexity and rapid global change. Faraway events are transmitted to corporate environments ever more rapidly due to the globalization of all markets, including capital and currency markets. Traditional instruments of environmental analysis usually have the company as the main focus, in the same way as scientists have made earth the center of the universe in centuries past.

A company-centered view of the world looks only at sales and labor markets.[16] In contrast, macroeconomic global models see companies as grains of sand and stick to forecasting only economic variables of national income accounting; looking even at a sector in terms of global trends is an exception. This strict division was useful while classic boundary conditions remained the same. Ever since local and global setbacks in trend have become an increasingly frequent occurrence and have been rapidly changing the 'environmental spheres' via their interdependence, this division—at least from a company's point of view—has been making less and less sense.

This increases the benefits gained from the development of global scenarios by means of global models. The only restrictive factor is translating them into effects for an individual company. As countries have been the addressees so far, their concerns have been represented the best. There are still hardly any instruments available for applying knowledge from global scenarios to the concerns of companies. Surprisingly, the environments of companies have proven more complex—at least in terms of creating images of them—than those of countries. Companies are subject to local, national and international developments, particularly trends of national and increasingly also international markets and sectors (cf. Figure 1.3). Therefore, the creation of corporate images within the scope of the objectives of global models has not even been attempted.

EXPANDING THE APPLICATION OF GLOBAL MODELS

While in the past, large, multinational corporations only looked for new markets, they have in the meantime developed into transnational corporations. They already distribute individual (elements of) products or process chains, depending on the local conditions offered by countries, because communication technologies and comparatively inexpensive and efficient means of transportation *allow* doing so in the global political landscape. This leads to market integration, increasingly affecting also small and medium-size companies. They depend more and more on global scenarios as a basis for developing their strategies. This is because such companies do not have the resources available for constantly adjusting to, and developing, their global sales and procurement markets and also because they are literally tied to national and regional developments, respectively. The pressures on second- and third-level suppliers reach entirely new proportions.

Therefore, it becomes important to couple different levels of observation in a company-specific manner by means of adequate models. This is a method for applying the grain-of-sand view of global and national models to companies and, conversely, the company-centered perspective to the developments of sectors, competition, and markets in order to create comprehensive environmental images. It is important to develop interfaces between companies such that they can meet their information requirements—basic data are available in abundance. In addressing this new audience, the task of global models continues to be the development of global scenarios so that the results can be used in scenarios for sectors or markets and eventually also companies. The procedure described in Part III of this book, which has in part been developed further at the SGZZ, has already repeatedly proven successful in specific applications.

NOTES

This chapter is based on Kummer, St. (Weltmodelle), 1995.

1. UNO, *World Economic and Social Survey*, New York (various volumes). An insight into the method of this econometric macromodel can be gained from the appendix of the 1994 UN report. The following quote should illustrate that working with this type of global model is hardly possible for individuals or even multinational corporations:

> The global model combines 79 national or regional models that are controlled by more than 40 national institutions. The models assume that existing or publicized macroeconomic policies will be implemented. The primary variables are merchandise trade and prices, as well as interest and exchange rates. . . . The model is solved via an iterative process, so determining endogenously the most important exchange rates, interest rates, and a complete matrix of trade flows and changes in price. A notable exception is the international price of crude oil, which has been kept as an assumption: for 1994 an average price of $14 per barrel was assumed for the average of the OPEC [Organization of Petroleum Exporting Countries) basket consisting of seven crude oil types. It is assumed that the price of oil will increase in 1995 by an amount that corresponds to the average price increase in dollars of industrial exports . . . which is an endogenous variable.

2. It was this association's objective to increase the public's awareness of global problems, after its members had detected first signs indicating that the prevalent demographic, economic, social, technical and ecological developmental trends in the 1950s and 1960s did not have only positive effects on 'starship earth.' It was financed largely through the 'Volkswagen Foundation.'

3. Cf. Augusto, A., Legasto, A., Forrester, J.W., and Lyneis, J.M. (*System Dynamics*), 1980.

4. Meadows, D. et al. (*Limits to Growth*).

5. Bossel, H. (*Modellbildung und Simulation*), 1992. As few as two nonlinear differential equations in a determined system can result in 'chaotic' behavior of the variables of state (i.e., with the right kind of trigger and arrangement of relationships).

6. For example, entire powers of 10 were omitted, the initial values chosen could not be retraced and nonsensical global population figures emerged when calculations were made back to the period before 1800.

7. 'Progress' would have to raise the limits in accordance with the increase in population. A heroic endeavor, considering that 1% population growth per year leads to a doubling in world population within 70 years.

8. Mesarovic, M. and Pestel, E. (*Wendepunkt*), 1974.

9. Kahn, H. et al. (*The Next 200 Years*), 1976.

10. Leontief, W. et al. (*Future*), 1977.

11. Linnemann, H. et al. (*MOIRA*), 1979.

12. Isolated measures, such as repeated 'gifts' or artificially low-priced food deliveries destroy local agriculture by removing local performance incentives. On the other hand, reduced consumption in affluent countries would cause prices to collapse in global agricultural production, so that production would eventually go down—with the result of globally reduced yields of food.

13. Bremer, S. et al. (*GLOBUS Model*), 1987.

14. Bremer, S. and Gruhn, W. (*Micro GLOBUS*), 1987.

15. Hughes, B.B. (*International Futures*), 1993.

16. The postulate upheld here of extending this narrow view is already part of the St. Gallen Management Model, where a company is seen explicitly as an element of a higher system; cf. Ulrich, H. and Krieg, W. (*Managementmodell*), 1974.

12

DELPHI TECHNIQUE

The increasing complexity of the issues involved in forecasting led to a search for new instruments for dealing with them as early as the beginning of the 1960s. At the forefront of these considerations was how knowledge, experience, and insights of a group of people could be combined such that more broadly supported answers could be given to the problems at issue. Work along these lines—such as the scenario technique—was advanced mainly by the Rand Corporation. Ultimately, such work is based on a philosophical foundation, as represented by Locke, Leibniz, Kant, Hegel, and Signer. The efforts at the Rand Corporation, under the direction of Helmer and Gordon, focused mainly on developing a method that allows structured communication within a group of experts (i.e., a method with which the most diverse developments and circumstances could be examined as to their future importance and probability of occurrence). Therefore, according to Linstone and Turoff (Linstone and Turoff, 1975, p. 3), a comprehensive definition of the Delphi technique is as follows: 'Delphi can be characterized as a method for structuring group communication in order that such a process proceeds efficiently and a group of individuals can work on the solution to a complex problem.'

Four prerequisites have to be fulfilled for making this structured communication process possible: (1) provision of basic information and knowledge via the participants; (2) determination of the views of all group members; (3) the possibility of revising individual assessments; and (4) anonymity of the individual answers. When looking at the Delphi technique as a communication process, it becomes apparent that there is virtually no area of human activity that is not suited for this method. Therefore, Delphi can by no means be used only for forecasting purposes. It is also used for working out historical facts, examining local and regional planning options, revealing the advantages and disadvantages associated with various policy options, and so on.

At any rate, the Delphi technique can be considered a first step in the direction of comprehensive, systemic approaches because of the explicit expansion of the base of experience and inclusion of various views in the investigation of a problem. Consequently, highly complex issues are worked on with the Delphi technique, characterized by great dynamics or a great degree of change—not least due to the long-term nature of the issues (Brockhoff, 1979). Addressed in particular are those areas that cannot be quantified easily or for which there is no, or only an insufficiently known, theoretical basis.

The Delphi method combines the advantages of a comprehensive interview with those of 'brainstorming.' This is accomplished because a wide selection of interested people can be included in this method and because a kind of remotely controlled consensus-building takes place by incorporating several rounds. In a communication process all participants are informed, anonymously and in the form of summaries, of the respective views of the other participants and have to examine them critically.

The Delphi process is today implemented in two different forms. The usual form, the classic Delphi technique, is led by a management team that develops a questionnaire and distributes it to the group of participants. The management team summarizes the results, on the basis of which it develops another questionnaire. This second questionnaire essentially includes the same questions, but with means and quartiles, giving participants the opportunity of adjusting their opinions on the basis of results presented as the group's average opinion. Therefore, this is kind of a synchronization process within the panel, whereby the communication process within the large group of participants is transferred, to a large extent, to the management team. This procedure is repeated three to four times.

The new form of Delphi technique is frequently referred to as Delphi conference. Here the management team is partially replaced by a computer, which is programmed such that it summarizes the group results and transmits them to the participants. It can also make additional information available and pass on critical comments made by participants.[1] The advantage of this procedure is that the delay via the management team is avoided, so making it a 'real time' communication system. However, the general conditions for this communication process have to be defined very precisely at the outset, a task that would otherwise be taken care of by the management team. The Delphi process normally consists of four very distinct phases, in both he conventional and computer-assisted form:

- The first phase consists of analysis of the investigation subject, whereby each participant contributes additional information to the pool of information that he or she considers crucial to the matter.

- The second phase is dedicated to the process of forming an opinion within the group. At issue is finding out where there is agreement or disagreement between participants and how they assess the importance, desirability, or feasibility of individual developments.

- If there is a major contradiction, then it is examined more closely, in order to record and evaluate the underlying factors for these differences.
- The last phase consists of a final evaluation by including the information compiled to this point. Also included are the fundamentals developed at the beginning, as well as those that were mentioned as feedback during the decision-making process.

At first glance, the Delphi method appears to be a very simple concept that is just as easy to apply. For this reason a multitude of Delphi studies have been carried out without really shedding light on the associated problems, which has led to the development of disappointing results in many cases.[2]

Without doubt the most important feature of the Delphi technique is that it allows introduction of a far broader spectrum of knowledge and experience into the formation of opinions as to future developmental trends. Therefore, the usually limited views of individuals during a communication and discussion process can be expanded decisively. However, the Delphi approach is not suitable as a substitute for conventional quantitative approaches used for assessment and forecasting of empirically clearly graspable and theoretically well founded phenomena, because with such approaches explicit reconstructability can be guaranteed.

Other criticisms of the Delphi technique relate mostly to the selection of a 'good' group of participants. This problem undoubtedly exists; however, it applies to formation of groups in general, irrespective of the means of communication chosen. Therefore, it is important that it be ensured that participants approach such a process with great sincerity and expert knowledge. At the same time, they have to be willing to put in the necessary time in order to be able to deal seriously with the factual issues discussed and information conveyed in the various rounds of the Delphi process. Another problem is that the Delphi process has to be precisely tailored to each of the specific factual issues in order to prevent the procedure from simply being transferred from one problem to another. This is because often explicit and limiting definitions have to be chosen for specific cases.

Finally, the interview has to be conducted in a professional manner. Due to its apparent 'simplicity,' interviews are often structured in a naive and amateurish way. That is, they already imply opinions via their line of questioning, instead of arguing in a factual manner. This means that in such cases the basic hypothesis of the Delphi method does not apply, which says that the probability of a future event's occurring is all the greater, the larger the number of people that believe in it and are convinced of it. In such a case increasing convergence of opinions is meaningless. To the contrary, it induces misunderstandings and false interpretations. That is, such opinions do not have to have come about via a real discussion of problems. Rather, the people being questioned gradually adjust to the opinion held by the majority.

During implementation of a Delphi study it will never be possible to avoid all problems. In particular, an intrinsic conflict exists when, on one hand, as wide a contribution of information as possible is expected from individual participants, and on the other, the communication process is to proceed efficiently. The leaders of each of the Delphi studies are obligated to minimize such problems as much as possible and to combine the various objectives targeted via the communication process within their respective Delphi processes. Balanced structuring of such a communication process is associated with a number of difficulties, despite the experiences gained by now with this instrument.

Professionally conducted classic Delphi investigations are associated with considerable effort on the parts of the management team and frequently also of the participants, if this process is to lead to meaningful results. Particularly with a view to the future, such an approach is presently the only workable route for areas where empirical basics are largely missing and particularly clear, scientifically reconstructable theoretical models are not available. Such problems arise mostly in connection with highly complex relationships, where it is therefore exceptionally difficult for the individual to develop a comprehensive view that includes all relevant problems. For all that, earlier studies at the beginning of the 1960s focused mainly on attributing probabilities of occurrence to conceivable futures (scenarios!), whereby the objective was the replacement of the otherwise predominant subjectivity in single-researcher assessments with group opinion.

NOTES

1. In this respect it is closely related to the scenario technique.

2. Typical examples are applications in the areas of milk consumption or development of tourism markets, for which the Delphi technique has proven unsuitable.

13
CROSS-IMPACT ANALYSIS

The experiences with the Delphi technique led to the realization relatively quickly that the formation of broader-based opinions via a communication process does indeed improve the assessment of future situations significantly. However, it was also realized that the fundamental orientation of the Delphi technique toward the evaluation of individual events, even when taking into account various individual opinions, will continue to provide dissatisfying results from a systemic point of view. This was based on the assumption that a specific event can occur only within the higher context of several events (i.e., the future is ultimately always determined by a group of several general conditions and developmental and general trends).

Very obviously, these considerations again open up the perspective toward a comprehensive view. At the same time the question is raised as to various futures and scenarios. This is done due to the realization that the future does not develop as independent individual events; rather, it results from the concurrence of various trends that influence each other. In addition, different importance has to be attributed to individual factors and variables within such a system, because these factors determine and influence each other to varying degrees at the same time. Based on these considerations, cross-impact analysis was developed—also at the Rand Corporation—which in the meantime can also be found in the European literature under a variety of names.[1]

Consequently, a common problem of the various applications of the Delphi and cross-impact techniques is recognizing basic relationships between possible future events. The existence of such relationships is the reason for the complexity of some biological or social systems and their sometimes counterintuitive behavior. Therefore, this parallelism in the systems view led to 'systems thinking' looking for, and finding, spiritual kinship in the ecological movement—particularly in German-speaking regions. This meant that in applications the foundations of cross-impact analysis (and also the Delphi technique), which were developed from a military planning perspective, were rejected.

It is usually difficult for an individual to retrace completely the impact within an entire system of changes in one of its elements. As mentioned in connection with complexity reduction, people tend to assume, therefore, that a system's individual parts are independent, and so they solve each of the segments individually. This mistake can be avoided using cross-impact analysis. It is attempted via this approach to record the reciprocal impacts of individual elements and so to take into account interactions between the system's elements. There are several approaches for assessing this cross-impact problem and also several schools of thought, which are based on the work of Gordon, Enzer, Dalkey, and Ayres. In the second issue of the journal *Futures*, which was published for the first time in 1968, Gordon and Haywood[2] described their fundamental work with this instrument.

This fundamental work with cross-impact analysis showed a series of mathematical/statistical, probability theoretical and consistency problems, such that this approach did not resurface again in the scientific literature until the mid-1970s in various forms and has since been used more widely.[3] Combination with cluster or factor analyses as well as the increased efficiency of modern data processing facilities allow increased use of this instrument in the background of various tools offered for dealing with this cross-impact problem. The classic method of cross-impact analysis is clearly recognizable in all these applications.

The first step is establishing the relevant developments (areas of influence, determinants, variables, etc.) that describe a specific system. Because it makes sense and in accordance with the Delphi technique, these factors as well as players in the system investigated are chosen by means of a communication process, usually in the form of a workshop. At the same time, a common language is developed within the work group that ensures a basic understanding between participants. Essential prerequisites for efficient communication ultimately taking place in the participating group are the building of a consensus on the above mentioned factors, their relative importance in the system, and their exact definitions.

The second step consists of developing the actual cross-impact matrix, which records the intensities and directions of reciprocal impacts between the variables observed. Usually, the determinants are established during another workshop. Originally, it was attempted to record these cross-impact parameters via the Delphi technique, frequently with meticulous precision. In the meantime it has been shown that a four-step scale is sufficient for attaining a maximum of information. This is because efficiency criteria must also play a crucial part in such a procedure, of course. In addition, the pretense—especially with a view toward a longer-term future—of decimal-point accuracy does not make much sense.

The cross-impact matrix, already described by Gordon and Haywood in 1968 in the previously-mentioned *Futures* article, is of particular importance for further development of this work in the direction of scenarios. This will allow working out in detail the roles and importance of individual variables and ultimately also the degree to which the entire system can be influenced by varying individual factors that have been recognized as crucial.

Therefore, the Delphi technique and cross-impact analysis are important building blocks for constructing scenarios on a comprehensive foundation. At this point we do not address the mathematical/statistical and probability theoretical basics in any detail; Linstone and Turoff's book provides all the fundamentals needed in practice.[4]

NOTES

1. Cf. among others, Vester, F. (*Sensitivitätsmodell*), 1992, Godet, M. (*Anticipation*), 1994; Gausemeier, J., Fink, A. and Schlake, O. (*Szenario-Management*), 1996.

2. Gordon, Th.J. and Haywood, H. (Initial Experiments), 1968.

3. From 1970 to 1972, W.A. Jöhr and this book's author investigated at times at the University of St. Gallen economic trends for Switzerland with respect to their interconnections by means of cross-impact analysis; in so doing, historical fundamentals, among other issues, had to be checked by means of the Delphi technique.

4. Linstone, H.A, and Turoff, M. (*Delphi Method*), 1975.

PART III

SCENARIOS FOR STRATEGY DEVELOPMENT

14

SCENARIOS AS A REFLECTION OF INTEGRATED MANAGEMENT

FOCUSING ON INDIVIDUAL FIELDS

Past division of social sciences into economics and sociology and of economic science into business administration and economics has, in turn, led to their respective division into increasingly specialized fields such as marketing or econometrics, leading to highly differentiated specialized knowledge. However, at the same time this prevents seeing things from a holistic point of view (Capra, 1988, pp. 203ff.). The management of operational processes, whether in companies, government institutions, or associations, always depends in the end on its integration into a macroeconomic and social framework. Inevitably, long-term managerial decisions have to be supported by information from a macroeconomic and social science perspective if they are to be targeted and promising.

This information requirement can—depending on the issue—be extremely extensive. Information has, in terms of space, to extend as far as global economics and in terms of subject matter as far as inclusion of a large number of social, political, technological, and economic aspects.

MANAGEMENT FROM A HOLISTIC POINT OF VIEW

The St. Gallen management concept builds on the systems approach developed by Hans Ulrich and his students at the University of St. Gallen. In this context, Ulrich has emphasized that the application of cybernetic thinking—as a subdiscipline of systems theory—to social systems is not unproblematic. 'Attempts at modeling social systems on the basis of mechanical cybernetics knowledge must fail necessarily. However, this could not prevent such attempts being made over and over again' (Ulrich, 1988, p. 217). Such a mechanistic method turned out to be wrong, in any event. Further development of systems theory has been orienting it-self on systems that can be characterized as viable. Therefore, living creatures constitute the elements of such systems, making obvious the connection with eco-nomic systems, whether national economies or companies.[1] The special character-istic of such social systems is the fact that they are not limited to changing only in accordance with built-in mechanisms; rather, they develop qualitatively; that is, they are systems that can be described as 'learning organizations' (cf. Senge, 1993).

Knut Bleicher extended this reference frame to 'integrated management' and, in accordance with the requirements of a paradigm shift, as far as a management con-cept that consciously tackles increasing complexity and dynamics. 'Its key ele-ments are a holistic view combined with the integration of various influences in a network of relationships. This provides a pattern of thought for dealing with sys-tems that aims at making it easier for executives to find their way towards a changed management philosophy and, during its implementation, to master the various design problems.'[2]

An essential feature of integrated management in Bleicher's understanding is a determinant, basic paradigmatic idea that governs decisions at the normative, stra-tegic, and operational levels. In this context Bleicher speaks of a management phi-losophy that is distinctly future-oriented in nature and defines a company's attitude to its role and behavior in society. Moreover, the process of a company's finding a purpose in its social environment is oriented toward the company's abil-ity to survive and develop and forms the basis for ideas as to its future positioning in both the economy and society. Thus, the issue of a company's usefulness to its essential reference groups finds its expression in a vision as to the circumstances and development of the company in its future environment. Naturally, these con-siderations also apply to government institutions, where, it should be noted, such fundamental ideas have so far barely taken hold.[3] Because the political horizon of such institutions tends to be only short term, their view of the essentials is often blocked.

STRATEGIC PLANNING AND SCENARIOS

Consequently, the process of strategic planning aims at facilitating a company's 'fitness' for coping with expected future developments by taking advantage of in-ternally available resources. Working with scenarios helps such a process because it allows a glimpse into the various futures—all of which are equally plausible and likely—so reflecting the inherent insecurities of a future-oriented view. No recipes for behavior are prescribed in this process; rather, it is acknowledged that success-ful strategies must be unique and original creations for each of the companies or institutions. This is the only means by which they can prevail against competition.

The scenario technique concentrates on developing processes that expand an organization's abilities to make available the necessary resources. In so doing, more importance is attributed to invention and innovation. Another focus is on mutually developing concepts and a language that can be regarded as prerequisites for such a process in an organization. The provision of a common communication platform usually proves to be a central difficulty, particularly during times of corporate crises. This is because the individuals concerned have differing perspectives and so perceive a problem/crisis differently. Accordingly, working with scenarios contributes to strategic planning in various ways:

- Scenarios structure events and patterns in a company's/institution's environment;
- Unavoidable insecurities are clearly identified;
- Scenarios allow a process of dialectic conversation in which various points of view arc contrasted with one another;
- In this way the knowledge and resources available within a company are included;
- The information required on external relationships and developments of the environment becomes apparent; and
- The necessary information is put in a transparent and implementable form.

USING SCENARIOS IN STRATEGIC PLANNING PROCESSES

By using scenarios in a strategic planning process, an organizational structure is created within an institution—directed at the long term—that makes it easier to cope with unexpected future shocks. There are also advantages in the short term because a company's ability to adapt to changes in the environment is improved by more intensive observation of its environment. At the same time, it should not be overlooked that a successful competitive strategy has to be an original, unique creation; only a 'unique' business idea can stand its ground successfully.[4]

From this perspective the scenario technique turns out to be the counterpart to integrated management because, in both cases, decisions are ultimately understood as choices between various alternatives; that is, the basic idea or vision is developed from a group of alternative future positionings of a company. This vision has to include simultaneously various images of the future within the macroeconomic environment. Therefore, strategic management ultimately includes working with strategic contingency plans relevant to a company. Their function is the registering of changes in the general conditions (i.e., the central factors and key internal and external relationships for the company's system) and making them available for decision making. As defined by integrated management, the resulting decisions have to be coordinated on all corporate levels. This is ultimately the function of a vision and management philosophy.

Thinking in terms of various futures, which is the special feature of the scenario technique, is a crucial facet of integrated management. In this context Ulrich speaks of the necessity of a systemic perspective, which he contrasts with the thus far commonly prevailing nonsystemic view (Ulrich, 1988, p. 223). In particular, he emphasizes that when describing nontrivial systems, holistic ways of thinking are necessary, which follow circular approaches and have integrating effects. Therefore, he also stresses that it is useless to model a social institution as a trivial input/output system and then try bringing it closer to reality by gradually introducing more variables. 'Such a model remains a trivial system, however one that is somewhat more complicated' (Ulrich, 1988, p. 224). The function of systems theory and cybernetics is not only gaining knowledge on the characteristics and behavior of complex systems but also deriving from it rules as to how to deal mentally and in reality with such circumstances. Working with scenarios is consistent with this systemic perspective and obviously focuses on those managerial levels that are relevant from a corporate policy point of view (i.e., normative and strategic management). Operative management, on the other hand, is concerned with carrying out 'day to day business.' At this level it is possible to continue using conventional forecasting approaches in accordance with the short term nature of the issues.[5] In so doing, the usual nonsystemic perspective is overcome by incorporating such approaches in normative-strategic managerial targets.

ON THE WAY TO A LEARNING ORGANIZATION

Working with scenarios leads to success when a company or institution succeeds in making adjustments such that it maximizes its chances of achieving its set purpose, no matter what the environment. This can ultimately be accomplished only by a learning organization. As discussed in Part I, a company or corporation has the dual function of preserving its viability and strengthening its ability to develop. In order to be able to make important decisions, corporate management has to understand both the organization itself and its environments.

A company's 'personality' is incorporated in its business idea. Its ability to survive and develop can be examined by comparing this business idea with assumptions as to the future development of its environments. However, the future is uncertain to a large degree, and alternative outcomes are possible. Using the scenario technique in a planning process does not mean predicting something that is unpredictable. Rather, several equally plausible futures are investigated. These represent the test criteria for the usefulness of a company's vision or business idea. Options for potential adjustments become evident by comparing these possible futures. At the normative level it is not efficiency criteria that are at the forefront but the effectiveness of corporate alignment.[6]

This means that working with scenarios greatly deepens the concerns of a learning organization. The use of visions and multiple images of the future supports the analysis of environmental development trends. At the same time, it commands thorough reflection on experiences gained thus far and the mental models used in the process (Espejo et al., 1996, p. 92). Assessment of a business idea by means of various images of the future permits development of various options as to future action. Table 14.1 illustrates the parallelism in mental structure between strategic planning and integrated management of a learning organization. Ultimately, both the strategic planning process and the use of scenarios are based on the idea that a company (institution) is a living and learning organization whose primary objec-

Table 14.1
Strategic Planning and Learning Organizations

Strategic Planning Phases	Features of Learning Organizations
• Objectives: initiated by (expected) developments in the framework or by internal pressure to strengthen the ability to survive and develop	• Implement driving force for the learning cycle
• Analysis of the organizational prerequisites for success, including adaptability	• Develop mental models and theories for the evaluation of the framework
• Analysis of present and future environments (scenarios of the framework) by taking into account uncertainties and alternatives	• Examine existing models and experiences; identify new patterns
• Examination as to whether the organizational prerequisites meet the requirements of the environmental scenarios	• Make the necessary changes in mental models
• Development of (corporate) policy measures for adjustment of fit	• Plan future steps
• Implementation	• Implementation

tive is preservation of its ability to survive and develop. This organism's environments are observed, via such an approach, on the basis of scenarios.

In a learning organization or company a constant cycle of experience assessment takes place in order to evaluate and improve future decision processes (e.g., during the process of strategy development). Following Senge and Kolb, this cycle is referred to as feedback loop of learning.[7] Figure 14.1 shows the elements of this feedback loop:

1. The starting point for learning are experiences that were of significance, at least in part, to the company. They are the results of past decisions or actions and include both problems and positive circumstances.

2. Criteria have to be established for evaluating these experiences. These are by no means final; they vary both with time and the level of decision making.

3. When examining these experiences (i.e., checking our actions in the light of the preceding criteria and environmental conditions) new, previously unnoticed patterns and developments become apparent. In cases where the expected effect of a decision has not materialized, the underlying mental model that guided our behavior does not agree with actual reality.

Figure 14.1
Feedback Loop of Learning

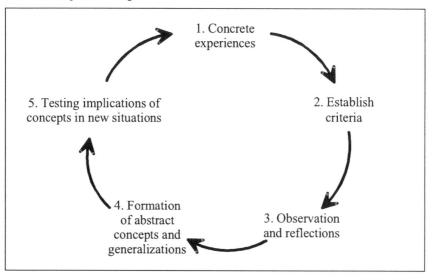

Sources: Following Kolb, D.A. and Rubin, I.M. (*Organizational Behavior*), 1991; Stucki, G. and Sangha, O., (Principles), 1998, p. 3.

4. When researching the reasons for such deviations,we develop new theories as to how our ideas about the environment have to change on the basis of observations and analyses. Finally, the old mental model and the new reality are integrated into a new theory.

5. New measures are taken on the basis of this new approach, such that the effects of this new theory can be tested in new situations via new actions.

Now we are back at the beginning of the feedback loop. New experiences are gained resulting from our actions and decisions, which again agree only in part with our expectations. In this way the cycle starts all over again; an organization is learning. Renewed assessment shows that our theory requires further development, so the process is continued. This feedback loop of learning can also serve as a holistic phenomenon to describe the process of strategy development as an integration of experience, plausibility, and action. Such a model is based on a continuous, step-by-step developmental process, instead of the idea that a correct answer exists. Therefore, such a process depends less on forecasts because the future's uncertainty and multivariety are included directly in the process.

NOTES

1. Ulrich distinguishes three levels. At the material level the focus is on analytical examination of material transformation processes (what is it composed of?); at the functional

level he looks at links and immaterial processes (how does it work?); and finally at the sense level the question is posed as to the purpose of a system; that is, the focus is on understanding (what sense does it make?); Ulrich, H. (Systemische Sicht), 1988, pp. 217ff.

2. Bleicher, K. (Konzept), 1996, p. 70. Here, Bleicher refers *expressis verbis* to Ulrich and Probst's work as described already in Part I of this book.

3. It is still open as to whether the rather promising approaches of so-called New Public Management will allow management of public institutions to depart from operative questions and to turn increasingly to normative and strategic tasks; cf. Schedler, K. (*Verwaltungs-führung*), 1996.

4. This original 'business idea,' which ultimately determines a company's or business unit's uniqueness, is the basis for prevailing in a market. It is based on the specific expertise available in each case; Heyden v.d., K. (*Scenarios*),1996, pp. 107 ff., 159ff.

5. Cf. Part IV.

6. The point is not doing things the right way but doing the right things.

7. Senge, P.M. (*Fifth Discipline*), 1993, pp. 233ff.; Kolb, D.A. and Rubin, I.M. (*Organizational Behavior*), 1991.

15

SCENARIOS AS INSTRUMENTS OF FORECASTING

THE TERM 'SCENARIO'

The term 'scenario' is used for creating pictures of several possible 'futures.' Due to the systemic view it is attempted to simultaneously take into account complexity resulting from a variety of factors and relationships, as well as great dynamics of change. Scenarios are possible images of the future whose function is the concentration of a variety of ideas and expectations. In order not to again restrict this knowledge prematurely, *no* probability of occurrence is attached initially to these individual images. In so doing, the systems approach requires application of several methods of futures research and detachment from the idea that forecasts are possible in this area. Scenarios consider many factors and relationships that go beyond a purely economic understanding of a system and include various fields of activity in society.

The term 'scenario' is presently 'fashionable' and in danger of decaying into a vogue word. It is a Late Latin expression for the location where a stage is set up. Today's usage of the term actually derives from theater language and describes the decor of a set (i.e., a 'scene'). The actual activities take place against this backdrop. In a theater their purpose is the creation of the right atmosphere for the audience.

Application of the term 'scenario' to economics and social sciences has been attributed to the futures researcher Herman Kahn. He worked for the Rand Corporation in Santa Monica, California, in the 1950s, a 'think tank' of the U.S. Air Force, which in addition to military future outlooks also dealt with economic, technological, and social perspectives. Besides the scenario technique, the Delphi technique and cross-impact analysis were, if not invented, at least further developed at that time (cf. Chapters 12 and 13). Kahn defined scenarios as follows: 'Scenarios describe hypothetically a succession of events with the objective of drawing attention to causal relationships and working towards decisions.' The central element of this definition is the hypothetical aspect (i.e., asking for conceivable alternative futures). In addition, the words 'succession of events' and 'causal relationships' emphasize the demand for logical consistency in a scenario. Finally, the reference to a basis for decision making stresses that scenarios have also to be quantified if they are to provide a useful basis for decisions. Additional attributes of scenarios are:

- Scenarios show environmental developments (i.e., do not deal with strategies for companies or national economies).[1]
- There are always several 'futures.' Which one of these occurs will never be known for sure. This is why scenarios are suitable for investigating alternative futures.
- No scenario will occur exactly as it has been described because scenarios have reciprocal effects on actual development.[2]
- Scenarios are particularly suitable for describing the many interconnected processes in the business world. They allow the combining of demographic changes, social trends, political events, economic variables, ecological conditions, and technological developments.

In the true sense of theater language a scenario reflects, therefore, a scene and the future development of events on a stage. Corporate management and (government) institutions, act against this set's backdrop. Scenarios allow inclusion of the various internal and external relationships: working with clients, suppliers, and associations and at the government level, with citizens, parties, unions, and other countries. In this way they meet the requirements of a holistic view of the system under investigation and ensure very complete insight into general conditions.

Therefore, scenarios show different futures, all of which are equally likely, and so open up to us choices with a view to the consequences of a decision. Instead of having to concentrate only on problems observed in past developments, expectations as to the future can be considered deliberately. This can be summarized as follows: scenarios open up choices by showing various futures, all of which are equally likely.

STRUCTURE OF A SCENARIO ANALYSIS

From the Scenario Cone to Scenario Space

The scenario technique can be well illustrated on the basis of the scenario cone (see Figure 15.1). The present is located at the narrowest (i.e., the starting point) of the cone. The widening cone represents the future's complexity and uncertainty. This is because the further we move from today's situation into the future, the greater becomes uncertainty (cf. Figure 2.3). At the same time, dynamics increase (i.e., changes in the structures of the system observed occur, and complexity of the subject observed becomes more important with increasing distance into the future).

Figure 15.1
The Scenario Cone

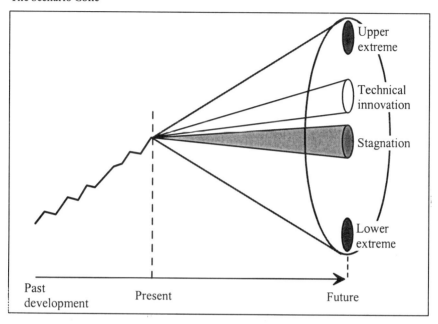

Source: Following Reibnitz, U.v. (*Szenario-Technik*), 1991, p. 27.

At the starting point of the cone the relationships in the system observed and the factors influencing them are known. This system is reflected in a company's output and position in the market and an economy's attractiveness of location and economic situation.

In scientific circles it is a controversial issue as to whether the cone's beginning can be depicted as a point, or whether it should be a plane that includes the various points of view of individuals, companies, institutions, political parties, and so on, when evaluating and interpreting the present and even the past (see Figure 15.2). There are already differing views of reality when perceiving the present, which are determined by different assessments.[3] It is exactly such perceived structures that often determine the choice of possible images of the future. Therefore, a crucial element of scenario thinking is realizing that the view of the future is often restricted by a specific view of the present. Such limitations have to be overcome if the field of possible alternatives is to be investigated fully. This has to be regarded as a critical element of scenario thinking.

Accordingly, the specific view at the starting point can influence the choice of scenarios. The subjectivity in stating a probability of occurrence becomes particularly apparent from the specific view held at the starting point. It also has to be considered that a scenario, labeled A in Figure 15.2, in its progression to A' does by no means have to be always desirable from a macroeconomic view. Therefore, possi-

Figure 15.2
Space of Possible Scenarios

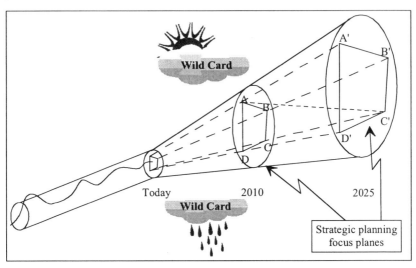

Source: Following Taylor, C.W. (World Scenarios), 1988, p. 4.

bly measures are taken at the macroeconomic level that 'redirect' development to C'. This circumstance ultimately makes it impossible to attribute probabilities of occurrence to individual scenarios because such a choice ultimately contains a subjective assessment of the field of observation. Consequently, the cone depicts the conceivable space of plausible futures, which is visualized via scenarios.

Following this line of thinking, it was derived from the classic point of view that it would be sensible to present forecasting results in the form of a 'developmental corridor' or 'scatter range' looking like a cone, because it becomes wider with increasing distance into the future. The width of this developmental corridor or cone depends on the following influential factors: the greater the influence of interference variables in the past, the greater the forecasting error that can be expected in the future (i.e., the wider a forecast's corridor or scatter range has to be); the more reliable a forecasting procedure is to be, the wider the forecast corridor or cone required and the more that possible future developments, despite their unlikely occurrence, have to be covered by the forecast; and the wider the forecast horizon, the wider the forecast corridor or cone has to be, because with increasing distance of a forecast into the future, the forecasting error inevitably also increases. Therefore, it was suggested that two instead of a single forecast value be provided to define the upper and lower limits of presumed development. This suggestion is based on the probability theory hypothesis that the statistical function, which best describes quantitatively past development, should also provide the most probable characterization of future development. In other words, the estimated errors that can be calculated for the past should also apply to the future.

However, with developmental corridors and cones—whose widths are determined through analyses of the past—the entirely wrong impression that actual development will in the end have to remain within the projected range can be created on the parts of forecast users. This diverts a forecast user's view from the much more important understanding that, especially in the long term, the decisive premises or general conditions for the development of the variable to be predicted can change.[4] Therefore, in our view forecasting possibilities cannot be improved by operating with widths or scatter ranges that have only subjective content based on probability theory at best, so providing no guarantee for their occurrence.

It is significant in this context that, particularly for longer-term alternative forecasts, results provided as figures probably lead to a better gauging, especially when making comparisons, of the consequences of such a development. However, the underlying assumptions and hypotheses are of central importance for such forecasts because they ultimately determine the result. In any event, it should not be the other way around, although this may still happen every once in a while.

'Wild Cards' as Potential Interference Variables

However, all futures that can possibly be conceived have not yet been captured. Developments and events that jump out of this cone, so to speak, and that do not seem very plausible from today's perspective are referred to as 'wild card' scenarios and are, by definition, outside the cone's margins (cf. Figure 15.2). These are serious, destructive, catastrophic, or anomalous events that are essentially not predictable. Such developments bring with them a massive change in the environment. Although an extremely small probability of occurrence must be attached to such events in the given circumstances, they nonetheless cannot be excluded. 'A wild card is a future development or event with a relatively low probability of occurrence but a likely high impact on the conduct of business.'[5] Wild card scenarios can become plausible at any time. Thus, if they penetrate the cone, the environmental assumptions of the scenarios in question will be altered to a great extent. They would also 'screw up' the logical progression of the scenarios within the cone until new recovery strategies, which can be regarded as driving forces for new scenarios, are developed that make allowances for the new trend.

Scenarios and Human Behavior

With such considerations it is important to take into account that the future comes about not only through the driving forces upon which each development is based but also through human decisions. Therefore, as a starting point for all future possibilities, realistic scenarios have to focus first on the current situation and underlying forces that have led to this condition. Second, a future scenario develops in response to the development of a group of determinant driving forces. However, this development does not occur only as a purely mechanical process based on past relationships. Rather, and third, the intentions and behaviors of people have to be considered.

It can be derived from the fact that the teleological concept of attractive and repulsive forces is introduced here that the concepts, symbols, and visions of possible future developments are not all equally attractive. Therefore, one future possibility will appear more attractive than another and so will move behaviors and policies more in this direction. Accordingly, negative images of possible futures will influence behavior such that undesired results are avoided. Consequently, a range of future scenarios from desirable to undesirable (scenario margins) is a useful approach for connecting future possibilities with the present. In this connection, attractive and repulsive forces can be the driving forces for scenarios as well as influence human decisions. In addition, wild cards will affect these trends. These are unexpected future events that—as in the past—can greatly influence a system's development; however, they can be predicted only with difficulty. Extreme events—world wars, availability of cheap fusion energy, fundamentalism as a global player, large-scale natural disasters, invasion from outer space—would have a great influence on the world's future; however, probabilities cannot be attached to them.

Variability with Time

As mentioned already and as also derivable from Figures 15.1 and 15.2, it is assumed that there are only minor changes in a system in the near future. The general conditions for the near future can therefore also be described with conventional, quantitative methods (cf. Figure 2.3). However, with increasing distance into the future, changes occur in the system that no longer allow a forecast as to its behavior. It is unknown what new factors will come into play, and it can no longer be answered conclusively as to the effects resulting from them in individual areas or the system as a whole.

If, at a future time, a cut is made through the cone, then at that time all possible and conceivable futures will be located on the intersecting plane. This means that, theoretically, a very large number of conceivable futures will result from diverting the 'cathode ray' of the 'Braun tube scenario cone' developed on the basis of the past. This picture also illustrates the increasing size of the plane of possible futures in the long term, which in the end cannot be tackled within the corporate planning process. However, when facing such variety, resignation and return to familiar extrapolation along with its pseudosecurity are, by no means, appropriate. Rather, it is essential to confront the uncertainties of the future consciously and to work out, from one's own point of view, various possible reactions for all cases that are, from today's perspective, particularly uncertain and especially relevant to the company.

Requirements for Scenarios

Experience with application of the scenario technique at the corporate level has shown that in the vast majority of cases it is sufficient to develop three scenarios.

This is because when working with scenarios, the efficiency principle must also apply such that only a limited number of futures can be worked out at any one time. These scenarios must meet the following criteria: the individual developments within the scenario must be consistent and cannot contradict each other; scenarios must be distinguished by sustainability and stability, and smaller changes in the general conditions must not lead to the building's collapse; and scenarios should have a wide scope and be designed in particular for those cases that would be especially 'painful' for a company. The purpose of this is to shed as much light as possible on the opposing margins of the scenario cone.

A Baseline Scenario as the Starting Point

As a first step, we recommend on the basis of our experience developing a baseline scenario as the starting point for alternative considerations.[6] In so doing, the main focus is on projecting the developments observed over the past 5 to 10 years into the future. Therefore, what is developed is not a static scenario but rather a continuation of both the dynamics observed previously in the change of structures or relationships and the development of key factors. In this way, one moves largely within known and familiar territory. Nonetheless, it is possible to point out problems that would result from continuing past behavior such that early indications as to possible problem situations and the necessary steps for solving them become evident.

In the baseline scenario, the relevant players, 'movers and shakers,' and mechanisms of effect of variables as well as their mutual relationships are determined simultaneously. Starting with the players, the central areas of influence of the system under investigation are analyzed initially and then concretized in the form of variables. The list of variables thus received serves in describing the system. The analyses that have to be carried out in this context allow setting up a system of effects. The use of a cross-impact-analysis allows for an assessment of the interrelations between the variables. Only knowledge about the relevant players, factors, and key relationships in such a system allows, ultimately, the development of informative and realistic scenarios that stand out through consistency and realism.

Following these considerations and the development of a baseline scenario, it is then important to derive one or two alternative scenarios. These are to shed light mainly on the cone's margins or should be designed for cases dealing with developments that are either serious and involve problems for a company or provide exceptional opportunities. Such scenarios allow reflection of corporate policy in possible environmental developments and can be tested for their usefulness and sustainability. They also provide a basis for developing contingency plans and so are of crucial significance for a company's ability to survive and develop. This was the case, for example, with the Royal Dutch/Shell group, which can be regarded as the pioneer for multiple planning methods. When the oil embargo was imposed in October 1973—a little earlier than expected—large sections of the company were prepared for 'rapids.' While crisis management was only beginning on the parts of previously incredulous politicians and other corporations, planners at Shell were already falling back on their contingency plans (Wack, 1984, pp. 84ff.).

Figure 15.3 illustrates schematically the procedure just described. Added to the baseline scenario is, at the levels relevant to each decision, additional information on alternative scenarios such that the overall view of all relevant internal and external relationships has to include the key factors and players.

Table 15.1 gives an example of the relevant levels of decision making and information, as well as the kind of information involved—in this case for scenarios at the macroeconomic level. Due to typographical constraints, this is a vastly abbreviated and simplified example. It illustrates the largely qualitative character of such an approach, while at the same time pointing out the requirement of consistency in the overall picture. It also illustrates the necessary range covered by such a systematic approach.

We are absolutely aware of the dangers associated with working with a baseline scenario. The greatest danger is that those participating in the process prefer such a scenario because its general conditions and relationships are well known. This is especially because one does not have to change oneself or one's behavior significantly, and everything can remain the same. Figure 15.4 shows that this path in particular will be the least successful in the long run. Nonetheless—especially at the political level—this path is extremely popular because adjustments to new circumstances can be avoided and, compared to an adjustment or alternative scenario, initially appears more promising. However, this line of thinking has to deal with the fact that even a well-thought-through base-line scenario does not at all always end in the long term in rosy futures. Rather, it is usually likely to indicate increasingly serious problems.

In addition, a baseline scenario allows not only checking past positioning but also a clean working out of relationships, factors, and players that determined past events and will only successively make room for other conceivable changes.

Figure 15.4 shows the development of two scenarios using economic policy as an example. In the basic scenario, defensive tactics ('everything remains at it was') supported, for example, by a government initially achieve short-term success. By contrast, in the alternative scenario there is initially a 'dry spell' due to structural adjustment (qualitative renewal of structures due to increased innovative activity). This 'dry spell' is characterized by low earnings margins, possibly losses, as well as limited scope for wage increases (i.e., altogether great demands on all employees and management in terms of adjustment). However, in the long term the situation is the reverse: in the alternative scenario there is continuous development on a qualitatively strengthened structural base. By contrast, in the long term there is an existential structural crisis in the baseline scenario requiring general rethinking in order to avoid disintegration phenomena.

Figure 15.3
Structure of a Scenario Analysis

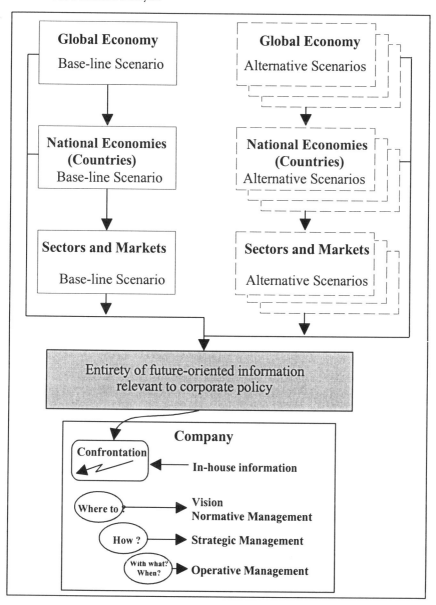

Source: Kneschaurek, F. and Graf, H.G. (*Wirtschafts- und Marktprognosen*), 1986, p. 92.

Table 15.1
Scenario Assumptions (Example: Baseline Scenario)

	Demographic Development	Sociopolitical Situation	General Economic Conditions	General Technological/ Ecological Conditions	Economic Policy Measures
Level 1: Global Economy	- Leveling off in population growth 		Million	Growth Rate %	 |---|---|---| | 1990 | 5283 | | | 1995 | 5687 | 1.73 | | 2000 | 6091 | 1.49 | | 2005 | 6491 | 1.38 | | 2010 | 6891 | 1.28 | | 2015 | 7286 | 1.20 | | | | 1.12 |	- Increasing role of market economic principles - Multilateral agreements to strengthen security policy - Delay in coordination of environmental protection	- Protections eliminated only slowly - Increased cooperation between developing countries - Increase in direct international investments	- Direct investments and transfer of know-how primarily between triad and its "clusters" - Coordination of global ecological projects takes great effort - Information technologies promote increase in productivity	- Increasing importance of World Trade Organization - Global market prices lead to pronounced structural shifts - MAI (Multilateral Agreement on Investment) implemented - First attempts towards Kyoto agreement continued
Level 2: Economic Regions	- Continued growth of Third World population - Significant differences in life expectancy |	1990	2000	2010	2015 | Developed abs. 1148.1 1186.9 1214.0 % 21.7 19.5 16.7 Developing abs. 4134.2 4904.4 6071.9 % 78.3 80.5 83.3 Western Europe abs. 378.8 389.6 388.6 % 7.2 6.4 5.5 GR % W. Europe 0.3 -0.0	- EU expanded, organization takes great effort, fluctuating dynamics, aging societies with pensioners' mentalities - Countries on eastern margin integrated; CIS functions as a joint between Europe and Islam, decreasing importance of Europe in decision-making bodies - Black Africa remains poorhouse - Fundamentalism locally confined	- Aging curbs dynamics in Southeast Asia - North/South American alliance strengthened - China's huge potential under constant threat of overheating	- Technology transfer into countries on eastern margin accelerated only slowly due to persistent uncertainties - Intensified research and development coordination in EU - USA remains prime technology power	- Density of regulation in EU decreases only slowly despite WTO - Market economic principles on the increase in eastern rim countries, association in EU region progressing - CIS a fickle partner showing latent danger of reversion
Level 3: National Economies	- Open policy towards non-residents in order to combat gaps in qualification Integration scenario: |	1990	2000	2010	2015 | Pop. ('000) 6750.7 7243.6 7443.3 7498.7 Foreign (%) 16.7 20.5 21.9 22.0 > 65's (%) 14.6 15.3 17.5 19.0 GR p.a. (%) 0.8 0.7 0.3 0.2 Load ratio 62.0 61.2 60.5 66.1 - Large increase in the load ratio	- Free rides with integration - Relative competitiveness strengthened only partially - Exodus of open minds weakens position (brain drain)	- Bilateral softening = delayed EU compliance - De facto EU member at approx. 2010 - Site attractiveness unbalanced, network partners unstable	- Acceptance of technology limited - Technology balance with other countries increasingly negative - Efficient use of resources and the environment becomes increasingly important	- Opportunistic implementation of deregulatory measures - EU economic policy de facto implemented - Monetary policy remains "independent" with close coordination - Social network becomes increasing burden
Level 4: Sectors	- Stagnation of birthrate in native population - Adaptation of qualification hierarchy to include nonresidents - Adjustment to EU labor market rules - Structural preservation policy to protect those who are inadequately qualified	- Liberalization vs. protectionism controversial due to regional equalization - Low acceptance of technology - Use of environmental technology sporadic - Panicipation weakened by doubtful partner in networks	- Partial exodus of companies - Lowering of barriers between markets intensifies pressure to adjust in sectors oriented towards domestic markets	- Resource intensive processes largely shifted to source - Willingness to cooperate under increasing pressure - Deregulations difficult to implement	- Promotion of science also to support regional structure - Protection of sectors softened by EU pressure - Internationalized sectors belatedly receive general conditions for promotion of site attractiveness

Figure 15.4
Advantages and Disadvantages of a Baseline Scenario

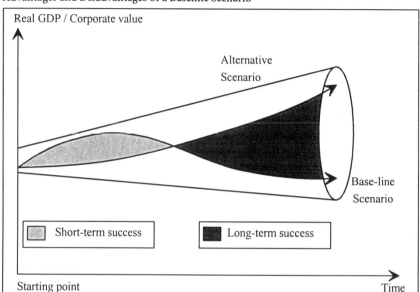

Differentiation from Planning

Occasionally the term 'scenario planning' is used in the literature in describing a traditional decision analysis method, the main purpose of which is estimating the probabilities of various futures. Such an approach is rooted in a rationalistic paradigm that works with a single criterion for evaluating options in order to determine the 'one correct answer' for each given case. A typical example for this procedure is the development of two sales budgets with either high or low turnovers. These can be regarded as possible lines of development in association with given probabilities of occurrence. The results of various corporate policy options can then be compared with 'scenario' targets (usually, three scenarios are used: high, low, and probable), whereby probabilities of occurrence are also determined for these scenarios. In this manner a quality measure can be calculated for each of these options, and eventually the one showing the best result is chosen. We consider using the term 'scenario' for such a procedure fundamentally wrong. Such 'scenarios' are none other than classic forecasts.

Scenarios do not want to predict; rather, they are instruments of knowledge. A method that provides high and low values does not expand our knowledge because no new concepts are incorporated in the forecasting process. This is because the creation of three futures in a single dimension, to which are attached subjective probabilities, is exactly the same activity, in terms of its concept, as developing a classic forecast. Such a procedure does not make us investigate conceptually different future paths.

In contrast, scenarios are a set of reasonably plausible, but structurally different, futures. These are developed on the basis of causal analyses, not of probability assumptions that reflect various interpretations of the factors driving the fundamental structures of corporate environments. Scenarios are developed as an instrument for considering strategic steps through comparison with structurally different, however plausible, images of the future. In order to be able to perceive them as different images, the same probability of occurrence has therefore to be initially attached to them.

NOTES

1. Cf. following section.
2. Cf. following section.
3. Cf. Berger, P.L. and Luckmann, Th. (*Konstruktion*), 1997.
4. In such circumstances it would be more useful to think about the possibilities of such a structural change and, if need be, to think alternatives through. This is better than indulging in false security regarding the probability of occurrence of a forecast by fixing developmental corridors or cones.
5. Rockfellow, J.D. (*Wild Cards*), 1994, pp. 14ff.
6. An opposing view is that one should work particularly with alternative scenarios that deviate from previous developments, because 'business as usual' would receive priority otherwise.

16

WORKING WITH SCENARIOS AT THE CORPORATE LEVEL

THE RELEVANCE CRITERION

'[A] system's intelligence and the corporate policy activities arising from it . . . ultimately·determine actual corporate development while trying to achieve a constantly changing fluid equilibrium between the external and internal worlds in the current of time between the past and the future' (Bleicher, 1996, p. 83). In so doing, increased environmental dynamics forces a company to confront the future in a timely and forward-looking manner. Systems theory and the obligation for holistic thinking have illustrated (Ulrich, 1988) that what matters is not reducing complexity through standardization; rather, complexity has to be tackled on a case-by-case basis and met with internal complexity. These experiences have shown clearly that the classic strategy of complexity reduction is unsuitable and has to be replaced instead with holistic thinking that takes into account the abilities of systems to survive and develop.

Therefore, it is essential for companies, as well as public institutions and other organizations, to develop in a timely manner relevant information on anticipated environmental changes. Forecasts that are expected to provide information as to what the future will be are usually used for this purpose. We have explained that 'knowledge as to the long-term future' cannot be attained via any of the available methodological approaches. In the end, people do not possess prophetic talents, even if some 'gurus' would like to make such promises. As the future will not develop along a linear and therefore clearly predictable pattern, even an abundance of irrelevant information cannot contribute to gaining a clear view of the relevant developmental trends in the environment. Therefore, traditional methods are more and more likely to fail.

STRATEGIC ORIENTATION IN THE LIGHT OF ALTERNATIVE FUTURES

The issue of relevant environmental variables and their selection (i.e., the question as to the correct trends because those are the ones that are actually relevant) is of particular significance, as each company has its unique environment. Because a company's business idea has to be unique if it wants to survive in the market, the information systems relevant to this company are also unique. The insights into a learning organization as previously described—a characteristic feature of a company capable of survival and development—indicate clearly that participation of the employees affected by strategic decisions in the normative strategic process is of central importance. This means that information about the future cannot simply be adopted passively but rather is essential to motivate those affected to actively participate in compiling it and to contribute their own ideas from the start.

A central feature of a strategic process so structured is that, with a longer-term horizon, the future can be projected only via several alternatives. This is because forecasting 'knowledge' is not available and because those involved in the process have different expectations of the future. Accordingly, the use of scenarios has to be the main focus in such a procedure. These activities aim at recognizing potentials that are opening up and at being better prepared for undesired events in order to be able to avoid surprises.

Successful application of the scenario method is based primarily on communication. This is because the number of determinants and the uncertainty of their development increase with greater distance into the future. At the same time, the individual is more and more challenged and eventually overburdened by perceiving and processing his or her future expectations (cf. Siegenthaler, 1993, pp. 51f.). A company's growth prospects, implementation of an innovation, and the developmental prospects of an economy or region depend on a great number of open-ended influences. Consequently, communication has the function of connecting the knowledge available in various minds so as to reveal as complete a picture as possible of both the initial situation and possible future changes. Mutual exchange of this knowledge—if necessary by drawing on expert knowledge in the environment of the company in question—allows targeted recognition of future changes and alternative developments in a company's environment. In this way—in contrast to the usual extrapolative view—fundamental changes in behavior and instruments can also be registered. To this extent, scenarios are the result of a process of discussion and formation of opinions within a group of employees. By generating a common vocabulary, they contribute fundamentally to ensuring communication—via a metalanguage—in this group.[1]

The corporate vision (i.e., the vision of normative management) has to be examined as to its usefulness and fit should various environmental scenarios occur. This again requires combining the entire management team's knowledge and must also ultimately entail communication of this information within the entire corporate hierarchy if the scenario process is to contribute to managerial improvement. In so doing, scenarios serve as a linguistic basis for recording the various points of view within the management team (see also Figure 15.2). Only when the various ideas of those involved in the process are compiled in a compatible form can common strategic priorities also be developed.

ASSESSMENT OF SUCCESSFUL STRATEGIC POSITIONS

Hence, in this developmental process of strategic management the focus is on the issue of the necessary, general, company-specific conditions that allow creation, maintenance, and exploitation of success potentials and determine the resources required for so doing. According to Gälweiler, success potentials are 'the whole structure of all product and market-specific prerequisites relevant to success in each case, which have to be in place at the latest at the implementation stage' (Gälweiler, 1987, p. 6). Pümpin expanded this definition under the term 'successful strategic positions' (SSP) (Pümpin, 1986, p. 33), beyond considering merely product and market-specific aspects, to relating it to essential aspects relevant to a company's competitiveness. These success potentials show the experience gained by a company over time with markets, technologies, social structures, and processes. They become evident through increased success relative to competitors in the market.

At this stage success potentials have to be examined as to their future usefulness in light of the scenarios developed. Consequently, scenarios have to make available the relevant information not only for such an issue but also for expected new success potentials, which are geared toward the development of capabilities that will be suitable in the future for achieving equivalent strengths also vis-à-vis competitors.

Accordingly, scenarios have the function of reflecting successful strategic positions in their respective environments and so of examining whether they can also guarantee in future, or in several futures, a company's sustained ability to survive and develop. Assessment of successful strategic positions is accomplished by means of various scenario images developed in the context of panel discussions of a management team assembled for this purpose. If necessary (i.e., when there are several SSPs in a company) such processes have to proceed both at the 'strategic business unit' (SBU) level and at that of the company as a whole (Heyden, 1996, pp. 75f.). Depending on the division, the summoned work groups have to carry out this discourse on the basis of the environments, determinants, and information relevant to their respective sections.

It can also be derived from the finding that a company's business idea has to possess a unique character in order to survive in the market, that companies having several divisions depend especially on scenarios tailored to their individual needs. Scenarios developed for an entire company are usually not sufficiently detailed to be able to strategically manage to a sufficient degree SBU's. However, scenarios for business units have to fit under the roof of macro-scenarios for an entire company and point to details as to respective markets, competitive technologies, and other environmental variables. In such a way one succeeds in introducing scenario thinking also at the level of SBUs and in strengthening the willingness to use scenarios widely.

SYSTEMS THINKING AS AN AID

'Suitable mental aids for structuring discussions are crucial to the success of a strategic conversation.'[2] Here, systems thinking provides us with important support.[3] In this context a system should be understood as a family of relationships. Therefore, relationships are more important in understanding the system than are the elements between which they occur. If we want to think 'in terms of a system,' it is necessary, first of all, to describe the entire field to be investigated (i.e., the future developments that we want to think about).

In order to recognize the most important factors in the, at first, seemingly inextricable tangle of interdependent details and to record systematically their relationships of effect, we employ a structured, but nonetheless open, procedure. The scenario technique as an applied form of systems thinking aims at attaining specific images of the future by condensing environmental information and putting it in concrete terms. Figure 16.1 shows seven steps, from describing a system to developing environmental scenarios. It should be kept in mind that the elements determine each other and form part of an iterative process.

'This procedure consists of three phases. For the 'system description' and 'set of variables' steps structured brainstorming techniques are used in order to first develop as complete and varied a picture of the environment as possible and to register all trends that are potentially relevant. In so doing, a common language is developed simultaneously among participants, which is a prerequisite for the functioning of a strategic conversation. The 'system criteria' and 'cross-impact matrix' steps aim at evaluating the aspects that make up a system. On one hand, all defined factors are assessed as to whether they can create an image of the system in-

Figure 16.1
Systems Thinking Proceeds in Three Phases and Seven Steps

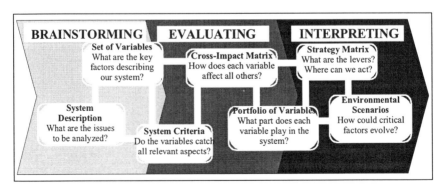

Source: Schlange, L.E. (Scenario Planning), 1995, p. 98.

vestigated, while on the other, the interdependencies between all factors are recorded systematically.[4] As for interpretation, the cross-impact matrix results are finally worked up in two forms. The system's 'portfolio of variables' provides information on the dynamic characteristics of the variables, while a 'strategy matrix' shows where we have to pay attention to strong levers during strategy development and how these can be influenced. In the final step 'environmental scenarios' are developed that record possible future developments of critical external factors.'[5]

IMPLEMENTATION

Recognition of relevant factors, analysis of alternative future images from the point of view of their relevance to a company-related environment, examination of normative and strategic ideas of management with respect to their usefulness as alternative images of the future, and discussion of possible measures: all these steps remain an academic exercise as long as the options obtained are not adopted or implemented. Such adoption and implementation require an intensive discussion among management as to the ideas compiled that focuses on how the company should prepare itself for the future and for various futures.

As various priorities usually emerge within a work group selected by management for evaluating these questions, these have to be brought closer to a consensus via further discussion so that planning steps can also be tackled eventually. In so doing, the focus must not be on continuing what existed and was familiar in the past but rather on working out specific contingency plans for 'worst case' developments and also on looking for new orientations toward newly discovered areas of opportunity. Therefore, it is important to also shed light on alternative developments (alternative scenarios) in addition to a basic scenario (cf. Chapter 15).

The point about this method is making lists of options available, checking them for overlap and contradictions, and tuning them to each other via strategy assessment. The purpose of this is emphasizing those options that are regarded as having particular priority by the persons involved in this matter. Here, especially strong agreement becomes evident with respect to the potential benefit of the planned managerial steps so as to be better able to face an uncertain future. In addition, such jointly developed strategies find greater acceptance, which significantly facilitates their introduction in a company. Specific project proposals or the process shown in Figure 16.1, can—in the case of unexpected results—be again quickly run through and checked as to their reasoning via an actual feedback process by means of analytically developed fundamentals. Both development and continued checking of a strategy always constitute an iterative process.[6]

A promising method requires inclusion of the knowledge spread across many people in a company about the relevant relationships, determinants, and developmental trends in the internal and external environments of the company in question. Combining the widely dispersed experiences and knowledge (insights) is necessary because, as experience has shown, this is the only way to succeed in both recognizing and shedding light on relevant conceivable alternative futures and deriving the necessary steps. Normative management and strategic management want to jointly bring about a situation where a company's future development is also influenced such that the future can be withstood as successfully as possible. A company's ability to survive and develop is therefore also guaranteed in a variety of environments.

The infrastructure necessary for mastering future tasks consists by no means only of material things. Frequently and even more so in the future, knowledge and skill constitute the decisive components for ensuring viability. This knowledge has to be combined with the development of strategic options that will become clear in the future so that the necessary measures in the areas of normative and strategic management can be developed that correspond to the company's vision. However, only implementation in the form of specific measures will guarantee that this sophisticated process will bear fruit for a company. For top management this means that, in addition to fully involving themselves in the process of developing normative and strategic guidelines, their full involvement is also required in implementing the options and obtained results.

NOTES

1. Cf. Schlange, L.E. and Sütterlin, R. (Zukunftsseminar), 1997, pp. 286f.

2. Schlange, L.E. and Sütterlin, R. (Zukunftsseminar), 1997, p. 286.

3. Cf. among others, Vester, F. (*Sensitivitätsmodell*), 1992, Gomez, P. and Probst, G. (*Praxis*), 1995, v. Reibnitz, U.v. (*Szenario-Technik*), 1991, Godet, M. (*Anticipation*), 1994.

4. Cf. Chapter 13.

5. Schlange, L.E. and Sütterlin, R. (Zukunftsseminar), 1997, p. 286.

6. Consequently, the idea has to be dropped for good that conclusive and final information on *the* development of a company's environment can be acquired by pushing a button, so to speak, and that the right decisions can be made for the company based on this 'knowledge about the future.'

17

INTRODUCTION OF SCENARIO THINKING IN CORPORATE POLICY

ADJUSTMENT OF CORPORATE CULTURE

We have illustrated that using the scenario technique in corporate policy has to be considered indispensable, particularly when it is affected by fast changing corporate environments and increasing complexity. In specific terms this means examining a company's vision, as well as the fundamentals of normative and strategic management, from the point of view of their usefulness by means of various scenarios. It has to be determined whether corporate policy is capable—also with fast changing environmental and various general future conditions—of ensuring the company's ability to survive and develop in the long term. Experience has shown that integration of scenario thinking in the planning process and corporate decision-making culture turns out to be a much greater challenge than most managers expect. The reason for this is that working with scenarios ultimately also has to fulfill efficiency criteria, and—this is particularly significant—that corporate culture has to be changed such that it is compatible with scenario thinking.[1]

The challenges emanating from a change in corporate culture represent a considerably more complex and difficult task than 'only' developing scenarios or ensuring that this technique is used for special strategic decisions. Why do even companies that take great pains in introducing the scenario approach in the making of their strategic decisions encounter such major difficulties? Many possible explanations have been offered. However, most managers experienced with this issue point out that this is a psychological and cultural problem. Most corporate cultures continue being oriented strongly toward quantitative analyses, preferably with decimal-point accuracy. By contrast, scenarios consist predominantly of qualitative considerations, which, of course, always have to be quantified in order that explicit conclusions and appropriate consequences can be drawn. A central feature of scenarios is that they discuss *various* possible future developments and present not only a single figure derived from a point forecast. This requires the willingness to change one's thinking fundamentally.

Many managerial decisions are still based on quantitative forecasts. For decisions at the operational level, the focus will continue to be on making decisions on the basis of such 'precise' information. However, at the strategic and normative levels of management, scenarios constitute a form of explorative images of the future, and anybody involved in this process is forced to understand the future and the decision-making process as a choice between alternatives. Therefore, scenarios force us to admit to a certain degree of incompetence.[2] Working with alternatives, understanding a decision as a choice between various possibilities, even thinking in terms of futures as a whole have thus far not been practiced much and are therefore difficult for many decision makers.

Consequently, introduction of scenarios in the planning process presupposes that corporate culture has to change significantly. The most important requirement is changing the system such that managers think through alternatives (futures, strategies, options) as a matter of habit before making a decision. This process not only is desirable but must necessarily and ultimately occur automatically. However, the necessary transition to such alternative thinking is difficult with the thought patterns that are customary today. Only conscious, recurring efforts toward reorganizing thought processes in this direction will, in the end, be successful, as has been shown so far by experience in companies that use scenarios to support their planning. This is because it is useless if this happens only at the managerial level and among a company's planning staff; this way of thinking also has to be introduced in operative and functional units.

At the same time, it is essential to depart from the idea that scenarios could simply be purchased somewhere 'ready-made' and that all requirements are therefore already fulfilled. Working with scenarios can, as with any other method, be successful only if the relevance criterion is fulfilled for each corporate issue (i.e., a clear decision focus is chosen). However, this does not mean uncritical acceptance of views held by whatever management is in place at any one time. Rather, scenarios should question conventional views, meaning that particularly the problem sources and issues regarded by management as latent dangers have to be incorporated in such an analysis. Therefore, management is required to participate in the scenario process to a large degree; in so doing, scenarios have to be adjusted to the requirements of the company-specific planning process. Here, the emphasis is on an explicit description of alternative bases for decision making. Only if this requirement is fulfilled can a company succeed in involving top management with full conviction and in implementing the scenario process as an efficient instrument for finding decisions.

AREAS OF SCENARIO APPLICATION

Since introduction of scenario thinking in a company is by no means an easy task, the initial steps in such a process turn out to be particularly meaningful.

Surely, scenarios can also be used for designing horror visions that would affect a company's environment enormously and endanger it extremely. Such a practice can be useful only in exceptional cases. Rather, the use of scenarios seems most suitable in circumstances that represent significant junctures for companies (i.e., when they can contribute to management instinctively and creatively at the same time). These circumstances are specifically chosen situations associated with the possibility of considerable increases in earnings. Such opportunities present themselves frequently when major investments are planned so that their usefulness, risks, and prospects can be examined. This leads to at least two obvious advantages: (1) central, long-term decisions are best suited to being evaluated by scenarios; and (2) because such an investment usually affects managers both in business units and in top management, two hierarchical levels are addressed at the same time. In addition, the use of scenarios in the entire company almost forces business units to also work with appropriately adjusted scenarios.

Another useful area of scenario application is the preparation of contingency plans. This is because it allows checking of the strategic importance of trends, uncertainties, and assumptions with respect to the future development of the general conditions of the company in question. An excellent method for doing this is developing alternatives to a basic scenario, on which, for example, present corporate strategy is based. It functions as a test of robustness for present strategies and strengthens at the same time the realization that other scenarios are conceivable. As illustrated in Figure 17.1, the main focus should be on making management realize that working with scenarios has to have pronounced repercussions for the existing strategic planning system, no matter what starting point is chosen. Figure 17.1 makes clear how much innovation has to be incorporated in the planning process, as scenarios have feedback on many areas of this process. During this planning process it is important to develop a precise schedule for applying scenarios that lays out which changes should occur and when. For this purpose an actual implementation plan has to be developed, as the use of scenarios in companies cannot occur arbitrarily.

CONVERSION INTO STRATEGIES

Some managers are so mesmerized by the development of scenarios that they forget that these images of the future are not an end in themselves. After all, they are merely a means for starting the thought process for new possibilities and options. Scenarios are an instrument for making better strategic decisions possible. However, it is precisely this connecting point between scenarios and strategy that seems to create the greatest problems for decision makers.

For many managers completion of a scenario is an anticlimactic experience. 'What now?' frequently describes the situation well. If a convincing answer cannot be given immediately, the result of all this work tends to disappear in a drawer. Consequently, the process of converting a developed scenario into a strategy proves to be an exceptionally important process. However, as experience has

Figure 17.1
The Use of Scenarios in Strategic Management

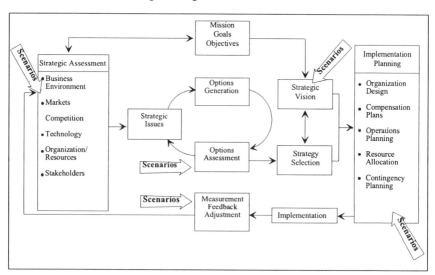

Source: Wilson, I. (Implementation), 1998, p. 358.

shown, this has to be learned with quite some effort and a great amount of time. Therefore, the development of scenarios will initially be tied to learning various basic techniques, which form the bridge between scenarios and strategy development (Wilson, 1998, p. 359).

COMMUNICATION, COMMUNICATION

A vital part of implementing the scenario process in a company is communication. If such fundamental change is intended and should take hold in a planning process or even the entire planning culture of a company, then the participants have to clearly define both the nature and purpose of such a change and communicate it properly to all employees concerned. Such communication has to meet the requirements of a variety of internal and, in part, external positions. Therefore, the opportunity to pass on the required information is of particular significance during the process of introducing scenario thinking in companies. In order to change the mental structures of corporate managers and planners, proponents of the scenario process have to first gain this group's attention and also keep it. The development of imaginative, yet plausible, scenarios for particular markets has proven a very good way of stirring the interest of operative management. As the term 'scenario' comes from the world of theater, the best scenarios resemble convincing 'stories about the future.' However, besides imagination there must not be a lack of logic, in order to point out new possibilities to the entrepreneurial mind. Accordingly, such 'scripts' require fascinating titles and gripping stories. They must stir the imagination and should also reflect the scenario's dynamics. Change is at the center, which means, at the same time, that not only a beginning and end should be shown but the entire developmental process in its future progression. Pierre Wack, one of the central personalities during introduction of the scenario planning process at Shell, called this process the development of a 'manager's mental maps of the future' (Wack, 1984, p. 62).

Particularly great attention has to be paid to the communication process. This is often overlooked when scenarios are used in a company for the first time. Participation of those concerned in workshops and seminars is a crucial instrument in introducing this process. Usually, scenarios and their effects are submitted in written form, customarily both as a comprehensive version and as an executive summary. However, experience of practically all experts with the scenario process has shown clearly that these written documents, while useful, have by no means the same significance as presentations and extensive discussions. Such communication has to occur at two levels in order to ultimately become part of a corporate culture. First, top management has to ensure with absolute clarity that the process of scenario planning is being pursued with complete sincerity. They must make clear not only how they use scenarios themselves in their own process of decision making but also how others should be using this procedure. Second, planning staff have to work out suitable 'step-by-step guidelines' on how scenarios are developed and best used.[3]

It cannot be emphasized enough that introduction of scenario thinking in a company's planning process has to include quite an extensive educational process at virtually all hierarchical levels. In so doing, the existing planning system has to be checked and appropriate guidelines have to be in hand on how scenarios can be used. Some of these educational steps can be carried out through books and other written material. Experience with adult education has shown, however, that success can essentially be guaranteed only with seminars and suitable interaction. Of particular importance is that the influence of scenario thinking should ultimately also be noticeable in other aspects of a company (e.g., management style and organizational culture). Hierarchical thinking and structures stand in actual contradiction to the scenario process, meaning that inclusion of all involved and their active creative participation promise the best results.

Due to the previously familiar nonsystemic perspective, reasoning errors tend to sneak into such a process, which have to be recognized and eliminated as soon as possible if such a method is to be promising. So, what has to be watched out for? According to Ulrich,[4] the following errors are frequently observed:

- *Thinking in linear causal chains.* These have a beginning and an end. However, dynamic systems are characterized by circular processes (i.e., positive or negative feedback loops). Successful strategies and system control measures are not possible without feedback loops.
- *Models lacking connection to problems.* Modeling based on systems theory is possible only by taking into account the key factors and relationships relevant to each prob-

lem. Such models do not provide any conceptual help until the problem for which they are to develop a solution is clarified (decision focus).

- *Inexpedient system definition.* A sensible definition of the system to be investigated comes about only on the basis of a definable target of knowledge or action. A purely economic definition, as is customary with classic economic models, is unsuitable for deriving rules of behavior for practical measures of economic policy or business management.

- *Reduction to simple systems.* Reducing an issue's complexity through suitable modeling undermines taking into account such complexity, which is crucial to understanding a system's behavior. Consequently, no realistic assumptions or research results can be derived.

- *Not taking into account structured complexity.* Social systems—national economies or companies—have structures. The individual parts of a system are characterized by specific behaviors that also have to be taken into account from a holistic point of view.

- *Mixing of various levels of a hierarchical system.* In order to understand a system defined at a certain level, it is necessary to conduct studies at least at the system's next higher and lower levels (see also Figure 1.3).[5] Social or macroeconomic influences on a company cannot simply be seen as isolated exogenous factors. They have to be recognized as elements of a complex, interconnected system of a higher order, which itself has to be studied as a whole system, as is done by means of the scenario technique.

- *Not taking into account the value level of social systems.* Many economic models are based on a one-dimensional/economistic view of people, which does not reflect day-to-day experiences or the many empirical investigations of values in today's society. We pointed out in Chapter 1 that people are at the center of economic activity, with its many interdependencies in a country's social, political, and organizational context. This means that an economic model also has to be based on the image of 'complex people.' Because social systems consist of people, they therefore have a value dimension. 'If this dimension is defined away due to a misunderstood endeavor toward scientific objectivity, then a social system becomes unintelligible and is reduced to a senseless mechanism.' (cf. Ulrich, 1988, p. 221)

These remarks on possible reasoning errors point out in particular that, when working with scenarios, strategy development is understood as a complex and interconnected system that management wants to intervene in for renewal purposes. Experience has shown that during this phase people are often too impatient, and, at the same time, mistakes made can no longer be eliminated in most cases. Only in exceptional cases do attempts at shortcutting or skipping the methodical steps outlined here not have negative consequences. Of greatest importance is inclusion of the specialized knowledge of all those participating in the task and their fully motivated involvement in developing such an instrument.

CHECKING AND UPDATING SCENARIOS

A good indicator of whether a scenario planning process has become part of a company becomes evident through the way that important participants handle checking and updating of scenarios. If scenarios are to contribute to a company's strategic process comprehensively and usefully, managers have to trust their continued relevance and attribute sufficient weight to checking their occurrence compared with actual events. Therefore, part of planning the implementation of scenario thinking in a company has to be showing how the scenario process can be attuned to the existing process of environmental analysis and its systems of observation. Such systems of observation are particularly useful when current events lead to junctures that scenarios have already identified as leading to various futures. By contrast, the analytical process can point out to companies previously unexpected developments. These are characteristic of, for example, successes of research and development or less clearly visible social and political changes that would produce the basis for entirely new scenarios. Observation and analysis are necessary for keeping the scenario process alive, for strengthening its relevance, and for making sure that it forms a central element of thought in a company.

Experience points to three additional procedures that make the scenario process dynamic and purpose-oriented (Wilson, 1998, p. 367): First, planning staff should plan workshops for scenario development such that their results flow naturally and completely into the usual planning cycle. Frequently, analysis of future environmental developments is planned for the beginning of the year; therefore, processing and tracking of scenarios have to occur in the fall. Second, it is generally believed that the greater the number of viewpoints expressed in a scenario process, the better the ultimately possible results. Including just planning staff is undoubtedly not a good idea. Therefore, management should include the ideas and experiences of marketing staff, technologists, the public relations department, and so on, every person whose experience can provide information as to the driving forces of scenarios. Such a broad base has two advantages: both scenarios and participants benefit from this process. Third, it is helpful to establish a provisional schedule for scenario revisions. Although detailed adjustment is usually necessary, experience in companies that have worked with scenarios for a longer period of time has shown that more radical reconsideration and possible restructuring of scenarios have to occur at intervals of three to four years. Of course, these revisions depend on the speed and occurrence of events, the insights of the original scenario, and, not least, the sector in which the company works.

Departure from the traditional planning process in favor of a scenario-supported strategic planning process requires transformation of corporate culture. Working with scenarios is not only a new planning instrument but a new way of considering future possibilities for companies and of making decisions that strengthen their abilities to survive and develop. Onetime use of scenarios requires considerably less investment than making them an integral part of the corporate planning process. Most problems arising in a company during introduction of a scenario plan are the result of misjudgments as to the extent and duration of the introductory effort necessary for changing, by means of this process, the procedures prevailing in the managerial process at any given time. Table 17.1 gives an overview of the steps of a scenario process in the form of a checklist that summarizes the preceding thoughts.

Table 17.1
Steps for Generating Scenarios

Step 1:	Objective of the scenario project; positioning in the institution; participants in the project. *What decision does management have to make?*
Step 2:	Establish players and variables to be observed. *What players and variables have to be taken into account?*
Step 3:	Division into logical subareas (subsystems). *What structure does the subject of investigation have?*
Step 4:	Establish system interrelationships (within and between subsystems); determine feedback mechanisms. *How is everything interconnected?*
Step 5:	Establish the relevant influential factors and their directions of influence *What are the determinants?*
Step 6:	Designate control variables. *How can they be influenced?*
Step 7:	Describe divergent scenario topics; record possible developments of the influential factors; assign consistent control variables. *What futures are possible?*
Step 8:	Choice of scenarios (a scenario); compile consistent sets of assumptions for the chosen scenarios; describe scenarios verbally. *What future do we choose?*
Step 9:	Quantifications of scenarios (the scenario). *What are the dimensions?*
Step 10:	Editing of a short report; workshops with all involved or affected; establish deadlines and responsibilities. *Who does what?*
Step 11:	Checking of scenarios and environments. *What is next?*
Step 12:	Tracking/updating of scenarios. *What has to be revised and when?*

NOTES

1. Cf. particularly Wilson, I. (Implementation), 1998, pp. 352ff.; Heyden v.d., K. (Business Idea), 1998, pp. 335ff.

2. The traditional definition of 'forecast' supports the following basic managerial precondition, that has been tested in practice for many years: I can make decisions on the basis of knowledge about the future. After all, the outstanding feature of a good manager is 'knowing' what is happening and therefore making the right decision. 'In the classic corpo-

rate culture intuition and vision were considered sheer heresy.' Graf, H.G. (Szenario-Denken), 1998, p. 66.

3. For details on this procedure, see Heyden v.d., K. (*Scenarios*), as well as Gausemeier, J., Fink, A. and Schlake, O. (*Szenario-Management*), 1996.

4. Ulrich, H. (Systemische Sicht), 1988, pp. 226ff.

5. Riedl, R., Biologie der Erkenntnis, Berlin/Hamburg, 1979, cited in Ulrich, H. (Systemische Sicht), 1988, p. 229.

PART IV

SHORT-TERM ECONOMIC
AND MARKET FORECASTING

18

INVESTIGATION SUBJECT
AND AIM OF PERCEPTION

THE ECONOMIC CYCLE PHENOMENON

One of the terms used most frequently in describing an economic situation and outlook continues to be 'business cycle.' In a 'favorable' economic situation the focus is on a positive assessment, whereas unpleasant circumstances and prospects are described during an 'unfavorable' economic situation. Likewise, 'business cycle' is one of the most misused terms and an important cause for a variety of misunderstandings in regard to a national economy's economic situation.

To begin with it has to be kept in mind that what is being described from a cyclical point of view are basically short-term phenomena associated with a country's economic activity. Therefore, the central focus is on the issue of fluctuations in the utilization of production capacity. Figure 18.1 shows a typical example of an economic cycle. However, in reality the notional existence of the most precise possible, three-year sinus curve can be excluded. From a longer-term point of view, 'business activity' is directed to the question of the development of production capacity (when looking at the dynamic behavior and development of potential output). Potential output is subject to greater changes only over the long term. In contrast, the focus with economic cycles is on whether this potential is actually being used at present and in the near future and also on the extent of fluctuation in the degree of utilization of an economy over the following year to year and a half.[1]

Misunderstandings associated with the term 'business activity' emerge when the cyclical short-term phenomenon is not clearly distinguished from the growth phenomenon, describing the long-term development of an economy's potential. This leads to confusion because the term 'business activity' is frequently used also to describe growth phenomena.

Figure 18.1
Typical Example of a Business Cycle

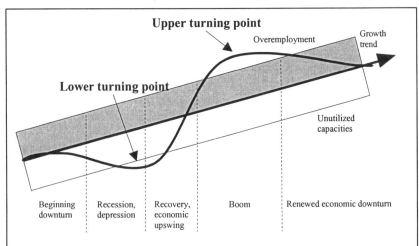

Source: Mettler, D., lecture notes, University of St. Gallen (HSG), 1991.

Cyclical fluctuations have to be clearly differentiated from long-term waves of growth, as shown for Switzerland in Figure 7.2. Kondratieff and van Duijn have shown empirically that economic growth also occurs in 'long waves.'[2] These extend over a period of 10 years or even several decades, in contrast to cyclical fluctuations (periods of 1 to 5 years). Cyclical fluctuations are a typical phenomenon of market economies. First, this is due to the great number of degrees of freedom available to a market economy's entities. Second, great complexity, assessable only to a limited degree, leads to misjudgments and so to fluctuations in the degree of utilization of available production capacities in individual companies and sectors. Through numerous feedforward and feedback mechanisms, a great number of positive and negative impulses influence the structures and modes of function and reaction of economic activities in a national economy, which are characterized by division of labor and global economic interconnections.

Therefore, cyclical development becomes evident—from a macroeconomic point of view—via those relatively short-term fluctuations in the degree of utilization of the production system, usually lasting several years. Market economies always tend to be subject to such fluctuations, varying in degree and intensity between countries. They are characterized at the level of individual sectors or markets by corresponding fluctuations in business that are tied to, although they do not necessarily coincide with, the macroeconomic cyclical trend.

THE ISSUE OF MEASUREMENT

According to the definition of cyclical fluctuations, it would be appropriate to measure them based on the development of the degree of utilization of potential output ('output-gap'), as shown in Figure 18.2 and discussed already in chapter 9. Consequently, it is assumed that the gap between actually realized gross domestic product (GDP) and full-employment GDP makes evident the extent to which a country's potential output is being utilized. However, there are considerable statistical problems associated with estimates of potential output.[3] This explains why such estimates of potential output are used in only a few countries as a basis for measuring economic trends. In the vast majority of cases economic trends are measured by means of the actual growth rates of real gross domestic product.

However, measuring an economic situation by means of growth rates of real GD—as shown in Figure 18.3—exaggerates cyclical fluctuations. This is because a decline in growth rates tends to give the impression of a worsening situation, even when growth rates remain positive. In the business world, economic cycles are felt in just this exaggerated form (i.e., as a change of change). A slowdown in growth rates triggers commentaries of concern, while in the reverse case, a decrease in negative growth rates already leads to positive expectations. This pronounced sensitivity of the business world (and consumers) to changes in economic situation is an essential factor further heightening short-term cyclical swings. It is particularly important to take this circumstance into consideration when interpreting results of economic surveys (see later). For example, a slight upturn is already hyped up into a success story, even when consumer sentiment is still downright chilly.

PROBLEMS WITH FORECASTING

It should be noted—particularly from the forecasting point of view—that the economic cycle problem (especially its effects on the economic situation and the labor market) becomes an issue mostly during times of slow economic expansion, while its negative features are hardly felt during times of rapid economic growth (see Figure 18.4). This is because during such times recessionary disturbances can be overcome quickly and easily due to the prevailing predominant forces of economic growth. The situation is totally different during times of slowed economic growth or stagnant economic development, when the forces of growth are not strong enough for absorbing recessionary cyclical disturbances. The susceptibility of affected national economies increases as their constitutional and structural defenses decrease.[4]

In addition, the following relevant circumstances have to be kept in mind: First, cyclical fluctuations can be explained by a complex interplay between impulses and amplifiers (Figure 18.5). A national economy is constantly impacted by a great number of influences, which show a positive or negative effect. Fluctuation is triggered when either positive or negative influential forces predominate.[5] In each highly developed national economy showing division of labor and international interdependence, such triggered movement has the tendency of self-accelerating and increasing beyond the measure of the original disturbance due to the influence of accelerators of economic activity. Figure 18.6 hints at the great number of impulses that impact a national economy and its companies. The shaded factors have

Figure 18.2
'Output Gap' 1985 to 1997

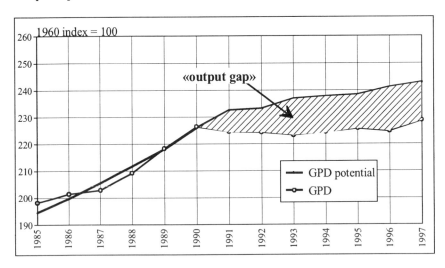

Source: Graf, H.G. (*K&P*), 1998, p. xiii.

Figure 18.3
Development of Gross Domestic Product, 1960 to 1997 (Average Annual Growth Rates in %)

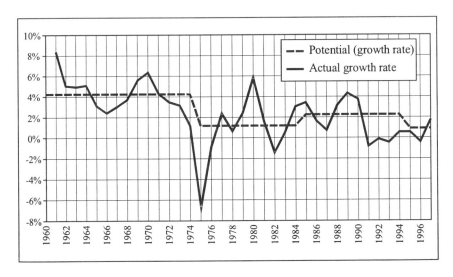

Source: Swiss Federal Statistical Office (*Yearbook*), various volumes.

Figure 18.4
The Relationship between Business Cycle and Waves of Growth

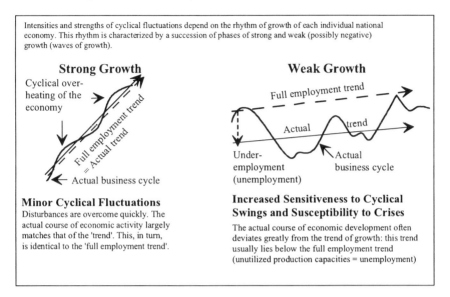

Source: Kneschaurek, F. and Graf, H.G. (*Wirtschafts- und Marktprognosen*), 1986, p. 101.

Figure 18.5
Basic Model of Cyclical Movement

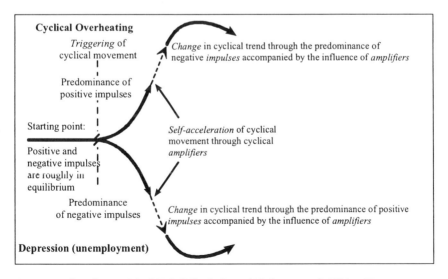

Source: Kneschaurek, F. and Graf, H.G. (*Wirtschafts- und Marktprognosen*), 1986, p. 98.

Figure 18.6
Impulses That Can Influence Companies and Trigger Cyclical Movement

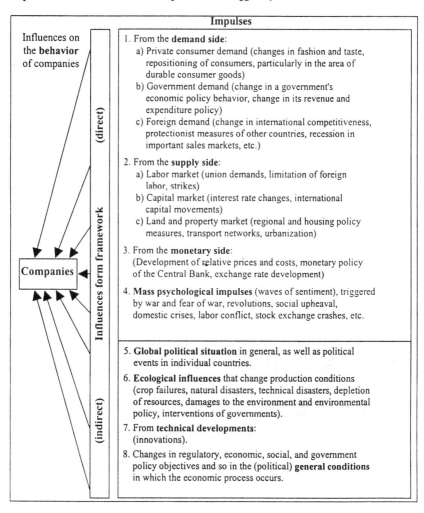

Impulses

Influences on the **behavior** of companies

Influences form framework

(direct)

Companies

1. From the **demand side**:
   a) Private consumer demand (changes in fashion and taste, repositioning of consumers, particularly in the area of durable consumer goods)
   b) Government demand (change in a government's economic policy behavior, change in its revenue and expenditure policy)
   c) Foreign demand (change in international competitiveness, protectionist measures of other countries, recession in important sales markets, etc.)

2. From the **supply side**:
   a) Labor market (union demands, limitation of foreign labor, strikes)
   b) Capital market (interest rate changes, international capital movements)
   c) Land and property market (regional and housing policy measures, transport networks, urbanization)

3. From the **monetary side**:
   (Development of relative prices and costs, monetary policy of the Central Bank, exchange rate development)

4. **Mass psychological impulses** (waves of sentiment), triggered by war and fear of war, revolutions, social upheaval, domestic crises, labor conflict, stock exchange crashes, etc.

(indirect)

5. **Global political situation** in general, as well as political events in individual countries.

6. **Ecological influences** that change production conditions (crop failures, natural disasters, technical disasters, depletion of resources, damages to the environment and environmental policy, interventions of governments).

7. From **technical developments**:
   (innovations).

8. Changes in regulatory, economic, social, and government policy objectives and so in the (political) **general conditions** in which the economic process occurs.

Source: Following Kneschaurek, F. (*Volkswirtschaft*), 1996, p. 340.

a predominantly long-term influence, while the upper half of Figure 18.6 shows mainly cyclical impulses.

Second, cyclical fluctuations are characterized by pronounced irregularity. The reason for irregularities in cyclical fluctuations is that the effect, in net terms, of the thousands of impulses impacting an economy does not change at a constant pace. Rather, it can be subject to abrupt changes. In addition, amplifiers do not always act in the same typified form, so leading to cyclical anomalies. This leads to the problem in economic forecasting of 'turning points' being predictable only with great difficulty (i.e., when there are other cyclical anomalies in addition to time irregularities). In particular, corporate decisions derived from wrong forecasts made with regard to turning points can have catastrophic consequences.

Third, individual sectors react to cyclical fluctuations in varying degrees because individual markets show differing sensitiveness to cyclical swings (cf. Figure 18.7). Production and employment of some sectors depend very strongly on changes in the macroeconomic situation; in contrast, others react less strongly, and some not at all. This diversity in behavior is due to varying sensitiveness of demand for the products and services of individual sectors during the course of economic activity. This circumstance also leads to differences in regional sensitiveness to cyclical swings, depending on the degree to which sectors, varying in sensitiveness to cyclical swings, are represented in a region.

Finally, it needs to be kept in mind that markets and products show different modes of reaction in cyclical and long-term areas, respectively. Often, pronounced sensitiveness can be perceived in the economic cycle, while in the long term (in the growth process) virtual synchronism of the respective market with macroeconomic development can be observed (see Figure 18.8). This demonstrates again that short and long-term studies cannot simply coexist independently (i.e., ultimately, short-term behavior has to also always take into consideration longer-term market reactions as well as be oriented toward the normative ideas of corporate management).

USE OF BUSINESS CYCLE FORECASTS

Business cycle forecasts can be used at two levels: as a basis for economic policy measures, in which case the focus is on localizing expected alternate economic situations and their relevant determinants and relationships such that 'correct' economic policy measures are also employed, and as a basis for corporate budgeting and (operative/short-term) planning processes. They form, as it were, the exogenous input variables for corporate market forecasts. In so doing, it has to be examined specifically in each case how the (behavioral) parameters could possibly change in the economic cycle investigated. With such approaches it is basically assumed that the parameters reflecting the structure of the system investigated remain constant. Therefore, from a variation in exogenous variables provided by business cycle forecasts, the corresponding market and product forecasts are usually derived directly. Accordingly, business cycle forecasts intended as input for

Figure 18.7
Typical Modes of Reaction of Markets in the Business Cycle

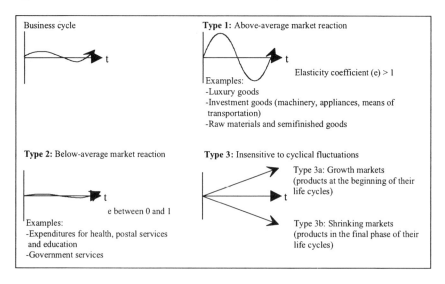

Figure 18.8
Annual Rates of Change of GDP, Building Investments, and Investments in Machinery
and Equipment

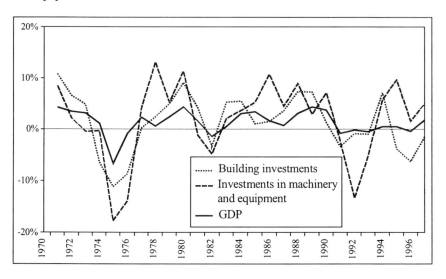

Source: Swiss Federal Statistics Office (*Yearbook*).

economic policy processes and corporate budgeting want to provide effectively a prognosis: 'This is how it is going to be!'

NOTES

1. The 'output gap' concept forms the connecting point between short and long-term views; cf. Chapter 9.

2. Kondratieff, N.D. (*Lange Wellen*), 1926, pp. 573ff., and Duijn, J.J. van (*Long Wave*), 1983.

3. Cf. Giorno, C.P. et al. (Potential Output), 1995.

4. The reason for this is, in particular, that in such cases the demand for labor is low, and so the ability to absorb released employees is restricted.

5. Here, the expectations of economic entities play a crucial part; cf. Jöhr, W.A. (Psychologie), pp. 157 ff., 1972.

19

BUSINESS CYCLE FORECASTING

BUSINESS CYCLE FORECASTING APPROACH

Business cycle forecasts attempt to predict fluctuations in the utilization of a national economy's production capacity one to one and a half years in advance. The reasons and determinants for cyclical fluctuations are explained in the previous chapter. The notorious irregularity of fluctuations makes this task particularly difficult. It is important to determine the turning points of the economic 'ups and downs' as exactly as possible and to identify the amplitude of fluctuation intensity. Both are difficult tasks because cyclical fluctuations in individual economic sectors have a different shape compared to the overall average, or the overall shape is the average of various sector-specific economic cycles. Some sectors are very sensitive to cyclical fluctuations, and others are less so; some respond immediately, and others only with a time lag. In particular, some markets clearly respond disproportionately in the hectic cyclical activity, while in the longer term they take a course proportional to that of macroeconomic development. Therefore, the important points about business cycle forecasts are, first, to accurately predict macroeconomic development (i.e., the general economic situation) and, second, to correctly determine the specific reactions of partial aggregates or markets of interest to a change in the general economic situation. At the macroeconomic level, labor market and foreign trade balance issues are addressed in addition to output development.

EXPLICIT AND IMPLICIT MODELS

As illustrated in Figure 19.1, the theoretical modeling approach is a first way of distinguishing business cycle forecasting methods. In the case of explicit models

Figure 19.1
The Most Important Methods for Forecasting Business Cycles

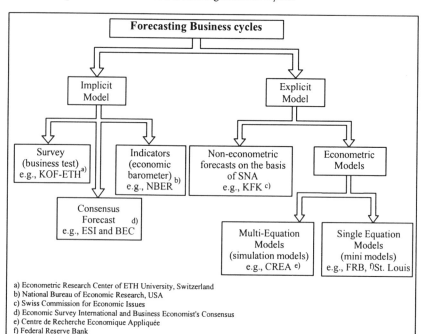

a) Econometric Research Center of ETH University, Switzerland
b) National Bureau of Economic Research, USA
c) Swiss Commission for Economic Issues
d) Economic Survey International and Business Economist's Consensus
e) Centre de Recherche Economique Appliquée
f) Federal Reserve Bank

the methodical approach is, in large part, intersubjectively reconstructable and so fulfills to a great extent the requirements of scientific methods. With implicit models the mechanism of effect, which ultimately indicates cyclical fluctuations, is not studied or explained in detail. Experience with implicit models has shown that such a method is suitable for registering cyclical fluctuations. However, neither the causes nor definition relationships are studied (i.e., theoretical considerations are part of the method or 'implicit').

BUSINESS CYCLE FORECASTING METHODS

Figure 19.1 gives an overview of the most important business cycle forecasting methods. The individual approaches are briefly characterized in the following sections.

Business Cycle Survey

Interviewing methods focus on asking groups of people of varying sizes their opinions as to facts relevant to the future. Most surveys are conducted on the basis of samples (i.e., a selection of a group of people). In terms of statistical/mathematical tools, knowledge of sample analysis and methods is required. This also presupposes a certain knowledge of probability theory in order to be able to determine the margins of error for estimates associated with random samples. Representative random samples aim at estimating results for an entire actual population.

However, most surveys are deliberate, not random. Also, an interview is often applied to relatively few elements of a population, which, however, have a dominating role in it (e.g., large corporations producing a large proportion of a sector's total output). Important macroeconomic conclusions can undoubtedly be drawn from interviewing such a group.

Nevertheless, such a group is representative only if changes are not expected in the size of corporate structures, and if greater differences in the development of individual company categories are not expected. In fact, a deliberate sample can be as good as a random one except that this cannot be proven.[1]

The so-called business cycle survey is a classic example of a (deliberate) sample survey. 'Representative' entities of industry, trade, business, finance, and the stock market are interviewed as to their opinions on the presumed development of economic activity and planned corporate policy measures (investment plans, stockpiling, personnel policy, etc.) taken with a view to such development. The procedure developed by Ifo, the Institute for Economic Research, Munich, was originally not intended as a means of forecasting. Rather, the plan was to develop a new and rapidly available source of information on the development of important economic data. This was done mostly with a view to the fact that official macroeconomic statistics, that is, as part of the National Accounts (SNA), are usually made available by statistics offices with a delay of six months or even longer. In due course, Ifo concentrated more and more on surveying companies and other economic players as to their future prospects and intentions. In this context, 'future' usually means the next quarter, occasionally the next two quarters. Since a business cycle survey also shows a delay due to the taking and processing of the survey with a projection horizon of one quarter, the lead time for publishing the results is frequently very modest.

The main advantages of the business cycle survey compared to approaches based on SNA are (1) that it is very up-to-date, as interview results are located at the current margin of economic activity and (2) that there is a breakdown into individual economic sectors, both in the industrial and increasingly also, in the service sector. In addition, business cycle surveys, due to their design, are very suitable for checking the quality of interview results, or answers given by those interviewed, by means of control questions. This is because contradictory questions in terms of their logic cannot be answered in the same way. In Switzerland, a business cycle survey is carried out monthly by the Economic Research Center (*Konjunkturforschungsstelle, KOF*) of Swiss Technical University ETH (KOF/ETH). In the case of industry checks, about 1,600 persons in executive positions are interviewed in voluntarily participating companies. A company's answers are weighted according to its number of employees. In addition, for sector results, companies are differentiated into small, medium-size and large companies, and each group is analyzed separately. Due to their significance in the population as a whole, these three levels are weighted before aggregating them into a sector result.

The psychological component plays a rather significant part in the economic cycle. For this reason, interviewing consumers or determining their sentiments also forms an essential element of assessing the economic situation and prospects. A consumer survey is conducted in Switzerland by the State Secretary for Economic Affairs (*seco*) every three months by calling more than 1,000 households in the German- and French-speaking parts of Switzerland. The collective index determined on the basis of the various questions is the calculated arithmetic mean of three questions: Swiss economic situation over the past 12 months; financial situation of the household over the past year; and financial situation of the household over the following 12 months. We are mentioning this consumer survey under the heading 'business cycle survey' as it represents a particularly important element when assessing economic prospects in virtually all countries using the business cycle survey. In both approaches the opinions held are generalized according to the law of large numbers and, in most cases, also quantified and so reformulated into forecasts.

Characteristic features of business cycle surveys are the short-term nature of statements and relative subjectivity of these outlooks. *First*, forecasting information based on opinions about the future is valid only for the short term (e.g., expected development of turnover, orders received, exports, or number of employees). Experience has shown that an extension of the interview's time horizon to several months leads to increasingly more speculative answers.

Second, decision makers in trade and industry are interviewed via the business cycle survey on a subject that they are interested in themselves, namely, the future of the environment relevant to them. This environment substantially determines their decisions and also has to determine them in the future. An individual's opinion as to the presumed course of his or her business is, in principle, subjective and dependent on moods. Only when an interview attempts to obtain information about certain specific measures and plans of companies or consumers can it guarantee an objective answer. For example, this applies to already decided investment projects or acquisitions of durables on the parts of consumers. Also in this case the future time horizon has to be relatively short in order to obtain concrete information. The starting point for this method is the notion that economic events are ultimately also determined by a great number of subjective behaviors. Therefore, when the scope of such a survey is wide enough, then the results represent sufficiently secured conclusions.

It is assumed that with such interviews they are well able to pick up on the prevailing sentiment and, above all, sentiment waves. This is surely correct. However, the real challenge with such instruments for registering sentiments is the correct interpretation of interview results. The important thing is recognizing the extent to which these sentiments are based on objective foundations, or whether they came about purely by speculation via mass psychological means. Undoubtedly, subjective elements of assessment and the optimistic or pessimistic moods caused by them play an important part in the business world. However, without a suffi-ciently objective basis they will not survive in the long run and are therefore usually toppled both rapidly and unexpectedly. Also, for example, in cases where a signifi-cant improvement in the economic situation is conjured up for the near future by the media and all authoritative institutions, and if such 'propaganda' is not fol-lowed by actual improvement in the labor market situation, then a setback in eco-nomic activity is virtually the inevitable outcome.

Consensus Forecasts

At the beginning of the 1980s the Ifo Institute developed another interviewing instrument that allowed very up-to-date assessments of the economic situations of Western industrialized countries. This was done particularly because relevant in-formation from official statistics was made available, if at all, after a delay of six months. Therefore, the Ifo Institute established a network of corresponding econ-omists and employees in international corporations and organizations who quarterly provide assessments of the current economic situations in their respec-tive countries as well as economic trend evaluations by means of questionnaires for the next six months. Such a qualitative assessment is similar to the business cycle survey and has definitely proven useful.

This instrument, the 'Economic Survey International' (ESI; recently renamed 'World Economic Survey' WES), has in the meantime been expanded to non-European countries and presently includes 1080 economic experts in 90 coun-tries and gives a good, up-to-date, and informative overview of the current global economic situation and economic outlook.[2] Such an approach is also used on a much smaller scale by other agencies under the term 'consensus forecast.' There is an increasing trend toward surveying quantitative orders of magnitude, rather than qualitative assessments. Instead of working with a scale of good, fair, and bad or better, unchanged, and worse, as in case of WES, gross domestic product, inflation, and unemployment growth rates are surveyed and also interest and ex-change rates (with a view to financial markets). In Switzerland, such a survey of around 30 experts is conducted every three months by Zürcher Kantonalbank under the title 'Business Economist's Consensus' (BEC). It deals with the eco-nomic situation and economic development prospects of Switzerland as well as various financial indicators.

Indicator Systems

Economic Barometers. Indicator systems that act as barometers for the economic situation and therefore also predict it to a certain degree can be used exclusively for cyclical economic forecasts. The first such attempt goes back to W.M. Persons, who developed an indicator system in the 1920s, widely referred to as 'Harvard Ba-rometer' in the literature, that was also intended for forecasting purposes. Persons started from the empirically supported experience that there are series of numbers that coincide with the economic cycle ('coincident series'), while others run ahead of it ('leading series'). There are also time series that lag behind the economic cycle ('lagging series'). Typical of coincident time series are the industrial production index and turnover of cargo by rail. Typical of leading indicators are orders received in industry and building permits. Typical of lagging indicators are development of wages and interest rates. As long as these developments are characteristic of the economic trend and are therefore 'typifiable,' then an indicator system that appropriately reflects the three groups of time series can, in fact, fulfill the function of a barometer, which also possesses certain forecasting characteristics.

Yet, the experiences with the Harvard Barometer (1929!) were highly disappointing, and so things became quiet around this procedure for some time. Not until the end of World War II did interest rise again in economic indicator systems, thanks to comprehensive studies by the American National Bureau of Economic Research. Today, such indicator systems exist not only in the United States, but also in practically all Western industrialized countries. Their abilities to describe economic trends and register them like barometers are undisputed. However, their abilities as forecasting instruments are extremely limited. This is due to the construction of indicators, which are established as follows:

- In the first step the course of each variable during past economic cycles is analyzed and recorded in the form of corresponding trends (specific cycles).
- In the second step all specific cycles are combined into a single 'reference cycle' through average calculation. This reference cycle reflects the 'typified trend' of the analyzed variable. It is obvious that the specific cycles deviate more or less strongly from the average values of the reference cycle.
- Finally, the reference cycles for the leading and lagging time series are compared to the reference cycles for the coincident series of numbers. That way, the 'lead' and 'lag' are determined for each individual case. With respect to forecasts, it is the typical lead of the leading indicators that is the most significant: the bigger it is, the greater is the forecasting potential of the corresponding time series.

The usefulness of the indicator process for forecasting purposes depends on the constancy of the leads and lags of individual indicators. However, this constancy, with very few exceptions, hardly ever exists. In addition, the following points should be considered:

- The lead is often so small that the turning point in the macroeconomic trend cannot be recognized in time solely on the basis of the course of the dominant indicators.
- The erratic movements of monthly series of numbers make it extremely difficult for the forecaster to distinguish between a change in direction due to cyclical causes and a more incidental short-term change of leading indicators. For example, a setback over the course of a few months is no guarantee that the turning point has been reached and surpassed and that there is now finally a downward trend. In the majority of cases it is possible to identify only in retrospect when the time series really reached its turning point.

- Specific cycles often differ substantially from reference cycles. However, since the entire indicator system is oriented toward reference cycles, its ability to provide information for forecasting purposes is relatively limited.

Diffusion Index. Because of the sobering experiences with the reference cycle system, another indicator system was developed (again by the National Bureau of Economic Research), which has in the meantime been introduced in several Western European countries as well as in Japan. It is the so-called diffusion index. The basic idea behind such indexes is interpreting varying numbers of indicators that shed light on the developments in all areas of a national economy. The index itself reflects the development of the percentage of time series showing a positive basic trend. Accordingly, the index always lies between 0 (none of the series show a positive trend) and 100 (all series show a positive trend).

It is easy to explain how the diffusion index mechanism works. During an economic upturn the percentage of positive figures increases continuously, while, conversely, an ever smaller number of indicators is negative. When the drive of the cyclical upswing slows down, the percentage of positive indicators decreases rapidly. This development indicates that a change in cyclical trend is imminent. Once this change occurs, the diffusion index drops to virtually zero.

The diffusion index has considerable advantages over the reference cycle system: it is exceptionally easy to determine and does not have to be corrected constantly like a reference cycle, because the average values applying to the reference cycle shift more or less strongly after every new economic cycle; it can include series of numbers that are relevant to the economic trend, even when these are not collected according to uniform criteria; and it is very sensitive to changes in economic trend and leads it, that is, in the United States, by an average of nine months.

At the same time the diffusion index is not without problems. Such an index works best when it covers as many series of data as possible, because its effect is then shown by the law of large numbers. Furthermore, the fact that 'economic weights' of individual series of numbers, represented in the diffusion index, vary greatly will then not have a significant impact. This explains why the National Bureau of Economic Research originally intended to build the diffusion index on several hundreds of time series of data. This does, in fact, increase the index's ability in providing information. However, the determination and interpretation of hundreds of statistical series of data are so time-consuming that the diffusion index goes out of date, so that its lead over the general economic cycle becomes relatively small. Often the diffusion index is not available until the change has already taken place from one economic situation to another.

Another aggravating factor is the fact that it is not always possible during ongoing preparation of the diffusion index to determine, with sufficient certainty, whether the individual series of numbers have a positive or negative trend. Irregular or erratic fluctuations, known only too well, make it difficult to determine whether the indicators investigated have already reached their turning points or not. Such a decision can often be made with certainty only in retrospect. However, such an *ex post facto* view is hardly useful to the forecaster.

The preceding considerations made the generators of such indexes reduce the number of series substantially. At present most countries operate with 20 to 30 individual time series. However, as the number of indicators is reduced, a new problem arises in turn, because the variables included in the individual series of numbers impact the economic cycle to greatly varying degrees. They are, however, included in the diffusion index unweighted, merely because it cannot be determined when they actually occur during the course of economic activity. This, in turn, reduces the diffusion index's ability in providing information, particularly when assessing imminent cyclical turning points.

These arguments apply particularly to countries that have expanded the diffusion index to some kind of 'cyclical warning index' as a basis for interventions designed to maintain and promote stability. The basic reasoning leading to such use can be summarized as follows:

- Margins of tolerance (between about 40% and 60% of the diffusion index) are set as targets.
- If the diffusion index remains within these margins of tolerance, then there is no need for increased activities designed to maintain and promote stability on the part of government. However, if the diffusion index exceeds these margins, then this will be seen as a signal that an unhealthy and undesired economic development is in progress, which calls for increased efforts toward maintaining and promoting stability.

This line of argument sounds logical. It is, however, not very useful to those making economic policy decisions. This procedure could be compared to a doctor's relying exclusively on a patient's temperature and blood pressure for diagnosing the course of a disease. Sensible stability policy requires thorough economic analysis (and forecasting) that responds to the forces behind each individual development (i.e., a *causal analysis*), which is exactly what an indicator system cannot provide. Such a system can indeed not provide any information on the interplay between the factors and forces relevant to an economic cycle. Therefore, it is more likely to cloud, rather than enlighten, the future. This criticism has to be taken even more seriously in light of the fact that anomalies in economic activity are increasingly becoming the norm. This means that individual cycles deviate increasingly from the typified economic trend used as a basis for the diffusion index.

Finally, economic indicators can at best serve as partial and complementary aids for assessing future economic situations. Under no circumstances can they function as independent bases for such forecasts.

Explicit Models

Business cycle forecasting models used in the System of National Accounts (SNA) are based on the assumptions described in Chapter 8 and particularly in

Figure 10.2. The national accounts system, particularly the utilization side and occasionally also the income side, form the definition basis for gauging economic development.

The individual components of the utilization side are initially predicted independently, sometimes by different institutions, and then successively adjusted to each other via an iteration process. It can be observed frequently that several methodological approaches are used for the individual components of the utilization side. For example, besides regression analysis for estimating private consumer demand (taking into account, among others, income, prices, etc.), surveys on consumer sentiments as part of a business cycle survey or survey results on the propensities of companies to invest are also used frequently. When estimating the development of public budgets, the focus is on budget information. Consequently, with such an approach the SNA provides structures of definition (i.e., form the explicit model for this approach).

The SNA is usually also at the center of econometric approaches. Here they provide the definition relationships between individual variables, which are recorded as individual equations and then solved simultaneously (cf. Chapter 8). At this point we would like to draw attention to the fact that econometric simulation models working with constant parameters (i.e., constant structures due to calibration on a period of the past) have only a limited forecasting horizon of one to two years. This is because it is assumed, by definition, that the structures observed during the calibration period will also apply in the future. However, structural change is a phenomenon inextricably linked to economic development so that with such an approach predictions are possible only for the short term, especially because the basic assumption of constant structures for several years to come is untenable.

In addition to 'big' simulation models, there are also so-called mini models for economic forecasting, which in most cases are based on one single equation. A typical example is the equation $Dy_{t+3} = a + bDM_t$, frequently used by the Federal Reserve Bank of St. Louis. It says that GDP development (y) is determined solely by the development of money supply (M), with a delay of three quarters. Such models definitely make sense if, on one hand, they make a sensible causal theoretical reference and, on the other, the focus is not on shedding light on every facet of the economic cycle phenomenon. Rather, the emphasis is on gaining only relatively rough indications as to macroeconomic developmental trends.

Forecasts are not an end in themselves; they have to achieve a task and are, at the same time, subject to the efficiency criterion. Construction of the most complicated model possible may be a challenge in itself. However, the effort that it takes has to be in relation to the return. Unnecessary inflation and complication of a model, which in the end do not provide additional information, are not practical from an economic point of view.

Most economic research institutes build their forecasts on the basis of combining all future-oriented information obtained via various methods. Experience has shown that noneconometric models (e.g., based on national income accounts) take into account results of business cycle surveys and sector- or market-specific interviews, as well as indicators (barometers). This happens particularly when these results have the characteristic of leading economic trends (building permits, presentation of industrial and commercial construction plans, orders received, etc.). To this end they frequently also use results of econometric simulation models in order to carry out the necessary consistency testing. Conversely, econometric models cannot get by without judgments based on estimates. These judgments can be facilitated considerably by existing information bases, namely, knowledge of previously effective functional mechanisms in the economic trend. Certain variables are also estimated (predicted) on the basis of business cycle surveys or economic indicators in order to trace the database back as closely as possible to the date of forecast preparation.

Wrong forecasts result mostly from the notorious unpredictability of cyclical fluctuations, which makes the prediction of exogenous variables and possibly also behavioral parameters extremely more difficult in the respective models. Therefore, observation and critical examination of assumptions and hypotheses (judgments based on estimates) on which the forecasts are based will always be crucial for the evaluation of such forecasts.

Official and semiofficial economic forecasts are in most cases publicized in a rather undifferentiated way by the mass media. Often they present only the final forecast results as figures with a 'tel quel' commentary. This frequently gives the impression that there is no agreement between economic forecasters and that their forecasts are hopelessly divergent. However, part of the misunderstandings has to be attributed also to the addressees of such forecasts, who themselves do not take the time to read the accompanying explanations and commentaries in the original version before passing judgment. Rather, they often believe that they can follow the naked numerical results or second-, third- or fourth-hand information while otherwise relying only on their own experience and intuition.

What Is Important?

In most industrialized countries the various institutes and institutions develop economic forecasts that are publicized via the media or 'in-house' circulars. In Switzerland at least 10 more or less official and publicly accessible short-term economic forecasts are available, which naturally rarely agree because they are based on differing approaches and assumptions. Because the general mood in a national economy represents an essential element during economic development and is subjectively felt and passed on, considerable leeway is often the consequence. This puts the user of such forecasts in the difficult position of having to choose the 'correct' economic forecast.

Table 19.1, taken from a daily newspaper, summarizes the economic forecasts for Switzerland for 1998. It shows, among other things, that the expected growth rates in part vary greatly, in terms of not only their absolute values, but even their signs (i.e., there are considerable differences).

Table 19.1

Comparison of Economic Forecasts for 1998 (Real Changes Compared to Previous Year in %)

	KFK[1] 1997	KFK[1] 1998	KOF[2]	BAK[3]	OECD	UBS[4]	Credit Suisse	Max.	Min.	Avg.
GDP and its components										
Private consumption	0.5	1.0	1.0	1.5	1.3	1.2	1.2	1.5	0.5	1.1
Public consumption	-0.5	0.0	0.4	1.0	0.0	-2.0	-1.0	0.4	-2.0	0.3
Fixed asset investments	-1.8	2.4	2.6	1.4	1.6	2.0	4.5	4.5	-1.8	1.8
of this: buildings	-6.0	0.0	1.4	-0.2	—	0.0	2.0	2.0	-6.0	0.4
of this: equipment	3.0	5.0	3.8	3.1	—	4.0	4.5	5.0	3.0	3.3
Exports	6.2	6.0	4.8	5.3	5.5	5.3	6.5	6.5	4.8	5.7
Imports	5.4	5.0	3.7	4.0	4.6	5.0	5.0	5.4	3.7	4.7
Total GDP	0.5	1.8	2.2	2.2	1.7	1.8	1.6	2.2	0.5	1.7
Other indicators										
Inflation	0.5	1.0	0.8	1.1	0.9	0.6	0.8	1.1	0.5	0.8
Yield—federal medium-term Notes	3.5	3.8	3.9	3.6	3.9	4.2	4.0	4.2	2.8	3.8
Unemployment rate	5.2	4.8	5.1	5.0	5.0	4.4	5.1	5.2	4.4	4.9

[1]KFK: Kommission für Konjunkturfragen
[2]KOF: Konjunkturforschungsstelle ETH
[3]BAK: Basler Arbeitsgruppe für Konjunkturfragen
[4]UBS: Union Bank of Switzerland

Source: Neue Zürcher Zeitung.

Choosing the 'right' economic forecast can be accomplished only on the basis of the underlying assumptions as to the relevant determinants of an economy's cyclical development, as shown, for example in Figure 10.2. Another problem in this context results from the fact that only in exceptional cases do the daily press and media provide information on the respective underlying assumptions. The solution, suggested in Table 19.1, of calculating an average for the various forecast figures and then working with this 'economic forecast,' has to be rejected categorically because this recklessly muddles the various assumptions.

In addition, it cancels the function of the fixed mechanisms of national income accounts. Therefore, while, for example, one economic forecast assumes an increase in the exchange rate of the Swiss franc, another assumes exactly the opposite. Consequently, calculating an average of the two is obviously useless.

Inevitably, one has to refer to the original publication in order to gain insight into the underlying causal relationships, methodical approach, and empirical foundation, as well as the assumptions made. When choosing a forecast, it is particularly important to pay attention to the requirements for complete reconstructability. This is the only way of duly scrutinizing possible ideas of one's own.

Experiences in using business cycle forecasts in operative management—and this is the only area where they provide useful information for a firm—will often be

critical for choosing economic forecasts for regular use. These experiences by forecast users are only in exceptional cases based on the decimal-point accuracy of the
prediction used. Rather, they are built on the relevant reasons, which were applicable to varying degrees, that led eventually to a result that was also quantifiable. It is
more critical that they have placed behavioral instructions accurately in operative
management than that they match precisely actual development. The reliance on
numbers, which can be frequently observed, is hardly relevant in this context.
There is all too often a tendency to judge a macroeconomic forecast in absolutist
form with the meticulousness of a pedantic number-splitter. Under a magnifying
glass a forecast that predicts an increase in real GDP of around 1% for the coming
year and another that forecasts an equally strong setback in economic activity,
seem worlds apart (see Figure 19.2, part a). In mathematical terms the difference
between the two is close to infinity (because the zero line is being crossed). If, however, in the year preceding the forecast the growth rate in real GDP was considerably below or above 1%, then both forecast values (cf. Figure 19.2, part b) are
virtually equally reliable, and the difference between the two forecasts (+1% and
-1%, respectively) becomes nearly insignificant. The direction of change was identified correctly at any rate, making it possible to draw the right corporate conclusions regarding production, personnel development, advance orders, and so on.

It has to be highlighted once again that it is also important for business cycle
forecasts to double-check the forecast statement. As has been shown in Part I, in

Figure 19.2
Decimal-Point Accuracy Required?

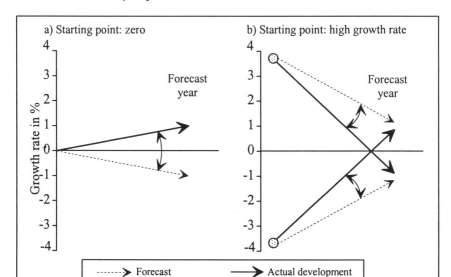

Source: Following Kneschaurek, F. and Graf, H.G. (*Wirtschafts- und Marktprognosen*), 1986, p. 108.

the case of business cycle forecasts, it cannot be excluded that they are normative in character. For example, wishes as to the effectiveness of economic policy measures influence the forecast, so limiting its usefulness. As a result, the question of 'who for whom' has to be raised in order to avoid possible distortions. It cannot be over-emphasized how important it is to be clear as to the underlying premises and not to lose sight of their actual objective for the correct assessment of forecasts and their further use within the scope of operative management. This objective is predicting, just as a weather forecast predicts the weather pattern of the future cyclical swings, especially an expected weather change. For short-term planning it is particularly important to know whether and in which form a change in the cyclical movement is imminent. In so doing, predicting the movement is more important than quantifying it as precisely as possible.

Business cycle forecasts are used in economic policy making and are required as a basis for preparing budgets and all other measures of operative management. In both cases they describe the short-term development of general conditions for an economy (international economic climate, probable development of one's own national economy in given general political conditions) or a company (development of income, propensity to invest, export opportunities).

BUSINESS CYCLE FORECASTING AND STABILITY POLICY

The function of business cycle forecasts within the scope of the stability policy is to contribute to achieving a country's stability goals (i.e., the lowest possible inflation, almost full employment and foreign trade balance).[3] A business cycle forecast wants to predict—by assuming the general political conditions set at the outset to prevail—whether during the upcoming one and a half years imbalances will develop in national economic development that endanger stability goals, so influencing policy toward a change that contributes to avoiding 'imbalances.' Because the previously mentioned amplifiers can lead to rapid self-acceleration of a movement already under way, drawing attention to such turning points in time is all the more important so that measures are introduced early enough that can mitigate possible instabilities.

Combating economic disequilibria, which become evident via unemployment, inflation or foreign trade imbalances, and associated currency problems, is one of the central tasks of economic policy.[4] Of course, economists are blamed for insufficient fulfillment of their stability policy tasks. Besides the accusation of missing or insufficiently secured analyses of the causes of economic instabilities, they are also charged with having the wrong theoretical ideas as to how a government should carry out stability policy. 'The often dogmatic controversy between classicists, neoclassicists, Keynesians, monetarists, and recently also supply-side theorists, fills entire bookshelves. So any hope of agreement in this matter is complete utopia' (Kneschaurek, 1996, p. 105).

This is not the place for a dogmatic historical discussion of economic policy approaches and instruments.[5] The dispute over the effectiveness of stability policy and the possibilities and limitations of the various economic policy interventions illustrates their difficulties. For business cycle forecasting this means that its importance also fluctuates, together with the margins for action granted to economic policy.[6] In addition, problems change over time so that theories, which in the past provided correct analyses, can turn out to be utterly false in a newly positioned economic environment. This circumstance again reflects the fact that the economic process ultimately revolves around people. People, however, do not necessarily behave rationally yet are in any event capable of learning and adjusting. Therefore, people's behavior—also in terms of their reaction to economic policy measures—cannot be finally predicted. Consequently, the effectiveness of the same stability policy measure at different times can be totally different in changed social environments.

Traditional instruments of stability policy for controlling demand are fiscal policy (i.e., variation of government spending and revenue) and monetary policy, which is essentially carried out by Central Banks via money supply or interest rate changes.[7] In this context, traditional demand control is confronted with several problems during application that strongly limit its effectiveness. First of all, there is the lack of differentiation of the two instruments: they are virtually always effective only at the macroeconomic level, that is, they cannot influence individual areas that might be particularly affected by instabilities. In this respect they are, therefore, a rather broad instrument—a kitchen knife instead of a scalpel. Furthermore, there is in fact a lack of instruments. Money supply management that affects the liquidity of the banking system ultimately influences loan demand in the same way as interest rate policy. It has been shown that monetary policy in particular has usually an asymmetric effect, that is, it is capable of slowing down a boom, while it can scarcely boost a bad economic situation. However, the time lags associated with using such instruments must be considered the worst problem. Not least, they have to be regarded as an information problem of business cycle forecasting, both in parliamentary democracy and in administration.[8]

The traditional approach of stability policy, with demand control as the most important instrument, has always been controversial. According to more recent models, an activist stability policy is ineffective at best. It is more likely to reduce welfare, because it delays or even prevents structural adjustments via the price mechanism and so increases, rather than decreases, fluctuations in the utilization of production capacity. According to this more recent theory, what matters is ensuring that the price mechanism works rapidly and effectively, because this accelerates adjustment processes and moves them in the right direction. When an active stability policy is pushed back, business cycle forecasts for economic policy purposes also play a less important role. This is because, according to modern theory, economic policy has to be obligated to play a stabilizing role, and continuity as well as credibility of economic policy are considerably more important than classic stability policy interventions. To date, this controversy has not been resolved. Furthermore, business cycle forecasting is called upon to indicate sufficiently early

possible breaches of targets, meaning that it really can remain open whether de-
mand-side or supply-side policy or both should be applied.

However, if it is assumed that economic policy authorities have no information
lead whatsoever (on the basis of business cycle forecasts), then it is obvious that
with such assumptions stability policy is not only ineffective but also unnecessary.[9]
Associated with this comes the demand for overthrowing economic policy, budget
restructuring, and deregulation, which has replaced the previous buzzword, 'fine-
tuning.' Instead, fiscal policy and monetary policy are seen—via the determinant
of investments—as influences toward a longer-term 'natural' growth rate. Only
when objections based on instability theory were raised did it become evident that
institutional, political, and sociopolitical considerations have to be taken into account more strongly in stability policy. This is necessary so that more importance
can again be attributed to stability policy within the economic policy spectrum and
so also to business cycle forecasting.

BUSINESS CYCLE FORECASTING AND COMPANIES

Irrespective of the fact that business cycle forecasting, as part of stability policy,
and the issue of its effectiveness and usefulness have assumed a significant role in
scientific discussions over the last two decades, business cycle forecasts as such
were, and still are, important input at the operative management level of companies (Menzl, 1988, pp. 265ff.). Competitive pressure associated with globalization
has become evident most of all through efforts toward better management of the
cost side via more efficient processes and rationalization, in order to increase the
competitiveness of one's own company. Concepts such as 'just in time' deliveries
depend on estimating sales potentials of products as precisely as possible, so mini-
mizing inventory carrying cost and optimizing the entire output chain. This has
led to the demand for corresponding proof of performance in association with increasingly short-term planning cycles. Added to this has been the demand for increasingly short-term economic forecasts. These are delivered on a quarterly basis,
if possible, and most recently even a monthly basis, so continuously providing new
information on the development of a company's environment. However, this also
leads to a massive increase in volatility (of assessment[10]) of the general macroeconomic conditions.

This procedure greatly increases a system's complexity, which can become so
extreme that the long-term strategic/normative focus of the managerial view is
lost. Ultimately, this puts in jeopardy the basic objective of corporate management, namely, increasing a company's ability to survive and develop in the long
term. Managerial processes and objectives, which orient themselves on a decidedly
short-term view, further aggravate this development.[11] For this reason we plead
also for favoring a steady course of action with business cycle forecasts. This means
that an annual business cycle forecast, with perhaps a semiannual review rhythm,
should represent a sensible compromise between too much volatility and sufficient
information for accurate planning.[12] In the context of market forecasts, described

in the following chapter, business cycle forecasts are rather important as planning input at the corporate level.

NOTES

1. In reality, the rules of probability calculation must be applied only to random samples.

2. Since the beginning of 2002, the WES is prepared in cooperation with the International Chamber of Commerce (ICC) in Paris and is partially funded by the EU-Commission.

3. For an overview cf. among many others, Dornbusch, R. and Fischer, S. (*Macroeconomics*), 1990, pp. 429ff., as well as Tichy, G. (*Konjunkturpolitik*), 1995, pp. 41ff.

4. This mandate is incorporated in the legal systems of most western industrialized countries. However, experience since World War II has shown that the governments and Central Banks of OECD countries succeeded only in exceptional cases in really fulfilling this mandate, even though a great number of instruments were employed, from 'laissez-faire' to stability policy, and from fine-tuning to 'concerted action' as proposed by the former German economics minister Karl Schiller. Furthermore, during a long-lasting economic prosperity phase (e.g., from 1983 to 1990) more than 10% of the Western European labor potential remained unemployed. The number of unemployed rapidly grew further with the start of the recession at the beginning of the 1990s.

5. For an overview, cf. Tichy, G. (*Konjunkturpolitik*), 1995, Bombach, G. (*Konjunkturtheorie*), 1991, W.A. Jöhr (*Konjunktur*), 1952.

6. This is particularly an ideological dispute over the function and meaning of government in a market-oriented system. In the end it addresses the various values as to whether, to what degree, and how government should handle stability tasks in general.

7. Cf., among others, Tichy, G. (*Konjunkturpolitik*), 1995, pp. 73ff.

8. For more information on the time-lag problem, cf. Schmid, H. (*Geld, Kredit und Banken*), 1997, p. 284.

9. The at present frequently upheld hypothesis of policy ineffectiveness increasingly determines public opinion and actual economic policy. This has become evident through increasing weariness of government and politics and an almost unlimited trust in the abilities of the market.

10. The new quarterly forecast can, after all, not contain the same information as the previous one!

11. This refers to the, often misunderstood, short-term maximization of corporate value under the buzzword 'shareholder value,' which stands in contrast to the originally long-term intention advocated in particular by Rappaport; Rappaport, A. (*Value*), 1986. It should not be overlooked in this context that with an excessively short-term view, a company's long-term generation of value is ultimately curtailed.

12. In this context the availability of reliable statistical data is also a limiting factor.

20

MARKET FORECASTING

INVESTIGATION SUBJECT AND AIM OF PERCEPTION

The distance into the future is not the only important differentiating criterion between forecasts. There are also significant differences in terms of content that have repercussions for organizational and institutional aspects when using such information in a company or government agency. Finally, a forecast's message is also not independent of the intended time horizon. Market forecasts are used in operative management. They want to provide instructions for action, which is clearly what their message focuses on. Market forecasts are based on empirical approaches, the vast majority of which include the relevant determinants of the markets studied and ultimately serve, if necessary, budget development as well as control. The main purpose of market studies is providing clues for planning and output, both in monetary and in physical areas (stockkeeping, delivery in advance, deployment of personnel, etc.). This is done on the basis of market volume forecasts and by assessing one's own competitive position.

Naturally, some lead time into the future is required also for such 'day-to-day business.' In industry it has been possible to shorten this lead time over the past few years through 'just in time' production. However, it must, nonetheless, ultimately extend at least half a year, more likely a year, into the future. Yet, the lead time varies greatly from sector to sector, which is also determined to a large degree by the type of product manufactured (daily necessaries, capital goods, services). Such planning steps certainly have to consider a company's strategic objectives, because nothing must be done in the short term that might do damage in the long run. Conversely, experience gained in the market has to be included in strategic considerations. Nonetheless, market forecasts are ultimately only of minor significance for a company's strategy creation process, a circumstance that has lately been taken much too little into account. Naturally, the operative objective of short-term profit maximization requires information other than the issue of a company's sustained ability to survive and develop.

MARKET FORECAST AND MARKET RESEARCH

When acquiring information on the development of markets, it is important to be aware of the difference between market forecast and market research. Classic market research investigates the buying behavior of consumers, either through interviews or through surveys at POSs ('points of sale'). This means that future-oriented intentions are occasionally asked for, especially in connection with interviews.[1] Results obtained in this way are qualitatively different in nature from those of market forecasts and, accordingly, have to be used differently. Surveys as to actual consumer behavior and corresponding observations at POSs mainly serve to improve assessment of one's competitive position. Information on individual buying behavior, collected more recently via modern cash register systems, undoubtedly reflects the behavior at each POS; however—as these systems are usually not connected between companies (exception: credit cards)—it cannot provide any information as to how discretionary income is used on the whole.

With a view to the periods of time at issue in operative management, which continue to span at least annual cycles, such information—considering the volatile behavior of consumers—is useful for a very specific, short time period and so is not reliable for annual planning or budgeting. Therefore, interviews on expected future consumer behavior are conducted as part of market research projects.

Interviews can basically cover only a relatively short period of time. It has been shown in virtually all countries that, especially with consumer surveys on larger purchases planned for the near future, if reliable answers are to be collected as to actual purchasing plans, then the time horizon should extend no more than half a year into the future. Beyond this time period each individual has a variety of dreams, such as purchase of an apartment, furniture, or car, that tend to exceed their financial capabilities considerably. In this respect market research results definitely represent a relevant and informative piece in the mosaic of market assessment in operative management. However, they cannot replace actual market forecasting, that is, the assessment of market volumes (requirements) and development of demand, connected, for example, to the development of income on the basis of economic forecasting.

SUBSTITUTION RELATIONSHIPS AND SALES POTENTIALS

Relationships with replacement goods always have to be considered when assessing a company's future sales potentials. This consideration has two facets. First, there is competition between the demand for one product group and the demand for other goods. This demand structure is by no means fixed (i.e., another product can—at relative short notice—be given significantly more weight in the consumer budget than has been observed previously). Expenditures for a product group of particular interest to us can be reduced overnight, so to speak, in order to acquire another, more attractive product. The issue here is shifts between individual groups of consumer goods, which usually occur only relatively slowly. However, these shifts sometimes also change direction at short notice. It has to be considered in this context that demand structures also differ greatly within countries and, of course, particularly between countries. For example, in Switzerland, the commodity 'housing' is of significantly different importance in the French-speaking part of the country compared to the German-speaking part. Therefore, commodities other than 'housing' have a much greater priority in the French part (i.e., a smaller proportion of the consumer budget is spent on the commodity 'housing' than in the German-speaking part of Switzerland). It is important to take these structural differences into consideration. A change in the direction of assimilating to the conditions in the German-speaking part of Switzerland, particularly in respect to this example, has recently been detected in consumer behavior in the French part.

Second, the replacement of the satisfaction of needs through different suppliers within the same product group has to be considered. This means that a competitor's offer perceived as qualitatively better can lead to a replacement of demand for the products of interest. However, ultimately what we are dealing with here is the consumer's perceiving better value for money, which triggers a shift in demand for goods of various suppliers.

With respect to using market forecasts, this basically means that due to these substitution relationships it is often not possible to think in absolute scales. Rather, the focus should be on working with market shares in order to also take into account from the beginning replacement possibilities within individual markets. For such a competitive analysis—primarily in the consumer goods area—market research results provide particularly important additional information that can make possible shifts in demand structure evident early enough. However, such issues are not assessed by starting from the future development of market potentials. The dimensional factor is a market volume fixed for a certain time or time period, which is why conducting such market research periodically, as well as processing it rapidly, is a '*conditio sine qua non.*'

'Prognosis is simply good analysis' (V.L. Bassie, p. 7). This remark essentially applies to all forecasting efforts. However, this is of fundamental importance, especially in the area of market research, where the focus is, ultimately on 'knowledge about the (foreseeable) future.' Reliable empirical data are required for assessing the future development of the market potential of a specific product or product group. This is required both for the product in question and for the factors determining this product line's sales. Only via detailed analysis of these relationships is it possible to understand market structures and the behaviors of players active in this market such that, ultimately, statements become feasible as to future developments.

DATABASE

The necessary data sets are made available through a national economy's descriptive statistics. In this context, it has to be stated clearly that no country has a statistics system that can provide complete and error-free information on every conceivable issue in the field of social science. It will always remain a dream to be able to empirically shed light fully on the theoretical ideas as to causal relationships in a market, including a comprehensive analysis of all aspects of the phenomenon under investigation. Of course, in this connection the question also has to be raised whether it is really desirable that anybody can receive information on anybody, including all actions, ideas, dreams, and desires. This fact and also the issue of being able to handle such a set of information have led to always working with models in market analysis and forecasting that render a simplified and abstract picture of the relevant relationships. These have to be constructed such that essential relationships or determinants are not overlooked through abstraction. Again, the main issue here is the problem of determining which information is relevant about the area under investigation.

Official statistics are, and remain to be, the central source of information for any work in the area of market analysis.[2] The results of official statistics provide basic information for the structural conditions of each market and, in part, also shed light on dynamic processes. There are also additional sources, such as market research or specific surveys at the association level or, if applicable, in the international area. No ideal solutions can be provided here, because each problem is a specific problem, since, after all, the business idea of the company investigated is unique. Therefore, there are no final pictures available that could be adopted as is. Due to limited availability of data, models, which form the beginning of such a process, usually have to be simplified further when the original theoretical model cannot be filled sufficiently with empirical information.[3] A great number of statistical methods are available for deriving planning bases and interpreting empirical information, which are characterized briefly in the following chapter. Of central importance in all cases is whether univariate or multivariate approaches should be used for such market forecasts (i.e., whether to work with causal models). This decision is, among others, also determined by the availability of data.

MARKET FORECASTING METHODS

Overview

Table 20.1 gives a systematic overview of forecasting methods. However, it does not go into detail as to the individual methods.[4] Some of the methods listed in the Table 20.1 have already been described in this book. We would like to concentrate in this chapter mainly on the difference between univariate and multivariate procedures so that we can give hints as to their usefulness within the scope of market forecasting for forecasting statements. This also includes methodical approaches at

Table 20.1
Overview of Forecasting Methods

Qualitative (subjective) methods	Empirical/formal (objective) methods		
Free estimate Survey Delphi method Cross-impact analysis Brainstorming Scenarios Science fiction	Univariate methods	Mulitvariate methods	
	Single equation models		Multiple equation models
	Naive forecast Calculation of mean Exponential smoothing Growth functions	Regression analysis Transfer functions	Iteration methods Simulation models System dynamics models Structural analysis
	Adaptive filters Spectral analysis Box-Jenkins method	Indicator method Cross section analyses Morphological studies	
Expert systems (eclectic methods)			

Source: Following Henschel, H. (*Wirtschaftsprognosen*), 1979, p. 17.

the macroeconomic level. By no means does this preclude, for example, the inclusion of small simulation models in market forecasting, assuming that sufficient data are available and the structure of the area investigated can be clearly reconstructed empirically. If the building permit for a specific sector of the construction materials industry, for example, turns out to be a suitable leading indicator, then market forecasting can definitely be developed with the indicator method.

Table 20.1 suggests a differentiation between qualitative and quantitative forecasts. However, such a differentiation does little in terms of clarifying methodical issues. A separation into 'quantitative' forecasts—based on numbers and with results also expressed numerically—and the rather subjectively, intuitively, and verbally expressed 'qualitative' forecasts is virtually impossible and often not even sensible. A procedure described as qualitative focuses to a large degree on considerations that cannot be easily quantified and for which the experience and intuition of the person or group in charge of this issue play a crucial role. Nonetheless, the actual foundation for such methods continues to be objective facts and numerically supported information on general conditions and specific fields.

Conversely, results of a quantitatively formulated forecast—if it is intended for specific applications and not to degenerate into a purely abstract mathematical-statistical pastime—always have to be supplemented by qualitative considerations, which have a considerable share in determining the quality of the data presented.

Pluralism of Methods in Expert Systems

It is no coincidence that a wide variety of forecasting methods are used in conjunction by experienced persons in charge of projects and analysis institutions. This is because they have come to the realization that a forecast's quality does not depend exclusively on the possibility of computerized processing of extensive numerical systems. Rather, it also depends on the quality of the underlying assumptions, estimates made during model development, and checking of parameters, as well as ultimately the qualitative interpretation of results through each of the persons in charge. In the end, qualitative methods (as listed in Table 20.1) also facilitate in the vast majority of cases the quantification of statements about the future (the Delphi method and cross-impact analysis are designed especially for processing soft information into quantitative data). The remaining qualitative approaches shown in Table 20.1 eventually also have to be quantified if a clear and unambiguous answer is to be ensured (e.g., the ability to differentiate between various scenarios). Only science fiction may be an exception here.

Working with a combination of several methods is often referred to as an 'expert system.' This involves an expert employing various methods, which he or she chooses due to their specific suitability for the problem in question. This is why the term 'eclectic methods' is also being used, which goes back to Greek philosophers known as eclectics (choosers). Their particular skill was choosing for synthesizing with their own teachings that with which they agreed from the most diverse teachings. By using this procedure in expert systems, the results worked out in detail via such eclectic methods (i.e., all available forecasts developed via the most diverse methods) are interpreted as far as they lead—in combination and after synthesis—to an improved forecast in the expert's eyes. Consequently, such approaches supplement and test each other. The diverse aspects that have to be taken into account in a market forecast sometimes necessitate using a variety of methods for assessing a situation in question.

NOTES

1. Cf. Weinhold-Stünzi, H. (*Marketing*), 1988, pp. 415ff., Kroeber-Riel, W. and Weinberg, P. (*Konsumentenverhalten*), 1996.

2. The forecast given here—'and remain to be'—is based on the assumption that effective data protection measures remain in force in our economies and are able to curb comprehensive 'data mining' to the point of consumers' becoming transparent.

3. Please see Figure 10.1.

4. Details as to methods for individual procedures are described among others in Kneschaurek, F. and Graf, H.G. (*Wirtschafts- und Marktprognosen*); 1986, Hüttner, M. (*Prognoseverfahren*), 1986; Brockhoff, K. (*Prognoseverfahren*), 1977; Winker, P. (*Wirtschaftsforschung*), 1997. In particular, we will not describe statistical/methodical/mathematical methods, as this would go beyond the scope of this book.

21

FORECASTING ON THE BASIS OF TIME SERIES ANALYSES

INHERENT LAWS DURING THE COURSE OF ECONOMIC ACTIVITY

This very popular method extrapolating past time series is based on the fundamental assumption that 'inherent laws' are effective during the course of economic activity, which will prevail again and again and steer the development of economically relevant variables onto certain 'predestined' courses. This has led to the conclusion that, once these inherent laws are successfully quantified through analysis of past developments and expressed in the form of an appropriate activity formula, we will then automatically also be in a position of being able to visualize future development. Forecasts based on such basic concepts are essentially built on an analysis of past activity. The results of this analysis are considered valid also in the future by means of an analogy conclusion. The mathematical-statistical tool required for this analysis is knowledge of time-series analysis, or breakdown of a time series into its components (trend, typical seasonal but still short-term fluctuations, business cycle and irregular influences), as well as typifying the first three components.[1]

MOST IMPORTANT AREAS OF APPLICATION

Experience has shown that the fundamental hypothesis on which time-series analysis is based (i.e., constancy of economic variables over time) does not apply to the economic cycle phenomenon. Therefore, time-series analysis cannot be used for economic forecasts from the outset. The reason for this is the irregularity of cyclical fluctuations (which cannot be taken into account via forecasting). In contrast, this hypothesis appears in most cases to be applicable to seasonal or thus far short-term cyclical fluctuations, as well as long-term developments (trends). Let us first look at short-term fluctuations having a distance into the future of less than one year and being subject to pronounced seasonal, monthly, weekly, daily, or hourly rhythms. The constancy of such short-term patterns of activity is obvious. Therefore, forecasts based on typified models of activity determined via analysis of the past usually provide very good results (see Figures 21.1 and 21.2).[2]

Longer-term developments of relevant economic variables, evident via trends, seem also to be subject to definite laws over the course of time. There are, in fact, numerous examples that seem to prove clearly that the developments of many variables are astoundingly regular in the long term insofar as they always fall on the trend again despite temporarily sustained short-term deviations. Even larger-scale political and economic disturbances do not seem to be able to throw a long-term trend off its course. It is as if it possessed magnetic power. Therefore, it is understandable that quite a few forecasters are tempted to extend a basic trend, determined on the basis of the past, through one stroke of a feather, so to speak. Indeed, why should a trend that has been very impressive in its regularity for years, even decades, suddenly deviate from its course?

The probability that the inherent laws, apparent through the constancy in trend, always win through again in the end is often considered greater than the probability that the future could lead to a fundamental change in a previous basic trend. An example may be useful in illustrating this point. The development of U.S. macroeconomic productivity (real gross domestic product per wage/salary earner) has shown a remarkably constant trend for more than 100 years, so it is not surprising that numerous economists see the influence of the innate and hardly changeable 'character' of the American economy as the reason behind this. By the way, similar ideas exist for other countries as well. For example, H. Kahn goes as far as saying that each country has 'its own' long-term course of development and that 'while it can depart from this course temporarily, it will always come back to it in the end.' Great Britain, whose growth rate had been hovering around 2% since 1860, achieved 3% growth after 1945. For British conditions this meant a considerable increase beyond the long-term benchmark, which was apparently only temporary. According to Kahn, Great Britain is and remains a 'two percent growth country.'[3]

TYPICAL TRENDS

It is generally accepted that there are different trends, the most important of which are shown schematically in Figure 21.3.

Linear Trend. A linear trend increases or decreases over time at constant absolute rates of change according to the basic formula:

$$Y = a + b X$$

where Y = the variable analyzed, a = the initial value of the trend (at x = 0), b = the absolute change of y per observation period, and X = the time unit (year, month,

Figure 21.1
Turnover in Retail Trade: Total Turnover from 1992 to 1996 on a Monthly Basis
(1949 Index = 100)

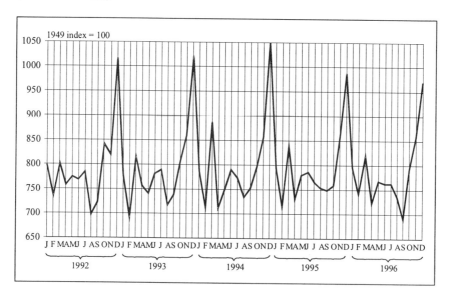

Source: Swiss Federal Statistical Office (*Yearbook*), various volumes.

Figure 21.2
Daily Load Curve: Power Consumption of Households (in % of Daily Peak)

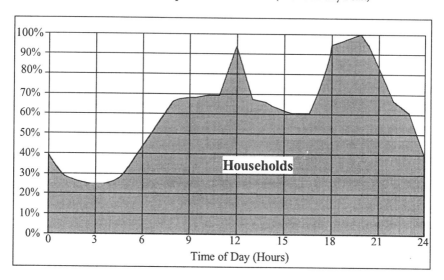

Source: Swiss Federal Office of Energy (*Statistic*), 2001, p. 54.

Figure 21.3
Statistic Curve Lines

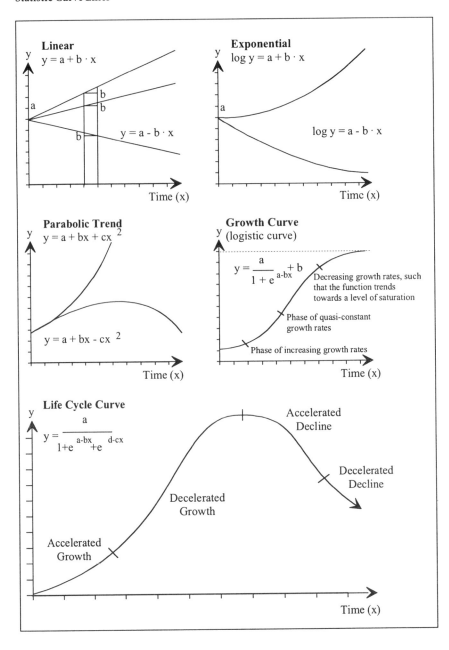

quarter, etc.), whereby x = 0 at the starting point and the time units are continuously updated (1, 2, 3, ... n).

Exponential Trend. This trend increases or decreases at constant percentage rates of growth (b), according to the formula:

$$\log Y = a + b \log X$$

On a logarithmic scale this trend is linear.

Parabolic Trend. This trend is consistent with the formula:

$$Y = a + b X + c X^2$$

This trend has the tendency of initially increasing or decreasing only slightly and then more and more so with time. The reason for this is parameter c, which due to multiplication with the squared time unit adds an increasingly strong upward or downward 'slant' to the trend.

Logistic Curves, Growth Curves. This trend is usually S-shaped, that is, moving from an initial phase into a dynamic phase in order to then enter into a new (stationary) equilibrium phase again in the end. It is consistent with the formula:

$$Y = a / 1 + e^{a \cdot bX} + b$$

Life Cycle Curves. These curves follow at first a growth curve trend. In a subsequent period the curve takes a downturn again. Its trend is consistent with the formula:

$$Y = a / 1 + e^{a \cdot bX} + e^{d \cdot cX}$$

Growth theory frequently operates with such depictions of trends. The difference between the logistic trend, moving toward saturation, and so-called life cycle curves is that with the latter—similarly to nature—no new stationary (equilibrium) phase occurs, rather, a downturn or waning of the variable in question. These curves are sections of frequency distributions, meaning that both approaches are closely connected or represent a transformation.

In all these cases forecasts are based on extrapolations of past trends. Therefore, it is important to first determine the 'typical' trend. In this context the phrase 'trend of the best fit' is often used (i.e., the trend that best reflects the previous trend of the analyzed series of numbers and is able—to use the language of econometrists—to most precisely 'remodel' it). This trend is then extrapolated into the future by assuming that the relationships so expressed remain the same and continue to exist in the same form in the future.

CRITICAL ASSESSMENT

As convincing as these considerations may be, they conceal to a large extent the problems that emerge during application of this method to specific cases. We illustrate this by the example of the development of the degree of Swiss motorization (see Figure 21.4). Let us go back to the year 1975. Due to the insecure oil market situation we have been given the task of carrying out a trend forecast for the degree of Swiss motorization until the year 2000. Annual data for the period from 1960 to 1974 are available as the empirical basis.

The scatter plot, as shown in Figure 21.4 a, suggests using a linear trend. The available information on the bracketed period precludes any other trend. Such an extrapolation would have turned out to be astoundingly accurate until 1985, despite two oil crises (in 1975 and 1979). In 1975, even a Sunday driving ban was twice imposed in order to reduce the threat of an oil shortage.

If a forecaster had been given the same task in 1986 (i.e., to forecast the degree of motorization until the year 2000 on the basis of available information for the 1960 to 1985 period,)then he or she would have been confronted with the fact that exceptionally rapid economic growth had been observed since 1983, which was very likely to continue. This continuation was due particularly to the liberalization of the European economies governed by a white paper published at the time. On the basis of this picture the continuation of the previously linear trend would have had to be seen as the lower margin of future development (Figure 21.4b).

Actual development is shown in Figure 21.5: after 1985 a pronounced slowdown becomes apparent in the pace of growth of the degree of motorization. In any

Figure 21.4

Development of the Degree of Swiss Motorization: The Forecasting Problem in 1975 and 1986

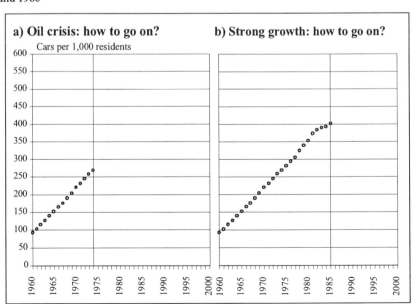

Source: Swiss Federal Statistical Office (*Yearbook*), various volumes.

Figure 21.5
Development of the Degree of Swiss Motorization, 1960–1996

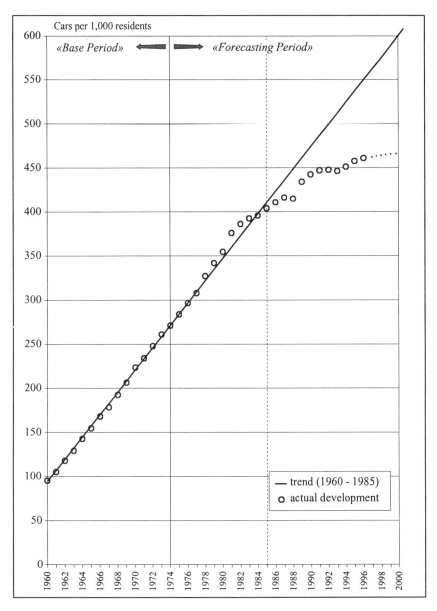

Sources: Swiss Federal Statistical Office (*Yearbook*), various volumes and SGZZ calculations.

event, the 15-year bracket period from 1960 to 1974 and subsequent period until 1985 did not permit concluding that a clearly flatter trend had to be expected after 1985. Furthermore, no indication can be found either in the 25-year bracket period (1960–1985) for using a logistic or parabolic trend as a forecasting basis. No other curve shape is likely to achieve the statistical test values shown by the linear trend.

A continuation of the trend for this bracket period until the year 2000 leads to a degree of motorization of approximately 600 cars per 1,000 residents. This is a scale reached, for example, in California and several other U.S. regions, so such a number should appear by no means completely implausible. Consequently, on the basis of the statistical control possibilities of the 1960 to 1985 database, there is no indication whatsoever that the trend will change. At any rate, the slowdown in degree of motorization growth observed after 1985 was not identifiable on the basis of time-series analysis alone.

The difference between the 'forecast value' for the year 2000 according to trend extrapolation (600 cars per 1,000 residents) and the expected value from today's point of view of around 500 cars per 1,000 residents is particularly significant because each of these two numbers has to be multiplied by the estimated number of residents for the year 2000, that is, 7.2 million.

The resulting 'forecasting error' amounts to almost 720,000 cars; that is, the level in 2000 turns out to be lower than would have been predicted with a linear function (on the basis of the 1960–1974 and 1960–1985 bracket periods). On average, 50,000 more cars would have had to be sold annually between 1985 and 2000 than has so far been expected.

Therefore, with a view to a forecast, the differences are extremely large. In addition, they are burdened with chance factors too great for them to be considered sufficiently secured bases for a longer-term forecast. In any event, this example clearly illustrates the problem with trend extrapolation. The uncertainty of this method increases greatly, particularly when analyzing the development of narrowly defined partial sectors of an economy or even individual markets. Even more sophisticated methods operating with nonlinear trends, logistic or life cycle curves, are hardly capable of reducing the danger of more seriously wrong forecasts.

NOTES

1. This method is described, in Hüttner, M. (*Prognoseverfahren*), 1986, pp. 11–73.

2. This book does not attempt to address these issues in detail and deals exclusively with problems of economic and market forecasting, as well as long-term forecasting.

3. Kahn, H. (*World Economic Development*), 1980.

22

OPERATING WITH GROWTH AND LIFE CYCLE CURVES

BIOLOGICAL PROCESSES AS A BASIS

Biological processes follow a certain rhythm in nature that can be described very well with growth and life cycle curves. The S-shaped growth curve depicts a graphical symbol of cumulative growth, while the rate of growth follows a bell-shaped curve (i.e., a life cycle curve). A good example for the development of a plant to its full height is the sunflower. Its growth follows an S-curve, by reaching about 15 cm in height in 7 days and up to 2.50 m in 70 days. About halfway, when the growth rate is highest, the plant has reached about half its final height at 1.25 m. To stick to this example, germination of the sunflower occurs on day 0, the greatest increase in growth rate can be observed around day 20, its maximum on day 35, and its greatest decrease around day 50; a standstill in growth is reached after 70 days. In this case, the life cycle curve reflects growth rates, and the S-curve describes cumulative growth, as shown in Figure 22.1.

APPLICATION TO ECONOMIC ISSUES

It has been attempted over and over again to also recognize such a cycle in processes of economic development and to derive a forecast for the future development of the variable investigated on the basis of such acquired knowledge. If such inherent laws are successfully understood, then the future is calculable, because natural growth acts as a basic law and applies to all processes within a society and so also to the economy. If, in addition, a fixed duration is successfully assigned to this life cycle, then it becomes easy not only to describe economic and technological developments but also to forecast economic processes. For example, Modis[1] has assigned uniform durations to the vitalities and creative powers of contemporary

Figure 22.1
Life Cycle and Growth Curves

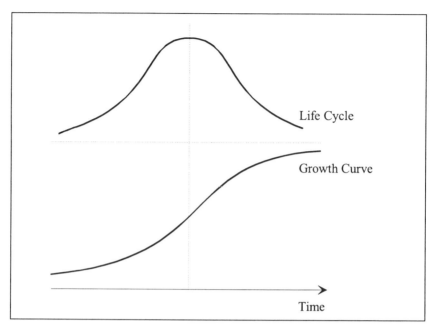

geniuses, and to populations of automobiles and fruit flies, all the way to the growth of annual energy consumption at the global level.

An example from Modis' book (Modis, 1992, p. 251) illustrates the use of such an S-curve with a view to airfreight turnover, according to which 90% of the saturation level in this area should be reached by the turn of the century (Figure 22.2). In this context we can also look at level of population and number of flights as a function of income (Figure 22.3). Consequently, Modis' observation means that, despite increases in income—aspired to and definitely noticeable in India and China—no further increase in airfreight traffic has to be expected despite the enormous weights of these economies in terms of their populations. Since such an idea is hardly defensible, Modis suggests in support of his thesis that a second S-curve succeeds the first one so repeating the trend to this point at a higher level (Figure 22.4). However, there are no clues for this on the basis of empirical data. Nonetheless, according to Modis, the 'chaotic' fluctuations, evident when reaching saturation level, indicate that such a process has to be expected.

PROBLEMS WITH LIFE CYCLES

As interesting as such considerations may be, and as fascinating as the description of a wide variety of processes in economics, politics, and cultural and social life may seem, extrapolations based on typified growth and life cycle curves are no

Figure 22.2
Slowdown in Growth of Air Traffic toward the Year 2000

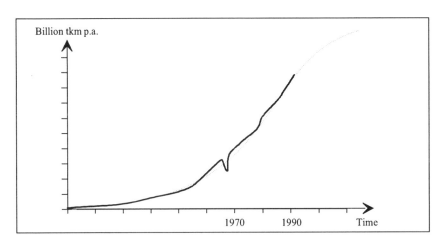

Source: Modis, Th. (*Predictions*), 1992, p. 251.

Figure 22.3
Relationship between Income and Air Travel around 1990

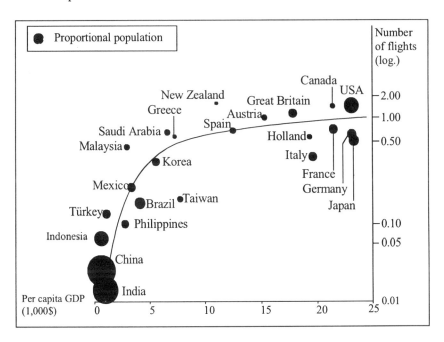

Source: Booz, Allen, & Hamilton, cited in *The Economist,* Vol. 353 (1993).

Figure 22.4
Natural Growth Alternating with States of Chaos

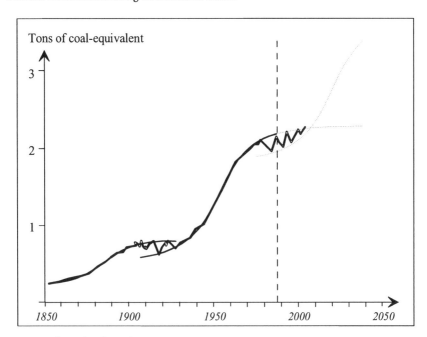

Source: Modis, T. (Predictions), 1992, p. 271.

less problematic than simpler extrapolation methods. Such processes—as presented by Modis—range from the lives of Bach and Mozart to the discoveries of Columbus, Gauss, and Einstein, from the extinction of dinosaurs, to the spread of AIDS, and from energy consumption, to Wall Street crashes. In the majority of cases statistical data are even not available for determining growth or life cycle curves. Available data cover only fractions of the entire developmental curves and so represent an extremely uncertain basis for extrapolation.

Additionally, many economic sectors and markets, are still far from their 'maturity stages.' Some of them are at the beginning of their developments. Good examples are biochemistry, genetic engineering, electronics, and communication technology. It would be irresponsible to attempt predicting the developments of these innovative sectors by extrapolating output or turnover data available so far. This is because their abilities to expand and potentials in terms of market expansion are still largely unknown, although they are of particular interest at this time. During the first, particularly dynamic phase of development, it is certainly not yet possible to speak of 'inherent laws' with respect to the variables investigated. In some cases there is continued growth for 10 or more years at the very high pace established during a company's start-up phase (e.g., microprocessor technology). However, a growth trend can also—even after a promising start—take a sudden downturn and reach the stagnation or even decline stage unexpectedly early.

There appears to be a phase in the long-term development of each economic variable (around the middle of the growth curve) during which its growth rate remains relatively stable. However, the duration of this phase is uncertain and varies depending on the investigation subject, such that an extrapolation relying on the presumably remarkable 'constancy of growth rates' can also lead to complete failure. Experience has shown that individual variables increase more rapidly during their phases of more or less constant development than does the economy as a whole. Consequently, it is unavoidable that growth of particularly rapidly expanding sectors will sooner or later have to adjust back again to the pace of growth of the entire economy.[2]

However, trying to determine how long this phase of above-average growth is going to last, solely on the basis of analysis of past development, is obviously difficult. In other words, it is hard to establish when the process of 'downward adjustment' will start along with the corresponding slowdown in economic growth.

Even when we are dealing with a single variable that appears to have reached or even surpassed the maturity stage, extrapolating a known growth curve proves to be problematic. The same problem applies to growth and life cycle curves and cyclical fluctuations. It is established that cyclical fluctuations are a characteristic feature of a free market economy and will remain so. Likewise, it is undisputed that individual economic variables—no matter at what aggregational level one may look at them—follow certain 'inherent laws' during their long-term developments, which can be illustrated conveniently via the concept of growth and life cycle curves. However, as cyclical fluctuations cannot be 'typified' and forecast due to their notorious irregularities in development over time, so future courses of growth and life cycle curves cannot be forecast by optimally describing mathematically and statistically their previously known courses and then extrapolating them.

After all, an intrinsic part of growth and life cycle curves is that the development of the variable investigated is a function of time. However, this must be excluded in economic relationships.[3] The period of time that elapses between market penetration, expansion, market saturation, decline, and disintegration is different for each economic variable. Even the saturation phase does not necessarily have to be followed by final disintegration. Rather, development can lead into longer-term stagnation, after which both a final setback and renewed growth are possible. In other words, more information is required for an informative projection—namely, on the actual determinants of the variables of interest to us—than just time-series analysis. This is so even if it has been able to apparently describe development to this point exceptionally well.

SUMMING UP

Let us bear in mind that it is not time that determines economic development, but rather its economic and noneconomic determinants. Trend extrapolation will provide only supportable results under so-called *ceteris paribus* conditions (i.e., when the influence of the relevant determinants of the variables to be forecast will be as strong in the future as it was in the past). However, this prerequisite does not have to be fulfilled by any means. It is met most likely at the level of macroeconomic aggregates (gross domestic product, national income, etc.). This is due to the fact that the development of these variables constitutes a resultant reflecting the influences of thousands and thousands of different individual trends, whose effect in net terms—and this is what counts, not the individual influences—is relatively constant. This explains why the development of aggregate variables frequently shows a regular and continuous trend. However, even such a trend is stopped abruptly by a trend setback. For this reason, in particular the extrapolation method cannot be satisfying because it is in no way able to recognize early enough imminent trend setbacks—which steer economic and market developments into entirely new directions—and consider them in a forecast.

The more that aggregate macroeconomic variables are broken down into their components, the more reservations there are about extrapolation as a method. It is hard to rely on this method, especially during times of fundamental and global structural change, because especially then the trend that best records and describes past development is the least suited as a basis for assessing the future.

NOTES

1. Modis, Th. (*Predictions*), 1992.

2. Otherwise,the share of these sectors in the entire national economic output would increase continuously (i.e., so fast, that no room would be left for other goods within a short period of time).

3. This does not refer to those variables that orient themselves, at the individual level, on a consumer's age. In that case, time (age) is one of the determinants for each individual's needs.

23

FORECASTS BASED ON THE
THEORY OF CAUSE AND EFFECT

THE BASIC PRINCIPLE

The term 'causal theoretical forecast' is used when variables to be predicted are put in a dependent relationship with their relevant determinants and are then predicted on the basis of this knowledge. These forecasts are also referred to as multivariate approaches because several (multiple) variables are investigated for their interrelationships via such a procedure, and a forecast is deduced on the basis of empirically determined relationships.[1] A step-by-step procedure is followed for such forecasts. First, the factors determining the developments of the variables investigated are established. Then it is attempted to establish the influence of these determinants in terms of degree and direction and to express them as quantitative behavioral and reaction coefficients. Third, a forecast is derived on the basis of the presumed (estimated) developments of the determinants of the variables to be predicted as well as the established parameters. Procedures based on this basic concept range from simple behavioral equations to comprehensive econometric models. In behavioral equations the development of the variable to be predicted is attributed to the influence of a single dominant determinant, while with econometric models the variables to be predicted are seen as variables of an integrated system of mathematical equations, which registers the interdependencies between the relevant variables and expresses them as behavioral and definition equations.

Irrespective of the complexity of the theoretical statement (model) used, such a forecast's structure essentially always remains the same. As shown in Figure 10.1, a causal theoretical forecast is always based on a theoretical concept that starts from certain ideas as to the economic variables relevant to forecasting and their interdependencies. On the basis of these fundamental theoretical ideas, a theoretical statement is derived in verbal or formal-mathematical form that describes the relevant functional relationships and relationships of effect. A simple example of such a theoretical statement (equation) containing only two variables (a determining explanatory [exogenous] variable and a determinate, dependent [endogenous] variable) is shown in the following example. Private consumption (C) depends on disposable personal income (Y) and the propensity to consume (c) (verbal definition) or per formal definition:

$$C = c * Y$$

Complicated models, which can contain up to 100 or more variables, have more theoretical statements (equations) that are connected with each other in the model. Otherwise, they are structured according to the same principles as the simplest equations.

For use in forecasts, these equations (models) have to be 'filled' with concrete numbers by means of available statistical data as well as results of statistical analyses. Statistical analyses are used for determining the interconnections and past behavioral functions relevant to each case. Using the preceding example, a quantified consumer function could look as follows:

$$C_t - C_{t-1} = 0.8 * (Y_t - Y_{t-1})$$

(= average propensity to consume: 80% of disposable personal income is being consumed)
or:

$$C_t = 0.8 * Y_t$$

Marginal propensity to consume: a change in disposable personal income by 1 unit (CHF, CHF million, CHF billion) leads to a change in private consumption by 0.8 units.
or:

$$C_t - C_{t-1} / C_{t-1} * 100 = 0.8 * Y_t - Y_{t-1} / Y_{t-1} * 100$$

Elasticity of private income: a 1% change in disposable personal income leads to a 0.8% change in private consumption.

Statistics provides the necessary test procedures for being able to assess to what extent quantitatively formulated descriptive statements are capable of capturing reality and what errors have to be estimated. Such errors arise when previous development is expressed by means of these descriptive statements.[2] Data processing systems are, in turn, capable of greatly facilitating quantification of the descriptive statements (models) as well as testing their relevance. Such numerically concretized descriptive statements (models) can be used both for analytical purposes (i.e., for testing theories empirically) and for forecasting purposes.

FORECASTS AND SIMULATIONS

Causal theoretical approaches can be separated into actual forecasts and alternative simulations. Those forecasts that in the forecaster's eyes indicate the most likely future development (similarly to weather forecasts) can be regarded as actual forecasts. Of course, these forecasts are not unconditional ('this is how it will be') but are conditional ('this is how it will be, if . . . '); that is, they are based on hypotheses as to the future development of the relevant determinants of the variable to be forecast. However, forecasters ascribe the greatest probability of occurrence to such hypotheses, similarly to a meteorologist's expecting that his or her hypotheses as to the shifts of weather fronts, future pressure and wind conditions, and so on will come true and so also his or her forecast. Market forecasts and short-term economic forecasts clearly belong in this category.

Alternative simulations assume that forecasts in the previously mentioned sense are not possible for the long term. This is because general conditions change, not only for national economies but, for example, also for foreign trade, in ways that cannot be assessed objectively via probability or plausibility considerations. Therefore, it is essential to consider alternatives, that is, to simulate various equally likely future situations—mostly with a view to their economic effects (cf. Part III of this book).

Judgments based on estimates are unavoidable when formulating actual forecasts. All explanatory, determining variables (i.e., disposable personal income in the earlier case) have to be predicted, unless they are determined endogenously in a model (i.e., from within the model). Nevertheless, a relatively large number of explanatory (exogenous) variables always remain in each equation or model. These variables have to be predicted by means of judgments based on estimates before it is possible to start working on the actual forecast. This is the fundamental difference between the forecasting and the analytical model. Although with the latter all explanatory variables are known and have to be used in the model as such for empirical verification, their future development is unknown and so has to be predicted.

In addition, it has to be decided in a forecasting model the extent to which the reaction and behavioral coefficients from empirical analysis of the past will also be valid in the future, or whether they have to be revised. Such decisions also amount to a judgment based on estimates, in which not only theoretical knowledge but also the forecaster's experience and intuition play an essential part.

The situation is similar with forecasting simulations. In our simple example the development of private consumption could be established on the basis of various propensities to consume or changes in disposable personal income. In order to provide these simulations with some real forecasting value, the alternatively chosen hypotheses must not be purely hypothetical in nature (which would definitely be acceptable within the scope of analytical simulation models) but should be applied to reality as much as possible. Selecting them from a virtually unlimited variety of theoretical alternatives again requires an individual judgment based on estimates. This judgment is of particular significance insofar as the final user of forecasts cannot be presented with an entire package of, in part, diametrically opposed forecasts. If alternatives must be presented, then it is important to concentrate on a few particularly important and realistic versions. Furthermore, only those variables and behavioral coefficients should be alternated whose future developments appear especially uncertain or that can be moved in various directions via political decisions. We have already addressed these issues in the context of discussing the scenario technique (Part III).

CENTRAL IMPORTANCE OF THE CAUSAL CHAIN (RELATIONAL NETWORK)

As shown in Figure 10.1, a theoretical statement's structure represents the first step of working with causal theoretical methods. The extreme importance of this step cannot be overemphasized. This step focuses on recognizing the relevant determinants for each of the market segments. It has to be determined at the same time which structural features characterize the subject of investigation. If applicable, it also has to be established whether key factors have to be taken into account that characterize especially the investigation subject and so make a specific forecasting approach imperative. We would like to illustrate this seemingly rather easy step by means of an equally simple forecasting problem. For this, we would like to go back to the earlier example.

It should be possible to predetermine relatively precisely new car sales in a country via the determinants of income and development of the population (capable of driving). Car sales can be measured precisely and are registered statistically on the basis of the number of new car registrations. The question remains, however, how many of these cars are merely replacements of discharged vehicles? Evidently, there are two demand components, namely, a demand for new or additional cars and a demand for replacement cars. Therefore, there are already two components of the investigation subject that need to be analyzed and forecast, because each component is dependent on different determinants (cf. Chapter 21).

Replacement demand is obviously a function of the stock of cars as well as their average useful lives. This means, however, that average useful life is the actual key factor in a forecast for determining replacement demand. Therefore, what is important at this stage of the causal chain is recording the determinants for a car's average useful life and analyzing, as well as ultimately predicting, changes in useful life due to, for example, general legislative or technical conditions as well as changing consumer preferences.

Similar reasoning can be applied to new and additional demand. The key factor in the demand for new or additional durables is the already achieved saturation level, which has to be considered both analytically and in terms of forecasting. In this example, achieved saturation is measured on the basis of the so-called degree of motorization (i.e., the number of cars per 1,000 residents). Prediction of this variable as well as multiplication of the change in this number by expected population development, allow for the estimation of new demand. Therefore, it is important to construct a separate causal chain for estimating the development of the degree of motorization and then to derive a forecast for the degree of motorization on the basis of a prediction of these factors.

The shaded part of Figure 23.1 illustrates the investigation subject's structure (the actual definition equations) while the connection between the key factors and their determinants reflects the behavior of the players in this market. For durables and also for capital goods, the relatively simple causal chain for nondurables has to be expanded into two strands. This is because, on one hand, it is always necessary to differentiate between replacement and new demand. On the other hand, the fo-

Figure 23.1
Modeling Approach (Car Ownership)

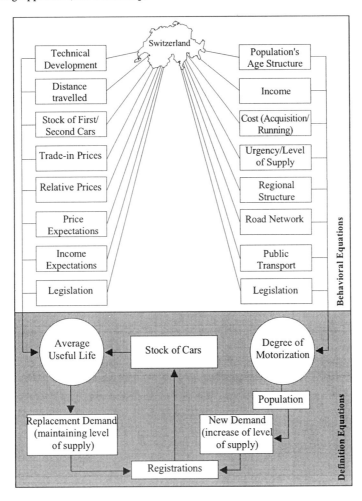

cus in determining additional demand has to be not only on consumption (= sales, or, in this case, new registrations) but also on achieved levels of saturation.

We would like to use this example to illustrate how the causal relational structure plays a central part in the process of causal theoretical forecasts. Each economic variable is obviously determined by a great number of political, social, ecological, technological, and demographic factors. Such additional influences have to be made evident in a causal analysis because irregularities in individual markets cause deviations from the expected causal theoretical development. This can be illustrated excellently by the already used example of the degree of Swiss motorization. Figure 23.2 shows the progression of the relationship between development of the degree of motorization and per capita gross domestic product, the latter in place of the development of income in Switzerland between 1960 and 1996. Obviously, even causal analysis reaches its limitations of reliability with only one determinant.

In this case, development was massively thrown out of proportion after 1974 in comparison with that observed previously by political events and demographic developmental trends. The oil crisis in 1975 led to a serious economic slump in Switzerland, giving rise to a decrease in the number of foreigners employed in Switzerland by about 300,000 persons. These seasonal and annual workers were usually significantly less motorized than Swiss citizens, especially because they transferred large parts of their incomes back to their home countries. This population decrease led—despite decreasing per capita income—to a strong increase in the average degree of Swiss motorization, which invalidates the hypothesis on which the analysis is based. According to this hypothesis, the degree of motorization increases with increasing prosperity according to a parabolic trend, which can clearly be proven empirically for the 1960 to 1974 period.

In the period from 1976 to 1982 an extremely strong increase in representation of the 20–24 age group could be observed, which greatly increased this age group's weight in the population and so gave rise to an apparently strong increase in the demand for cars. In addition, this development coincided with completion of the first sections of a national highway network, as well as the availability of affordable four-wheel drives. This enabled larger parts of the rural population—also in mountain regions—to acquire cars. Since 1983, development has apparently gone back to the basic relationship in accord with the 1960 and 1974 trend pattern, although at a significantly higher level. The recessionary development after 1990 shows the typical ratchet effect with respect to consumer spending (the degree of saturation has not decreased despite stagnating or slightly decreasing incomes). However, the quieter demographic development did not lead to swings like those after 1974.

The model taken into account ultimately in behavioral equations has to consider equally availability/quality of data and efficiency of the forecasting process. We would like to stress that, in the end, the simplest possible approaches should be used because any complication immediately means increases in cost. After all, the forecast is not a means in itself but rather fulfills a service function in the planning

Figure 23.2
Relationship between Degree of Swiss Motorization and per Capita Real Gross Domestic
Product

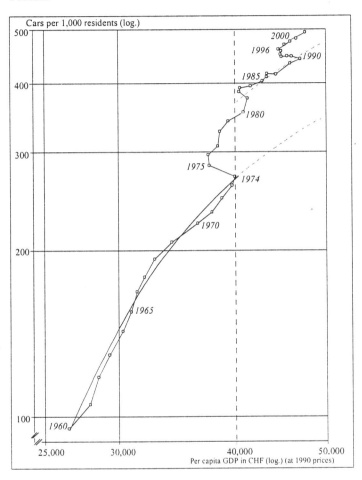

Sources: Swiss Federal Statistical Office (*Yearbook*), various volumes and SGZZ calculations.

process, which also has to be subject to cost and efficiency criteria. However, the causal chain's structure must not suffer under these restrictions because only knowledge of the entire causal chain and the degree of ultimately unavoidable abstraction via the model used makes adequate interpretation of the results possible.

CRITICAL ASSESSMENT

Our considerations thus far indicate possible sources of error that can occur with a causal theoretical forecast. These can be due to:

1. Theoretical reasoning. This case arises when the underlying theory has gaps (i.e., not all relevant interdependencies have been considered), or when it is inconsistent (by containing errors of logic), irrelevant (with a view to the forecast to be made), or unrealistic (by not reflecting at all, or only inadequately, the realities of the business world).

2. Quantification of theoretically derived statements (models), especially numerical registration of all variables and relationships relevant to forecasting. A quantified model can never fully reflect reality. Consequently, operating with models leads to more or less already flawed results during analysis. These flaws come about by comparing actual past developments of relevant economic variables with those calculated by means of the model.

3. Misjudgment of exogenous variables, as well as behavioral and reaction coefficients, relevant to forecasting. The greater the number of variables and considered interdependencies between them (i.e., the greater the model's complexity) the greater is the danger of such misjudgments. Experience has shown that the danger of cumulative errors is greater than the chance that they neutralize each other in terms of their effects.

NOTES

1. For an overview, cf. Backhaus, K. (*Multivariate*), 1996.
2. For an overview, cf. Bohly, P. (*Statistik*), 1989.

24

Transformation of Market
Forecasts into Corporate Decisions

INFORMATION BASE

At the beginning of this book we demonstrated the significance of executive information and its integration into the managerial process (see Figures 1.1 and 1.2). Short-term market forecasting focuses on information for operative management (i.e., the information base required in 'day-to-day business' and planning for about one year in advance). Table 24.1 shows the sphere of data for assessing the environment, from which the relevant information has to be obtained for the issue under consideration. The central problem that must be coped with in this context is not a lack of information but rather the necessity of filtering out from the abundance of available information what is relevant to the managerial decisions under consideration. Figure 24.1 gives an overview of the available information and its use in such a decision-making process. This figure is not exclusively tailored to acquiring information for operative management but is rather of a more fundamental nature such that it can also be applied to strategic and normative issues. The information shown in the economic environment box is of particular significance in the area of operative decision making. These two lists in table and figure 24.1 make very clear the central role of management as a filter for choosing relevant information.

Figure 24.2, in attempting to list the various sources of environmental information for a company, illustrates this flood of information even more clearly, and this list is not even complete. In this context it should be kept in mind that part of the information can turn out to be rather contradictory. Conversely, even agreement as to future events by no means indicates that it is correct. Therefore, targeted processing of information is of crucial importance in this process. It needs to be clarified which causal chain has to be called upon for the business segment in question.

Table 24.1
Set of Data for Assessing the Framework from an Operative Point of View

Overall Development	Economic situation
	Foreign trade
	Currency, etc.
Sales Markets:	Volumes
	Potentials
	Demand structures
	Regional differences, etc.
Supply Markets:	Raw materials, energy, special materials (e.g., speculative goods, licenses)
	Capital, etc.
Labor Market:	Structures
	Availability of individual categories
	Wage levels
	Degree of organization, etc.
Unusual technological developments	
Unusual economic developments (e.g., sectors)	
Unusual social developments	

In so doing, it can be excluded that all relevant information for a specific issue can be worked up in clear form. Consequently, the focus has to be on filling the model (i.e., a simplified image of reality produced during the development of the causal chain) with information. This has to be done such that a decision can be made that does the situation justice and corresponds to the operative objectives but is ultimately also in keeping with normative objectives.

STEP-BY-STEP PROCEDURE

In working out quantitative targets in a company's central business segments, a step-by-step procedure again turns out to be useful. This is shown in Figure 24.3. It is most important to work out clues as to the developmental trends in the environments relevant to the company. Of greatest importance is the choice of forecast for the relevant determinants based on the causal chain. These determinants are laid out for the macroeconomic level and have to be differentiated, if necessary, by country and sales region.

Usually, market forecasts relate to central aggregate economic variables that determine relevant markets. In addition to economic aggregates, it is also often important to consider population development and structure issues, because economic

Figure 24.1
Crucial Role of Environmental Information in the Corporate Decision-Making Process

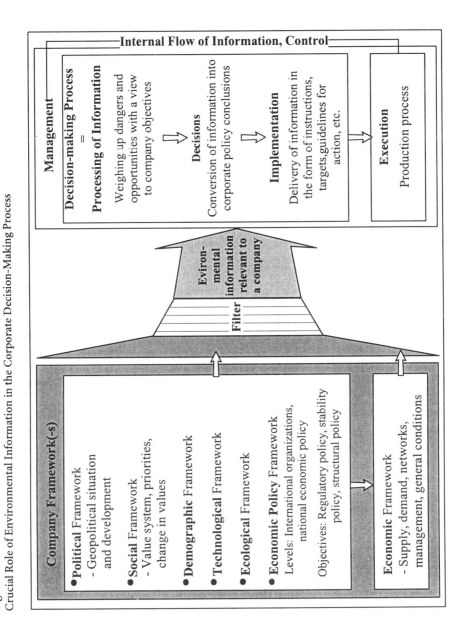

Figure 24.2
Corporate Management Flooded with Future-Related Information

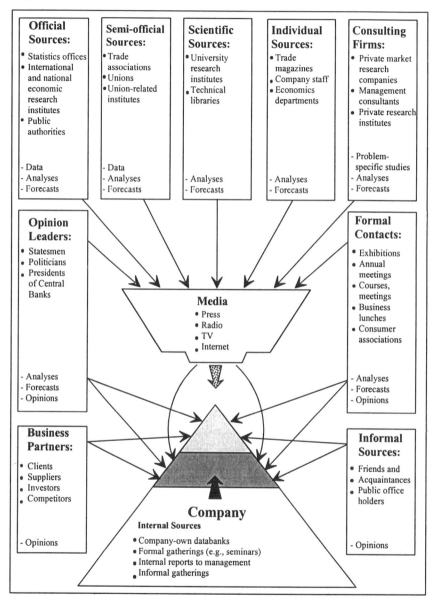

Source: Kneschaurek, F. (*Volkswirtschaft*), 1996, p. 23.

Figure 24.3
From Forecast to Corporate Planning

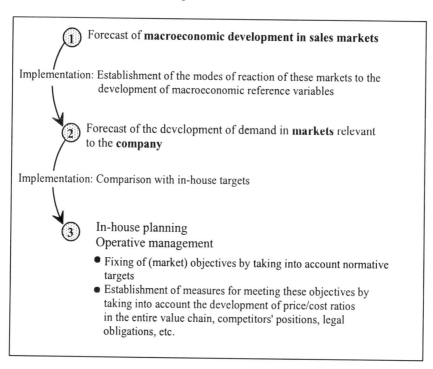

Source: Following Kneschaurek, F. (*Volkswirtschaft*), 1996, p. 328.

activity is also always directed at people. As a rule, demographic processes are characterized by comparatively slow developments so that they often are of little significance in operative management. However, there are market and business segments in which demographic influences show effects also in the short term.

MODES OF MARKET REACTION

In a first implementation step, the question as to how the markets of interest react to changes in macroeconomic determinants has to be answered. It has been pointed out that, as a rule, each market reacts in a very specific (statistically measurable) way to changes in the macroeconomic determinants relevant to that market. Determining and typifying these reaction parameters of individual markets to changes in their determinants, on the basis of empirical analyses, are the essential element of such implementation and have to be done in a company-specific way. It should be emphasized again that the business segments of individual companies are unique in character (i.e., reactions of their markets have to be studied and established individually). The individual modes of market reaction are influenced by the levels of economic development of individual economies and by the structural and institutional situations of the markets of individual countries.

In addition, one has to pay attention to the fact that there are often great differences in the short- and long-term responsiveness of individual markets. This means that the information required for operative management is established on the basis of relatively short-term responsiveness, while when analyzing markets for strategic decisions, one usually has to work with other elasticities (coefficients). Figure 18.7 shows the different modes of market reaction during the course of economic activity. It has to be emphasized that the responsiveness of individual business segments or products (product groups) cannot be taken ready-made from some statistical yearbook. Rather, it is the job of market analysis to work out such information.

Figure 24.4 shows these procedural steps in a simplified diagram. The company used as an example produces four goods in the area of food (A, B, C, D). During the development of the causal chain, the total volume of personal consumer spending on food has been determined as the most important direct determinant. This is because there are substitution relationships at play within the mix of goods consumed that are reflected in various sensitivities (reaction coefficients of individual goods of the entire supply of food). Since the component 'consumer spending on food' is not listed in official economic forecasts, the causal chain has to be extended backward (i.e., to personal consumption as a whole and ultimately to macroeconomic development).

The reaction parameter between the individual steps of this model is elasticity (e). It shows the dependent variable's relative change in relation to the determinant's relative change; an elasticity of 0.5 means that with a 1% change in the determinant, the dependent variable changes by 0.5%. As can be seen from the figure, the forecast then progresses step by step: from gross domestic product to private consumption (e = 0.6), from there to food consumption at the macroeconomic level, and from there to individual product segments, each with different elasticities.

ADJUSTMENT OF TARGETS

Starting from projected market developments, the next step consists of determining the actual objectives for the planning process. Other factors of immediate concern to the market (cost/price ratios, positions of competitors, etc.) are also considered more carefully in this implementation step. Of particular importance in this step are the company's objectives, which can be derived from market share studies. The procedure shown in Figure 24.4 looks rather complicated. This process does in fact require a considerable amount of time (and cost) because it has to be completed for each specific business segment of a company (i.e., there are no fixed recipes available that could take this job off a planning manager's hands).

Due to the obviously great efforts associated with compiling such information, the process of converting results of macroeconomic environmental forecasts into corporate conclusions turns out to be blocked relatively often from the start. This

Figure 24.4
From Economic Forecast to Budget (Simplified Diagram)

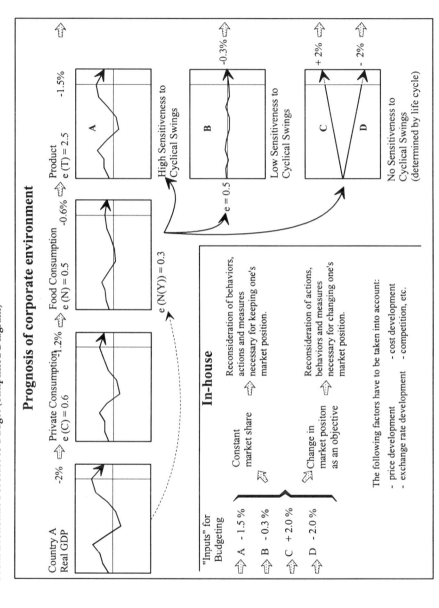

happens despite the fact that most of these relationships can be checked statistically and can, for example, also be compared internationally.[1] In this context, it is also important to keep in mind that during development of the causal chain, soft, qualitative information is not integrated into the model due to its lack of quantifiability. However, these factors have an effect nonetheless, which can be taken into account adequately only by informed developers. Therefore, empirical calculations are always only part of planning. Consideration of qualitative factors and interpretation of quantitative results built on it represent an essential step in the development of market projections.

ORGANIZATIONAL ASPECTS

In terms of its organizational/institutional manifestation, the corporate planning process depends to a large extent on the company's size. Therefore, a small company's planning process is often coped with in an unstructured fashion, which is not problematic due to the transparency of a frequently limited product range and sales territory. Contrastingly, within the planning process of larger companies an organizationally and institutionally clearly specified agenda has to be followed if it is to be used in a targeted manner for the entire company. Staff and line personnel have to work together in the planning process of a larger company. At the normative/strategic level top management is called upon to cooperate closely and discuss issues in order to determine the company's objectives and establish its strategy and policy in light of the various scenarios (cf. Part III). In contrast, carrying out detailed work in the empirical area in operative management is mainly the job of staff personnel.

Figure 24.5 illustrates these organizational aspects. It is obvious that line positions are of crucial significance during establishment of the business segments to be investigated, while actual implementation is taken care of mainly by staff personnel. The category 'external specialist' does not mean calling in a management consultant in each case. All that we wish to indicate with this description is that additional information on the environment has to be acquired externally. A statistical yearbook, a trade association publication, or theoretical textbook may provide completely sufficient information. Of major importance are informing line personnel in time and particularly also involving them in the selection of fundamental assumptions as to the development of the corporate environment. Therefore, selection of the 'right' economic forecast should by no means be done only by staff personnel, because line personnel may be of an entirely different opinion and are ultimately responsible.

With respect to organization/institutional procedures, it is important that a control system be installed for this process of information gathering and processing. It has to be determined whether actual development follows the forecast trends, whether the targets are being met, and particularly what the causes are for possible deviations. It is customary to blame false macroeconomic forecasts for

Figure 24.5
Who Does What?

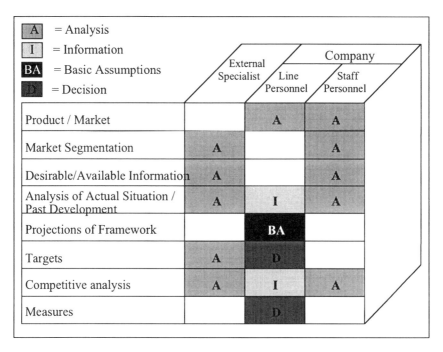

	External Specialist	Company — Line Personnel	Company — Staff Personnel
A = Analysis, **I** = Information, **BA** = Basic Assumptions, **D** = Decision			
Product / Market		A	A
Market Segmentation	A		A
Desirable/Available Information	A		A
Analysis of Actual Situation / Past Development	A	I	A
Projections of Framework		BA	
Targets	A	D	
Competitive analysis	A	I	A
Measures		D	

such differences between targets and actual development. While this may be applicable, it is not inevitable by any means because deviations can also arise during adaptation of a macroeconomic forecast to markets and a company's product lines. This can happen either because consumer behavior has changed or because market responsiveness has departed from the margins observed previously.

Such control is relatively easy with consumer goods, particularly daily necessities, because no time lags have to be observed. However, such control is often considerably more difficult with capital goods or raw materials. This is because, on one hand, a time lag can be observed between order and delivery, and, on the other, warehouses function as buffers, meaning that market reaction occurs initially not only with a delay but often also disproportionately. It is also important in this case to get a good hold of company-specific market particularities in order to recognize such interconnections early on and so consider them in the decision-making process. Such control work is of such importance because it is the only way of successfully improving each process. So much is often concealed by attaching blame solely to macroeconomic projections that difficulties, problems, and changes occur during the implementation process, which can definitely be recognized via such control. These can then be taken adequately into account during the following years so that the planning process as a whole is improved.

Figure 24.6
Use of Short- and Long-Term Forecasts in a Company

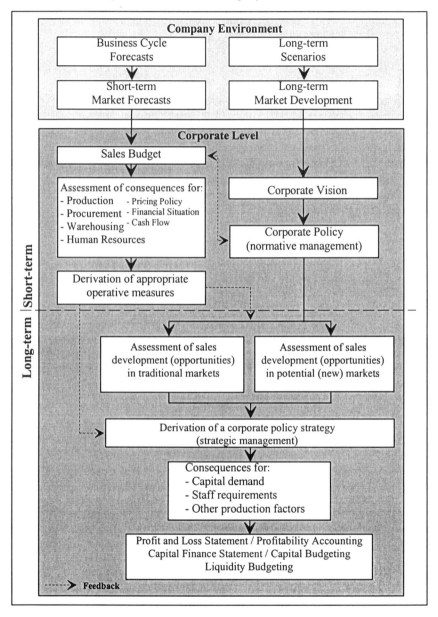

FEEDBACK TO NORMATIVE MANGEMENT

Since the nature of forecasting problems changes depending on the level of management, it is therefore useful to strictly separate the individual levels. Nonetheless, there has to be feedback between a normative orientation and operative planning. To that extent, short-term forecasting and planning cannot get by without considering the long-term macroeconomic development of a national economy or company, and vice versa.

Consequently, short- and long-term planning processes have to be connected within a company (i.e., short- and long-term forecasting cannot be used independently of each other). These interconnections are shown in Figure 24.6. Also pointed out are the areas in which environmental information for the various fields of corporate activity can be used. This is in order to draw attention to the fact that it is also important here to make all forecast uses dependent on the task under consideration. Consequently, specific information has to be provided in each case by the forecast, be it for the short or long term, which has to cover individual business segments or specific areas of supply markets. The planning process is—like integrated management—an intricate and complicated whole, in which the problem at hand and the various messages of forecasts have to be clearly taken into account.

The customary idea that it would be possible to somewhere obtain a forecast specifically customized on one's needs and to use it—without further trouble, preferable putting it under one's headrest at night—for providing the necessary planning targets is misguided and the primary reason for many people to (still) 'turn up their noses' at future-oriented thinking.

NOTE

1. The use of electronic data processing or personal computers (PCs) and dedicated software can also support the necessary procedure of working out in detail a causal chain for acquiring the appropriate data and for processing and interpreting these results. However, this cannot in the end simplify it very much.

25

In Place of Closing Remarks: What Must Be Looked Out for in Economic Forecasting?

This book aims mainly at making it easier for readers to assess forecasting efforts and to recognize the possibilities and limitations of forecasts. It does not intend to provide instructions for producing forecasts, which is evident from the lack of reference both to methods and description of the steps necessary for empirical economic research.

For the purposes of a brief recapitulation, the following checklist summarizies the most important points that one should look out for when using economic forecasts. The aspects mentioned in part refer to sections of the book and in part provide supplementary information for the actual evaluation of economic forecasts. Neither is the checklist complete, nor does it list definitively all issues associated with forecasts. Company-specific topics or issues, which are of particular significance for an individual national economy and so on, can hardly be included in such a widely applicable overview. Rather, the following compilation intends to draw attention to the most important traps and misunderstandings still associated with forecasts in order to contribute to dealing with forecasts such that their possibilities and limitations are taken into account. A first overview has to consider points 1, 4, and 9 specifically.

1. Which economic phenomenon is being addressed?
   - Is it a business cycle forecast? (quarterly/annual values)
   - Does it focus on (long-term) economic growth?
   - Are structural issues at the forefront?
2. What are the empirical bases of analyses?
   - Official national statistics
   - Official international statistics

- Comparability (basis for constant prices, exchange rates, purchasing power parities, etc.)
- Trade association statistics
- Official surveys (full/partial surveys with projections)
- Private survey/poll (sample survey, representativeness, expert selection)
- 'Own calculations'/estimates

3. Which forecasting methods are being used?

- (Trend/times-series) extrapolation
- Causal theoretical approach
- Econometric model
- Survey

4. Which assumptions is the forecast based on? (completeness/relevance)

- General conditions
- Definition model (equations)
- Behavioral parameters (structural constancy with parameter constancy!)
- Are changes in behavior being taken into account?

5. How applicable is the forecast to reality?

- Have the relevant general social and political conditions been covered?
- Have all subsystems been covered, and are their interrelationships evident?
- Have simulations been carried out under '*ceteris paribus*' conditions?
- Are the results determined by euphoria or end-of-the world sentiments?

6. Precision of the forecast

- Decimal-point accuracy
- 'When in doubt: mumble!'
- Frequency of revisions

7. Are references made to interpretation and the limitations of statements?

- Is reference made to particularly important uncertainties?
- Are references made to results or assumptions that are particularly relevant and therefore have to be watched closely?
- What are the forecast's limitations (in terms of time and subject matter)?

8. Is attention being paid to trend setbacks ('wild cards')?

- Long-term issues
- What triggers are conceivable?
- Self-destructive mechanisms (of longer-term forecasts)

9. How independent is the forecast developer?

- Who produced the forecast for whom? (trade association/political point of view?)
- Does it focus on changing behavior?

10. What is the forecaster's reputation?
   - Independence
   - Personality
   - Position
   - Experience

BIBLIOGRAPHY

Alesina, A., Roubini, N., and Cohen, G.D. (*Political Cycles*): *Political Cycles and the Macroeconomy*. Cambridge, MA, 1997.

Amara, R. and Lipinski, A.J.: *Business Planning for an Uncertain Future—Scenarios and Strategies*. New York, 1983.

Angermeier Naumann, R.: *Szenarien und Unternehmungspolitik*. Munich, 1985.

Atteslander, P. (*Sozialforschung*): *Methoden der empirischen Sozialforschung*, 7th ed. Berlin/New York, 1993.

Augusto A., Legasto, A., Forrester, J.W., and Lyneis, M. (*System Dynamics*): *System Dynamics*. Amsterdam, 1980.

Ayres, Robert V.: *Technological Forecasting*. New York, 1969.

Bächtold, R.V.: *Wirtschaftsprognostik*, Vol. 1. *Grundlagen*. Bern, 1992.

Backhaus, K. (*Multivariate*): *Multivariate Analysemethoden: eine anwendungsorientierte Einführung*, 8th ed. Berlin, 1996.

Barro, R.J. and Sala-i-Martin, X.: *Economic Growth*. New York, 1995.

Basseler, U., Heinrich, J., Koch W. (*Volkswirtschaft*): *Grundlagen und Probleme der Volkswirtschaft*, 15th ed. Köln, 1999.

Bassie, V.L.: *Economic Forecasting*. New York/Toronto/London, 1958.

Beck, U. (*Globalisierung*): *Was ist Globalisierung?*, 2nd ed. Frankfurt, 1997.

Beck, U. (*Risikogesellschaft*): *Risikogesellschaft: auf dem Weg in eine andere Moderne*. Frankfurt, 1986.

Bell, D.: *The Coming of the Post Industrial Society*. New York, 1973.

Bell, D.: *Towards the Year 2000: Work in Progress*. Cambridge, 1968.

Bell, W.: *Foundations of Futures Studies*, 2 vols. New Brunswick, NJ, 1997.

Berger, P.L. and Luckmann, Th. (*Konstruktion*): *Die gesellschaftliche Konstruktion der Wirklichkeit*, 5th ed. Frankfurt, 1997.

Bernstein, P. (*Risk*): *Against the Odds. The Remarkable Story of Risk*. New York, 1996.

Binswanger, H.C., Geissberger, W., and Ginsburg, T. (*Wohlstandsfalle*): *Wege aus der Wohlstandsfalle*. Frankfurt am Main, 1979.

Binswanger, H.C. (*Geld und Natur*): *Geld und Natur: Das wirtschaftliche Wachstum im Spannungsfeld zwischen Ökonomie und Ökologie.* Stuttgart, 1991.

Binswanger, H.C. (Wachstum): Geld und Wachstumszwang, in Binswanger, H.C. and Flotow von, P. (eds.): *Geld & Wachstum: zur Philosophie und Praxis des Geldes.* Stuttgart, 1994, pp. 81–124.

Bircher, B.: Wirtschaftliche Umwelt-Informationen—Erwartungen der Unternehmensplanung, in Graf, H.G., Meier, A., and Wuffli, H.R. (eds.): *Praxisorientierte Volkswirtschaftslehre,* commemorative publication for F. Kneschaurek. Bern, 1988, pp. 243–264.

Bleicher, K. (*Normatives Management*): *Normatives Management.* Frankfurt/New York, 1994.

Bleicher, K. (*Konzept*): *Das Konzept Integriertes Management,* 4th ed. Frankfurt/New York, 1996.

Bleicher, K., and Berthel, J. (*Wissensgesellschaft*): *Auf dem Weg in die Wissensgesellschaft.* Frankfurt, 2002.

Bodkin, R.G. et al. (*History*): *A History of Macroeconomic Model-Building.* Aldershot, 1991.

Bohley, P. (*Statistik*): *Statistik,* 3rd ed. Munich, 1989.

Bombach, G. (*Konjunkturtheorie*): *Konjunkturtheorie einst und heute.* Konstanz, 1991.

Bombach, G. (*Zyklen*): *Zyklen im Ablauf des Wirtschaftsprozesses—Mythos und Realität,* WWZ offprint No. 10. Basel, 1992.

Bossel, H. (*Modellbildung und Simulation*): *Modellbildung und Simulation.* Braunschweig/Wiesbaden, 1992.

Bossel, H. (*Simulationsprogramm*): *Die neuen Grenzen des Wachstums, Einführung zum Simulationsprogramm für MS-DOS mit SimPAS.* Stuttgart, 1992.

Bremer, S. et al. (*GLOBUS Model*): *The GLOBUS Model: Computer Simulation of World-Wide Political and Economic Developments.* Boulder, CO, 1987.

Bremer, S. and Gruhn, W. (*Micro GLOBUS*): *Micro GLOBUS: A Computer Model of Long-Term Global Political and Economic Processes.* Boulder, CO, 1987.

Brockhoff, K. (*Prognoseverfahren*): *Prognoseverfahren für die Unternehmungsplanung.* Wiesbaden, 1977.

Brockhoff, K. (*Computerdialog*): *Delphi-Prognosen im Computerdialog.* Tübingen, 1979.

Bruckmann, G.: *Langfristige Prognosen.* Würzburg, 1977/1978.

Brümmerhoff, D.: *Volkswirtschaftliche Gesamtrechnungen,* 5th ed. Munich, 1995.

Brunetti, A. (*Politics*): *Politics and Economic Growth: A Cross Country Data Perspective.* OECD Development Centre, Paris, 1997.

Buchinger, G.: *Umfeldanalysen für das strategische Management.* Vienna, 1983.

Butler, W.F. and Kavesh, R.A.: *How Business Economists Forecast.* Englewood Cliffs, NJ, 1966.

Capra, F.: *Wendezeit,* 8th ed. Bern, 1984. (Original title: *The Turning Point: Science, Society and the Rising Culture.*)

Capra, F.: *The Web of Life: A New Synthesis of Mind and Matter.* London, 1996.

Cazes, B.: Continuité et mutations dans l'histoire de la pensée prospective, in Hatem, F.: *La Prospective. Pratiques et Méthodes.* Paris, 1993.

Commission on the Year 2000: *Working Papers.* Boston, 1965.

Dalkey, N.C.: *An Elementary Cross Impact Model.* RAND Report R-677-ARPA, May 1971.

Davis Floyd, R.E.: Storying Corporate Futures: The SHELL Scenarios, in *International Journal of Futures Studies,* Vol. 1, 1996.

Dayal, R.: *A Quantitative View of Future World Economic Development.* Diessenhofen, 1980.

Delhees, K.H.: *Zukunft bewältigen*. Bern, 1997.

DIW (*Deutschland 2010*): *Entwicklung von Bevölkerung und Wirtschaft in Deutschland bis zum Jahr 2010*. Berlin, 1997.

Dornbusch, R. and Fischer, S. (*Macroeconomics*): *Macroeconomics*, 5th ed. New York, 1990.

Drucker, P.E. (*Post-Capitalist Society*): *Post-Capitalist Society*. New York, 1993.

Drucker, P.E.: The Global Economy and the Nation-State, in *Foreign Affairs*, Vol. 76, No. 5, (1997), pp. 159–170.

Duijn, J.J. van (*Long Wave*): *The Long Wave in Economic Life*. London, 1983.

Enzer, S.: *Delphi and Cross-Impact Techniques: An Effective Combination for Systematic Future Analysis*. Institute for the Future WP-8, June 1970.

Espejo, R. et al. (*Learning*): *Organizational Transformation and Learning: A Cybernetic Approach to Management*. New York, 1996.

Fahey, L. and Randall, R.M.: *Learning from the Future, Competitive Foresight Scenarios*. New York, 1998.

Flechtheim, O.K.: *Futurologie, Der Kampf um die Zukunft*. Cologne, 1970.

Fleiner-Gerster, Th.: *Allgemeine Staatslehre*, 2nd ed. Berlin, 1995

Forrester, J.W. (*World Dynamics*): *World Dynamics*. Cambridge, 1971.

Fourastié, J.: *Die grosse Metamorphose des 20. Jahrhunderts*. Düsseldorf, 1964.

Frey, B. S. and Kirchgässner, G.: *Demokratische Wirtschaftspolitik: Theorie und Anwendung*, 2nd ed. Munich, 1994.

Fulda, E., Härter, M., and Lenk, H.: Prognoseprobleme, in Szypersky, N. and Winand, U. (eds.): *Handwörterbuch der Planung*. Stuttgart, 1989.

Galbraith, J.K.: *Economics and the Public Purpose*. Boston, 1973.

Galbraith, J.K. (*Uncertainty*): *The Age of Uncertainty*. London, 1977.

Gälweiler, A. (*Unternehmungsführung*): *Strategische Unternehmungsführung*. Frankfurt, 1987.

Gausemeier, J., Fink, A., and Schlake, O. (*Szenario-Management*): *Szenario-Management*, 2nd ed. Munich, 1996.

Gerfin, H.: *Langfristige Wirtschaftsprognosen*. Tübingen/Zurich, 1964.

Geschka, H. and Hammer, R.: Die Szenario-Technik in der strategischen Unternehmensplanung, in Hahn, D. and Taylor B. (eds.): *Strategische Unternehmensplanung*, 4th ed. Heidelberg/Vienna, 1986.

Geus, Arie de: Planning as Learning, in *Harvard Business Review*, March/April 1988, pp. 70–74.

Giorno, C.P. et al. (Potential Output): Potential Output, Output Gaps and Structural Budget Balances, in *OECD Economic Studies*, No. 24, 1995.

Godet, M.: *Scenarios and Strategic Management*. London, 1987.

Godet, M.: (*Anticipation*): *From Anticipation to Action*. Paris, 1994.

Godet, M.: *Creating Futures*, Paris, 2001.

Gomez, P.: *Modelle und Methoden des systemorientierten Managements*. Bern/Stuttgart, 1981.

Gomez, P. (*Frühwarnung*): *Frühwarnung in der Unternehmung*. Bern, 1983.

Gomez, P. and Probst, G. (*Praxis*): *Die Praxis des ganzheitlichen Problemlösens*. Bern, 1995.

Gordon, Th.J. and Haywood, H. (Initial Experiments): Initial Experiments with the Cross-Impact Matrix Method of Forecasting, in *Futures*, Vol. 1, No. 2, 1968.

Gordon, Th.J., Rochberg, R. and Enzer, S.: *Research on Cross-Impact Techniques with Applications to Selected Problems in Economics, Political Science and Technology Assessment*. Institute for the Future R-12, August 1970.

Görzig, B. et al. (*Produktivität*): *Investitionen, Beschäftigung und Produktivität*, Beiträge zur Strukturforschung Heft 108, Deutsches Institut für Wirtschaftsforschung (DIW). Berlin, 1988.

Graemiger, A.O.: Umfeldinformationssysteme für mittelständische Unternehmungen, dissertation, University of St. Gallen, 1994.

Graf, H.G.: Gesamtwirtschaftliche Entwicklungsszenarien für Europa bis zum Jahr 2020, *Dokumente des SGZZ*, No. 5, St. Gallen, May 1983.

Graf, H.G.: Mögliche Entwicklungen Europas bis zum Jahr 2020, in Agustoni, H. and Schnyder, M. (eds.): *Angst abbauen, Hoffnung säen*. Munich, 1985.

Graf, H.G.: *Einzelhandel Schweiz 2000, Eine Delphi Studie*. St. Gallen, 1987.

Graf, H.G. (Instrument): Volkswirtschaftslehre als prognostisches Instrument, in Graf, H.G., Meier, A. and Wuffli, H.R. (eds.): *Praxisorientierte Volkswirtschaftslehre*, commemorative publication for F. Kneschaurek. Bern, 1988, pp. 29–53.

Graf, H.G.: *Wirtschaftliche und gesellschaftliche Entwicklungsszenarien bis zum Jahr 2025*. Bern, 1988.

Graf, H.G.: Scenarios for Future Freight Traffic and Emissions, in *ECMT (OECD): Freight Transport and the Environment*. Paris, 1991, pp. 39–55.

Graf, H.G.: *Branchenszenarien für die Schweiz—Alleingang vs. EG-Beitritt*. Chur, 1994.

Graf, H.G.: Grundlagen von Wirtschaftsprognosen, in *Mitteilungen des SGZZ*, Vol. 19, No. 13, March 1994, pp. 20–27.

Graf, H.G.: *Ökonomische Rahmendaten und Perspektiven für die Schweiz*. St. Gallen/Bern, 1995.

Graf, H.G.: Herausforderungen an die Ökonomie, in *Mitteilungen des SGZZ*, Vol. 22, No. 1, 1997, pp. 1–10.

Graf, H.G.: Politikberatung: Diskussionsbasis oder Argumentationshilfe, in Schmid, H. and Slembeck, T. (eds.): *Finanz- und Wirtschaftspolitik*, commemorative publication for A. Meier. Bern, 1997, pp. 489–515.

Graf, H.G.: Quantifizierung qualitativer Annahmen in den SGZZ-Perspektiven, in *Mitteilungen des SGZZ*, Vol. 22, No. 4, 1997, pp. 13–21.

Graf, H.G. (*K&P*): *Konjunktur & Perspektiven*, SGZZ. St. Gallen, 1998.

Graf, H.G. (Szenario-Denken): Szenario-Denken durchdringt die Unternehmenskultur, in *Thexis*, No. 2, 1998, pp. 64–67.

Graf, H.G. (*Wissensgesellschaft*): . . . *und in Zukunft die Wissensgesellschaft*. Chur/Zurich, 2001.

Graf, H.G. (Sektor): Szenarien einer Entwicklung zum quartären Sektor, in Bleicher, K. and Berthel, J. (*Wissensgesellschaft*), Frankfurt, 2002.

Graf, H.G. (*Global Scenarios*): *Global Scenarios: Megatrends in Worldwide Dynamics*, Chur/Zurich, 2002.

Graf, H.G. and Weber-Thedy, W.: *EG'92: Szenarien für Europa und die Schweiz*. St. Gallen, 1989.

Graf, H.G. and Mettler, D.: *Branchenmässige Simulation von Europaszenarien*. Chur, 1991.

Greene, W.H.: *Econometric Analysis*, 3rd ed. New Brunswick, NJ, 1997.

Gwartney, J.D. and Stroup, R.C. (*Public Choice*): *Economics. Private and Public Choice*, 8th ed. Orlando, FL, 1997.

Hamilton, H.R.: Scenarios in Corporate Planning, in *Journal of Business Strategy*, Vol. 2, No. 1, 1981.

Hatem, F.: *Econometric Analysis*. Paris, 1993.

Hatem, F. (*Prospective*): *La Prospective. Pratiques et Méthodes*. Paris, 1993.

Hayek von, F.A. (Muster): Die Theorie komplexer Phänomene, in Hayek von, F.A., Kerber,W. v. (ed.): *Die Anmassung von Wissen*. Tübingen, 1996, pp. 281–306.

Heil, J.: *Einführung in die Ökonometrie*, 5th ed. Munich, 1996.

Helmer, O.: *Looking Forward: A Guide to Futures Research*. Beverly Hills, CA, 1983.

Henderson, H. (*Win-Win World*): *Building a Win-Win World: Life beyond Global Economic Warfare*. San Francisco, 1996.

Henschel, H.: *Wirtschaftsprognosen*. Munich, 1979.

Herrera A., Skolnik H. et al. (*Grenzen des Elends*): *Grenzen des Elends*. Frankfurt, 1976.

Heyden v.d., K. (*Scenarios*): *Scenarios: The Art of the Strategic Conversation*, Chichester, 1996.

Heyden v.d., K. (Business Idea): Articulating the Business Idea, in Fahey, L. and Randall, R.M. (eds.): *Learning from the Future*. New York, 1998, pp. 335–351.

Holub, H.-W. (Wirtschaftsforschung): Empirische Wirtschaftsforschung auf Abwegen? Problematisches 'Modellieren auf der Basis von Modellen,' in *NZZ*, December 13, 1996.

Holub, H.-W. (Replik): Empirische Wirtschaftsforschung auf Abwegen? Eine Entgegnung . . . (reply to G. Kirchgässner), in *NZZ*, March 4, 1997.

Holub, H.-W. and Schnabel, W. (*Input-Output*): *Input-Output-Rechnung: Input-Output-Analyse: Eine Einführung*. Munich, 1994.

Hughes, B.B.: *International Futures*. Boulder, CO, 1993.

Hüttner, M. (*Prognoseverfahren*): *Prognoseverfahren und ihre Anwendung*. Berlin, 1986.

Iklé, F.C. (Social Predictions): On the Epistemology of Social Predictions, in *Working Papers of the Commission on the Year 2000*, Vol. 3. Boston, 1965.

International Commission on Peace and Food: *Uncommon Opportunities*. London, 1994.

Jäger, Th. and Piepenschneider, M.: *Europa 2020, Szenarien politischer Entwicklung*. Opladen, 1997.

Jantsch, E.: *Technological Forecasting in Perspective*. Paris, 1967.

Johnson, H.T. and Kaplan, R.S. (*Relevance*): *Relevance Lost: The Rise and Fall of Management Accounting*. Boston, 1987.

Jöhr, W.A. (*Konjunktur*): *Konjunkturschwankungen*. Tübingen, 1952.

Jöhr, W.A. (Psychologie): Zur Rolle des psychologischen Faktors in der Konjunkturtheorie, in *Zeitschrift des Ifo-Instituts für Wirtschaftsforschung*, Vol. 18, 1972, pp. 157–184.

Jonas, H.: *Das Prinzip Verantwortung*. Frankfurt, 1984.

Judt, T.: The Social Question Redivivus, in *Foreign Affairs*, Vol. 76, No. 5, 1997, pp. 95–116.

Jungk, R.: *Der Jahrtausendmensch*. Munich 1973.

Jungk, R. and Mundt, H.J.: *Modelle für eine neue Welt: Der Griff nach der Zukunft*. Munich, 1964.

Jungk, R. and Mundt, H.J.: *Modelle für eine neue Welt: Unsere Welt 1985*. Munich, 1964.

Jungk, R. and Mundt, H.J.: *Wege ins neue Jahrtausend*. Munich, 1964.

Jungk, R. and Mundt, H.J.: *Modelle für eine neue Welt: Perspektiven, Prognosen, Modelle, Bericht der Kommission für das Jahr 2000*. Munich, 1968.

Kahn, H. (*World Economic Development*): *World Economic Development (1980–2000)*. Vienna, 1980.

Kahn H. et al.: *The Next 200 Years*. New York, 1976.

Kahn, H. and Wiener, A.J.: *The Year 2000: A Framework for Speculation on the Next Thirty-Three Years*. New York, 1967.

Kennedy, P.M. (*Rise and Fall*): *The Rise and Fall of the Great Powers: Economic Change and Military Conflict from 1500 to 2000*. New York, 1987.

Kennedy, P.M.: *Preparing for the Twenty-First Century*. New York, 1993.

Kindleberger, C.P. (*Crises*): *Manias, Panics, and Crashes: A History of Financial Crises*, 3rd ed. New York ,1996.

Kirchgässner, G. (Modelle): Empirische Wirtschaftsforschung auf Abwegen? A Reply to H.W. Holub, in *NZZ*, January 9, 1997.

Klein, L. and Lo, F.: *Modelling Global Change*. Tokyo/New York/Paris, 1995.

Kneschaurek, F.: Szenarioanalysen, in Buchinger, G. (ed.): *Umfeldanalysen für das strategische Management*. Vienna, 1983.

Kneschaurek, F.: *Wirtschaftliche Perspektivstudien*. St. Gallen, 1988.

Kneschaurek, F. (*Volkswirtschaft*): *Unternehmung und Volkswirtschaft*, 4th ed. Zurich, 1996.

Kneschaurek, F. and Graf, H.G. (Arbeitsgruppe Perspektivstudien) (*Entwicklungsperspektiven*): *Entwicklungsperspektiven der schweizerischen Volkswirtschaft bis zum Jahr 2000*, 13 different partial volumes between 1969 and 1978.

Kneschaurek, F. and Graf, H.G. (*Wirtschafts- und Marktprognosen*): *Wirtschafts- und Marktprognosen als Grundlage der Unternehmungspolitik*, 1st ed. St. Gallen, 1984.

Kolb, D.A. and Rubin, I.M. (*Organizational Behavior*): *Organizational Behavior: An Experimental Approach*. Englewood Cliffs, NJ, 1991.

Kondratieff, N.D. (Lange Wellen): Die langen Wellen der Konjunktur, in *Archiv für Sozialwissenschaft und Sozialpolitik*, Vol. 56, 1926, pp. 573–609.

Königswieser, R., Haller, M., and Maas, P. (eds.) (*Risiko-Dialog*): *Risiko-Dialog: Zukunft ohne Harmonieformel*. Cologne, 1996.

Kramer, E.A. (Wirtschaftsrecht): Entwicklungstendenzen des Wirtschaftsrechts im ausgehenden Jahrhundert, in Kramer, E.A. (ed.): *Zur Theorie und Politik des Privat- und Wirtschaftsrechts*. Basel, 1997.

Kroeber-Riel, W. and Weinberg, P. (*Konsumentenverhalten*): *Konsumentenverhalten*, 6th ed. Munich, 1996.

Kromrey, H. (*Sozialforschung*): *Empirische Sozialforschung. Modelle und Methoden der Datenerhebung und Datenauswertung*, 2nd ed. Stuttgart, 1983.

Krugmann, P. (*Expectations*): *The Age of Diminished Expectations*, 2nd ed. Cambridge, 1996.

Krystek, U. and Müller-Stewens, G. (*Frühaufklärung*): *Frühaufklärung für Unternehmen: Identifikation und Handhabung zukünftiger Chancen und Bedrohungen*. Stuttgart, 1993.

Kummer, St. (Weltmodelle): Arbeiten mit Weltmodellen—Lernen und Voraussagen, in *Mitteilungen des SGZZ*, No. 3. St. Gallen, 1995.

Kusnets, S. (*Concepts*): *Concepts and Assumptions in Long Term Projections of Income and Wealth*. Princeton, NJ, 1954.

Laszlo, E.: *Goals for Mankind*. New York, 1977.

Laszlo, E. and Bierman, J.: *Goals in a Global Community*, 2 Vol. New York, 1977.

Leemhuis, J.P.: Using Scenarios to Develop Strategies, in *Long Range Planning*, Vol. 18, No. 2, 1985, pp. 30–37.

Lendi, M. (*Nationalplanung*): *Nationalplanung, Lecture notes*. ETH Center, Zurich, 1995.

Leontief, W.: *The Structure of the American Economy, 1919–1939: An Empirical Application of Equilibrium Analysis*, 2nd ed. New York, 1951.

Leontief, W.: *Studies in the Structure of the American Economy: Theoretical and Empirical Explorations in Input-Output Analysis*. New York, 1953.

Leontief, W. (*Input-Output*): *Input-Output Economics*. New York, 1966.

Leontief, W.: *The Economic System in an Age of Discontinuity: Long-Range Planning or Market Reliance*. New York, 1976.

Leontief, W. et al. (*Future*): *The Future of the World Economy*. New York, 1977.

Linnemann R.E. and Klein, H.E.: The Use of Multiple Scenarios by U.S. Industrial Companies: A Comparison Study, 1977–1981, in *Long Range Planning*, Vol. 16, No. 6, 1983.

Linnemann H. et al. (*MOIRA*): *Model of International Relations in Agriculture*. Amsterdam, 1979.

Linstone, H.A. and Turoff, M. (*Delphi Method*): *The Delphi Method*. Reading, PA, 1975.

Lyons, G.M. and Mastanduno, M. (eds.): *Beyond Westphalia*. Baltimore, 1995.

Makridakis, S. and Weelwright, S.C.: *The Handbook of Forecasting*. New York, 1982.

Marx, K. (*Kapital*): *Das Kapital: Kritik der politischen Ökonomie*, facsimile edition of the first edition published in 1867. Düsseldorf, 1988.

McRae, H.: *The World in 2000*. London, 1994

Meadows, D. et al.: *Limits to Growth—A Report to the Club of Rome*. New York, 1972.

Meadows, D. et al.: Limits to Growth. Technical Report, unpublished, 1972.

Meadows, D. et al. (*Beyond*): *Beyond the Limits*. Post Mills, VT, 1992.

Meier-Schatz, Ch. (Wirtschaftsrecht): Über Entwicklung, Begriff und Aufgaben des Wirtschaftsrechts, in *Zeitschrift für Schweizerisches Recht*, Neue Folge 101 I (1982), pp. 267ff.

Menzl, A. (Konjunkturprognose): Was kann die Volkswirtschaftslehre für den dispositiven Bereich einer Unternehmung leisten?, in Graf, H.G., Meier, A. and Wuffli, H.R. (eds.): *Praxisorientierte Volkswirtschaftslehre*, commemorative publication for F. Kneschaurek. Bern, 1988, pp. 265–277.

Mesarovic, M. and Pestel, E. (*Wendepunkt*): *Menschheit am Wendepunkt*. Stuttgart, 1974.

Meyer-Schönherr, M.: *Szenario-Technik als Instrument der strategischen Planung*. Ludwigsburg/Berlin, 1992.

Millet, S. and Honton, E.: *Managers Guide to Technology Forecasting and Strategic Analysis*. Columbus, OH, 1991.

Modis, Th. (*Predictions*): *Predictions, Society's Telltale Signature Reveals the Past and Forecasts the Future*. New York, 1992.

Morgenstern, O.: *Wirtschaftsprognose*. Vienna, 1928.

Morgenstern, O.: *Über die Genauigkeit wirtschaftlicher Beobachtungen*, 2nd ed. Würzburg, 1965.

Naisbitt, J.: *Global Paradox*. London, 1994.

OECD (*Economic Outlook*): *OECD Economic Outlook*, No. 62. Paris, 1997.

OECD: *The World in 2020, towards a New Global Age*. Paris, 1997.

OECD (Lesourne, J.): *Interfutures, Facing the Future, Mastering the Probable and Managing the Unpredictable*. Paris, 1979.

OECD (*Technology*): *Technology and Industrial Performance*. Paris, 1996.

Oh, K.-U.: *Methoden und Ergebnisse der Langfristprognose*. Meisenheim, 1976.

Ohmae, K.: *The End of the Nation State*. New York, 1995.

Olson, M.: *The Rise and Decline of Nations*. New Haven, CT, 1982.

Oppenländer, K.H. (*Wachstumspolitik*): *Wachstumstheorie und Wachstumspolitik*. Munich, 1988.

Pestel, E.: *Jenseits der Grenzen des Wachstums*, 2nd ed. Stuttgart, 1988.

Popper, K.R. (Logik): Die Logik der Sozialwissenschaften, in Adorno, Th.W. et al. (eds.): *Der Positivismusstreit in der deutschen Soziologie*. Neuwied/Berlin, 1969, pp. 103–123.

Pümpin, C. (*Erfolgspositionen*): *Management strategischer Erfolgspositionen*, 3rd ed. Bern, 1986.

Rappaport, A. (*Value*): *Creating Shareholder Value: The New Standard for Business Performance*. New York, 1986.

Reibnitz, U.v. (*Szenario-Technik*): *Szenario-Technik*. Wiesbaden, 1991.

Rescher, N.: *Predicting the Future. An Introduction to the Theory of Forecasting*. New York, 1997.

Riklin, A. (Wissenschaft): Wissenschaft und Ethik, in Riklin, A. (ed.): *Verantwortung des Akademikers*. St. Gallen, 1987, pp. 9–38.

Rockfellow, J.D. (Wild Cards): Wild Cards, Preparing for 'The Big One,' in *The Futurist*, January/February, 1994, pp. 14–19.

Rostow, W.W.: *The World Economy, History and Prospect*. Austin, TX, 1978.

Rostow, W.W. (*Stages*): *The Stages of Economic Growth: A Non-Communist Manifesto*. Cambridge, 1962.

Rothschild, K.W.: *Wirtschaftsprognose*. Berlin, 1969.

Ruggles, R.: *Long Range Economic Projections*. Princeton, NJ, 1954.

Ruth, M., Hannon, B. and Forrester, J.W. (*Modeling*): *Modeling Dynamic economic Systems*. New York, 1997.

Schedler, K. (*Verwaltungsführung*): *Ansätze einer wirkungsorientierten Verwaltungsführung*, 2nd ed. Bern, 1996.

Schips, B. (Aufbau): Ökonometrische Modelle, in *Hochschulinformation*, No. 1, 1979, University of St. Gallen.

Schips, B.: *Empirische Wirtschaftsforschung*. Wiesbaden, 1990.

Schlange, L.E. (*Umfeldinformationen*): *Die Umsetzung von Umfeldinformationen in unternehmungspolitische Entscheidungen*. Dissertation, University of St. Gallen/Bamberg, 1992.

Schlange, L.E.: Szenario-Planung—Quo Vadis?, in *Zukünfte*, No. 11/12, 1995.

Schlange, L.E. (Scenario Planning): Scenario Planning, Systems Thinking and Futures-Oriented Learning in the Electric Utility Industry, in Institute for Prospective Technological Studies (IPTS) (ed.): *Scenario Building. Convergences and Differences*. Seville, 1995, pp. 95–105.

Schlange, L.E. (*Zukunftsforschung und Planung*): *Zukunftsforschung und Planung—Zur methodischen Gestaltung prospektiver Wahrnehmungsprozesse*, Forschungspolitische Früherkennung (FER) des Schweiz. Wissenschaftsrats, Bern, 1995.

Schlange, L.E. and Schüller, A. (eds.): *Komplexität und Management*. Stuttgart, 1994.

Schlange, L.E. and Sütterlin, R. (Zukunftsseminar): Das Zukunftsseminar, in *ZFO Zeitschrift Führung und Organisation*, May 1997, pp. 284–289.

Schmid, H. (*Geld, Kredit und Banken*): *Geld, Kredit und Banken*, 3rd ed. Bern, 1997.

Schmidheiny, St. (*Kurswechsel*): *Kurswechsel: Globale unternehmerische Perspektiven für Entwicklung und Umwelt*. Munich, 1992.

Schnaars, S.P.: How to Develop and Use Scenarios, in *Long Range Planning*, Vol. 20, No. 1, February 1987.

Schultz, R.: *Quantitative Entscheidungsunterlagen auf der Grundlage von Szenarien*. Wiesbaden, 1987.

Schumpeter, J.A.: *Business cycles*, 2 Vol. New York/London, 1939 (rev. ed. published in 1964).

Schumpeter, J.A. (*Kapitalismus*): *Kapitalismus, Sozialismus und Demokratie*, 4th ed. Munich, 1975.

Schumpeter, J.A. (*Entwicklung*): *Theorie der wirtschaftlichen Entwicklung*. Düsseldorf, 1988, new edition of the 1912 1st.

Schwaninger, M.: *Managementsysteme*. Frankfurt/New York, 1994.

Schwartz, P.: *The Art of the Long View*. New York, 1991.

Schwarz, B.: *Methods in Futures Studies*. Boulder, CO, 1982.

Senge, P.M. (*Fifth Discipline*): *The Fifth Discipline*. London, 1993.

Servan-Schreiber, J.-J.: *Die amerikanische Herausforderung*. Hamburg, 1968.

Shani, M. (Futures Studies): Futures Studies versus Planning, in *Omega*, No. 5, 1974.

Siegenthaler, H. (*Krise*): *Regelvertrauen, Prosperität und Krisen*. Tübingen, 1993.

Slaughter, A.-M. (World Order): The Real New World Order, in *Foreign Affairs*, Vol. 76, No. 5, 1997, pp. 183–196.

Sombart, W.: *Allgemeine Nationalökonomie*. Berlin, 1960.

Sorrosal, A. and Sütterlin, R. (Verantwortung): Globalisierung und ethisches Vakuum— neue Verantwortung auf neuen Spielfeldern, in *Mitteilungen des SGZZ*, Vol. 23, No. 1, 1998, pp. 24–36.

Stephan, G. and Ahlheim, M.: *Ökonomische Ökologie* Heidelberg, 1996.

Stephan, G. and Previdoli, P.: *Die volkswirtschaftlichen Auswirkungen der Energieinitiative: eine empirische, dynamische Gleichgewichtsanalyse*, by order of BEW. Bern, 1996.

Stockholm Environment Institute (SEI)/United Nations Environment Program (UNEP, Global Scenario Group): *The Sustainability Transition: Beyond Conventional Development*. Nairobi, 1996.

Stucki, G. and Sangha, O. (Principles): Principles of Rehabilitation, in Klippel, J.H. and Dieppe, P.A. (eds.): *Rheumatology*, 2nd ed. London, 1998, No. 3, Section 11, pp. 1–14.

Swiss Federal Office of Energy (*Statistic*): *Schweiz. Elektrizitätsstatistik 2000*. Bern, 2001.

Swiss Federal Statistical Office (*Yearbook*): *Statistisches Jahrbuch der Schweiz*. Bern/Neuchâtel, various years.

Swiss Federal Statistical Office (*National Income Accounts*): *Volkswirtschaftliche Gesamtrechnung. Methoden und Konzepte*. Bern, 1997.

Taylor, C. W. (*World Scenarios*): *Alternative World Scenarios*. Strategic Studies Institute, U.S. Army War College, Carlisle Barracks, PA, 1988.

Teichmann, U.: *Grundriss der Konjunkturpolitik*, 5th ed. Munich, 1997.

Theil, H. (*Econometrics*): *Principles of Econometrics*. North Holland/Amsterdam/London, 1971.

Thurow, L.: *Head to Head: The Coming Economic Battle among Japan, Europe, and America*. New York, 1992.

Tichy, G.: *Konjunktur: stilisierte Fakten, Theorie, Prognose*, 2nd ed. Berlin, 1994.

Tichy, G. (*Konjunkturpolitik*): *Konjunkturpolitik: Quantitative Stabilisierungspolitik bei Unsicherheit*, 3rd ed. Berlin, 1995.

Tinbergen, J.: *Reshaping the International Order*. London, 1977.

Toffler, A.: *Future Shock*. New York, 1970.

Ulrich, H.: *Unternehmungspolitik*, 2nd ed. Bern/Stuttgart, 1987.

Ulrich, H. (Systemische Sicht): Unternehmung und Volkswirtschaft in systemischer Sicht, in Graf, H.G., Meier, A. and Wuffli, H. (eds.): *Unternehmung und Volkswirtschaft*, commemorative publication for F. Kneschaurek. Bern, 1988.

Ulrich, H.: Von der Betriebswirtschaftslehre zur systemorientierten Managementlehre, in Wunderer, R. (ed.): *Betriebswirtschaftslehre als Management- und Führungslehre*, 3rd ed. Stuttgart, 1995.

Ulrich, H. and Krieg, W. (*Managementmodell*): *St. Galler Managementmodell*, 3rd ed. Bern, 1974.

Ulrich, H. and Probst, G. (*Anleitung*): *Anleitung zum ganzheitlichen Denken und Handeln*. Bern/Stuttgart, 1988.

Ulrich, P.: (*Wirtschaftsethik*): *Integrative Wirtschaftsethik. Grundlagen einer lebensdienlichen Ökonomie.* Bern, 1997.

United Nations Development Program (UNDP): *Human Development Report.* New York, several volumes.

UNO (*World Survey*): *World Economic and Social Survey.* New York, several volumes.

UNO et al. (*National Accounts*): *System of National Accounts 1993.* Brussels, 1993.

Vallender, K.A. (*Wirtschaftsfreiheit*): *Wirtschaftsfreiheit und begrenzte Staatsverantwortung,* 3rd ed. Bern, 1995.

Venzin, M.: Crafting the Future. Dissertation, University of St. Gallen/Bamberg, 1997.

Vester, F.: *Neuland des Denkens.* Stuttgart, 1980.

Vester, F. (*Sensitivitätsmodell*): *Sensitivitätsmodell Prof. Vester®.* Munich, 1992.

Wack, P.: *Scenarios: The Gentle Art of Reperceiving.* Cambridge, MA, 1984.

Wack, P. (Uncharted Waters): Scenarios: Uncharted Waters Ahead. *Harvard Business Review,* Vol. 63, No. 5, 1985, pp. 72–79.

Wack, P.: Scenarios: Shooting the Rapids. *Harvard Business Review,* Vol. 63, No. 6, 1985, pp. 139–150.

Walter, H.: *Wachstums- und Entwicklungstheorie.* Stuttgart, 1983.

Walter-Busch, E. (*Organisationstheorien*): *Organisationstheorien von Weber bis Weick.* Amsterdam, 1996.

Weber, K.: *Wirtschaftsprognostik.* Munich, 1990.

Weinhold-Stünzi, H. (*Marketing*): *Marketing in 20 Lektionen,* 16th ed. St. Gallen, 1988.

Wells, H.G. (*Anticipations*): *Anticipations.* Paris, 1900.

Wells, H.G. (*Découverte*): *La découverte de l'avenir.* Paris, 1902.

Whiston, T.: *Uses and Abuses of Forecasting.* London, 1979.

Willke, H. (*Systemtheorie*): *Systemtheorie,* 3 Vols. Stuttgart, 1991–1996.

Wilson, I. H.: Scenarios, in J. Fowles (ed.): *Handbook of Futures Research.* Westport, CT, 1978.

Wilson, I. (Implementation): The Effective Implementation of Scenario Planning: Changing the Corporate Culture, in Fahey, L. and Randall, R.M. (eds.): *Learning from the Future.* New York, 1998, pp. 352–368.

Winker, P. (*Wirtschaftsforschung*): *Empirische Wirtschaftsforschung.* Berlin, 1997.

World Commission on Environment and Development: *Our Common Future.* Oxford, 1987.

Zalm, G. (*Scanning*): *Scanning the Future.* The Hague, 1992.

Zey, M.G. (Macroindustrial Era): Macroindustrial Era: A New Age of Abundance and Prosperity, *The Futurist,* March–April 1997, pp. 9–14.

INDEX

About the Author

HANS GEORG GRAF is President and CEO of the Center for Futures Research in St. Gallen, Switzerland, and Professor of Economics at the University of St. Gallen.